The Day Our World Changed

December 7, 1941
Punahou '52 Remembers Pearl Harbor

John B. Bowles, Editor

Ice Cube Books
North Liberty, Iowa 52317

THE DAY OUR WORLD CHANGED:

DECEMBER 7, 1941 PUNAHOU '52 REMEMBERS PEARL HARBOR

ISBN 9781888160116
Second Edition
Library of Congress Control Number: 2010926251

Ice Cube Books (Est. 1993)
205 N. Front Street
North Liberty, Iowa 52317
www.icecubepress.com

The paper used in this publication meets the minimum requirements of the American National Standard for Information Sciences—Permanence of Paper for Printed Library Materials, ANSI Z39.48-1992

planes on cover drawn by: Lindsay Yedlosky—age 6 (lower drawing) & Brittany Yedlosky—age 11 (upper drawing).

Manufactured in the United States of America

Note: this book was previously published in 2004
© 2004 John B. Bowles & Eric C. Gross, Editors
ISBN 1-888160-02-0
Library of Congress Control Number: 2003105312

A portion of the sales from this book go to the Punahou school in the name of the Class of '52.

Table of Contents

"We are under attack, take cover. This is no drill, it's the real McCoy!" Radio similar to the one many of us heard the news of the attack over. (photo courtesy of Jody Everett.)

Prologue—

I had the idea for this project in 1996. I was sitting in the small Chester R. Nimitz Museum in Fredericksburg, Texas, surrounded by memorabilia from the Pacific Theater of World War II. My thoughts wandered back to the morning of December 7, 1941. We looked out from our Honolulu home atop Maunalani Heights at Japanese planes flying over Kaimukī against the backdrop of Diamond Head. To our right, dark smoke billowed from Pearl Harbor fires.

We had left Japan for Hawai`i in 1936 because of the military buildup there and now war was upon us. I thought about my family's story of what happened that day and how our lives were forever changed by the events of the days, months and years that followed. Then I wondered what my Punahou School classmates ("The Motley Crew of '52") had experienced on December 7, and why their families had come to Hawai`i. I collected a few stories and was amazed at the differences in content, style of writing, and factors that affected each family. I expanded the project by inviting all our classmates to share their memories of that day and their family histories for our 50th Punahou reunion in Honolulu in 2002. The response was overwhelming and 86 indicated an interest in contributing their stories for this book.

Although these are stories of the same historical event, they reveal a wide range of personal feelings and experiences greatly influenced by where we lived, what our parents did, and why and when our families came to the Islands. They demonstrate a diversity of heritage, culture, and life experiences held together by the common threads of the vivid memories of that day and that time-period. All of us attended Punahou School and all were in the same class at some time during our school years—a few from kindergarten to graduation in 1952, a few just one year, but most for several years. Although we all spent time in Hawai`i, not all were there on that day. Nevertheless, we remember it well.

Diamond Head from Maunalani Hts with superimposed Japanese planes depicting our view on December 7, 1941. (Unless otherwise noted photos are by J.B.Bowles; this photo was taken in the 1940s.)

As six, seven and eight-year-olds on December 7, 1941, we are among the youngest who directly remember the experiences of that day and the days that followed. Somehow, it seems important to us to record our stories as we remember them because history is about personal experiences and the feelings they evoke, not just events recorded in textbooks. Furthermore, history tends to repeat itself so there often are opportunities to learn from "today's" events in order to prevent "tomorrow's" difficulties. Historical events also often show parallels that can enable us to focus more clearly on certain aspects that are especially damaging to both individuals and groups. As we reflect on the aftermath of "September 11th," for example, we can clearly see the parallels between treatment now of those from Middle East origins and the Japanese then living in Hawai`i.

Our Punahou Kindergarten class 1939 (unknown photographer).

Many of us living in Hawai`i at that time were conscious of the reaction against Japanese in general, and some of our stories allude to the personal struggles of local Japanese families, especially regarding country loyalty. The last story about the Mori family illustrates the cross-generational difficulties many local Japanese families encountered as well.

After we graduated from Punahou in 1952, we went our own ways, dispersing to live and travel throughout the world. We made our livings and raised our families differently. Yet despite (or perhaps because of) these differences there has always been a pervading sense of connectedness. Through the years this feeling of "extended family" has strengthened, aided in part by technological advances in communication. Perhaps this collection of stories will provide another link for us to remember the unique time and place we shared with each other and with those who have crossed over.

Mahalo nui (big thank you) to my classmates for sending their recollections of December 7, 1941—*The day our world changed.* A very special aloha to my former Texas neighbor, Heather Penne, for her dedication to the project and for doing the layout for our 50th reunion stories. Kit Smith, Bobbie Carter Reed, Terri Miller, Greg Seastrom and Helen Bowles Nicholson did general editing and Corinne Kong checked the spelling of the Hawaiian names, among other things. Shannon Heath Wilson helped me articulate my feelings, and Muriel Matson gave the energetic push when I felt overwhelmed. Justin Esquivel drew the maps, Amanda Moreland did some of the typing, and Ellen McGillivray Luhrs helped with the marketing. I am grateful for Ralph Ingram's historical framework in the Introduction, and Luella Kurkjian (Hawai`i State Archives) for locating many of the photos; she, Kylee Kurita (Punahou School Archives), Judith Bowman (U.S. Army Museum of Hawai`i) and DeSoto Brown (Bishop Museum), kindly gave permission to use numerous photos in this book. Others too numerous to name helped in a variety of ways. Mahalo nui to my coeditor and friend, Eric C. Gross (Iolani '65) for the many long and stimulating discussions; the help and dedication of the publisher, Steve Semken cannot be overlooked. Not to be lost in the shuffle but without whom this project could not have transpired, are the classmates and others who generously donated enough money to meet the initial publication costs. Finally, thanks to my wife, Gay, for her patience when I was preoccupied with this book.

Mahalo nui and aloha—John B. Bowles

Introduction—

Tuesday morning, September 11, 2001, was a morning just like any other—feed the cats, clean their litter boxes, and check the day's business news...but then, the "day of infamy" of this 21st century began to unfold. At first, I thought my television was mistakenly turned to the science fiction channel, yet a quick check and the second plane crashing into the World Trade Center confirmed the ugly, tragic reality. For some reason, my thoughts retreated to that warm, balmy Sunday morning, now more than sixty years in the past, when another day of infamy challenged a previous generation of Americans.

Prior to December 7, 1941, the United States was immersed in the Great Depression. Her citizens were not deeply concerned with foreign affairs. The general consensus was that the United States should remain isolated from world affairs. In other words, America was in a lethargy of isolationism; Pearl Harbor would change that feeling virtually overnight.

Not many Americans were aware of the diplomatic negotiations that transpired between Japan and the United States. In reality, since the administration of Theodore Roosevelt (1901-1908), both nations had become colonial rivals in the Pacific. From Japan's intrusion into Korea during the late nineteenth century to the emergence of the United States as a colonial power after the Spanish-American War in 1898, Japan and the United States were on a collision course in the Pacific that would culminate at Pearl Harbor.

At the conclusion of World War I, the United States possessed colonial interests throughout the Pacific—the Philippines, Guam, Johnston, Wake, Midway and the Hawaiian Islands. During that war, Japan, as an allied nation, obtained former German colonies in the central Pacific—the Marshall and the Marianas Islands, but it was during the 1930s, when Japan began to acquire territory through military aggression, that the administration of President Franklin Roosevelt became concerned. In 1931, Japan acquired Manchuria by force, then annexed northern China in 1937, seeking expansion in order to become the dominant nation throughout the Far East. As an island nation, Japan was lacking the natural resources she needed to fuel her industrial and military complex that centered on the Imperial Navy. Sea power became important as the means by which Japan could support expansion, as well as protect her colonies and the lines of supply and communication.

Japanese naval theorists like Admiral Isoroku Yamamoto, the architect of the Pearl Harbor attack, were impressed by the publications of Admiral Alfred Thayer Mahan, who emphasized sea power relative to colonial expansion. Beginning in the 1930s, Japan started an aggressive program of naval expansion in defiance of the disarmament treaties of 1922 and 1930. The Japanese stressed the use of the torpedo in coordination with cruisers, destroyers and the all-important aircraft carrier. It would be Japan's carriers that would run unchallenged across the Pacific from Pearl Harbor until the Battle of Midway in June 1942.

For the students attending Punahou School, a private institution established in 1841, world events were of no major concern. John Bowles, then in the third grade, was more preoccupied with how his beloved St. Louis Cardinals were going to perform during the coming 1942 major league baseball season. Considering the addition of a young outfielder from Pennsylvania that Brooklyn fans would later refer to as "The Man," things were looking good. However, John's parents and grandparents, who had lived in Japan, were certainly aware that relations between Japan and the United States were precarious.

Malcolm Ing, a Chinese American, was driven to church that Sunday by his mother. When they arrived, they were informed of the Japanese attack. Ing figured initially that the navy was holding extra gunnery practice, but on a Sunday morning Ing recalls his father, a doctor, serving in the emergency room of a local hospital and returning home that evening smelling of disinfectant. For the next six months, the Ing family, like many others, would be glued to their radios awaiting news on the progress of the war. After a series of depressing reports, Ing remembers hearing in June 1942 the report of the victory at Midway.

Korean American Jackie Young was seven years old on the day of the attack. She was having breakfast when she observed people in panic pointing at the sky. Going outside, she could see smoke billowing from Pearl Harbor in the distance and heard the buzzing of planes. People were saying words she had never before heard—"attack" "war" and "Japs." For Young, the events she witnessed brought an abrupt end to her calm and predictable life. After December 7th, the threat of poisoned water, invasion and espionage dominated all conversation.

Like September 11th for the current young generation, Pearl Harbor became the foremost childhood memory for these Punahou students. Such was the case for Fred Hundhammer, Jr., the son of a Honolulu automobile salesman. He recalls sighting with toy weapons at some of the Japanese aircraft as they flew low over the tree house in his back yard en route to Pearl Harbor. Hundhammer's family would later express concern for the two Japanese maids they employed. Fear of an American backlash was foremost in their minds.

The aforementioned are just a brief sampling of the personal recollections that comprise this book. One will find similarities to the reactions of Americans regarding September 11th; just ordinary people from every walk of life who saw, heard, even smelled their lives undergo major changes overnight. After Pearl Harbor, blackouts were common across the United States; Americans of Japanese heritage were looked upon with disdain; the nation unified towards the defeat of a common enemy; world events came to the forefront; fear of a Japanese invasion of the United States mainland persisted and Americans of all ages asked the question, "What can I do?" This collection of memoirs will allow one to discern the reactions of elementary-school-aged youngsters to modern war and to see the role they and their families would play in the defeat of a common enemy. The common enemy, Japan, later to include Germany and Italy, unified the nation. Just as Admiral Yamamoto predicted, the "sleeping giant" had awakened.

—Ralph Ingram, Prof. of History, The Pacific & WWII, Texas State University, San Marcos, Texas

Our symbols of tranquility before December 1941—Diamond Head, Waikīkī, and coconut palms. (1950s postcard).

Punahou School

According to legend, an old Hawaiian couple lived in Mānoa and had to travel far for water. They prayed for a spring. In a dream, they were told to uproot the stump of an old hala tree. Doing as they were told, they uncovered a spring of clear, sweet water, which they named Ka Punahou, the New Spring. This spring feeds the Lily Pond that became the focal point of the Punahou campus.

Punahou School was founded in 1841 to provide quality education for the children of the Congregational missionaries. It is the oldest private school west of the Rocky Mountains.

Today, Punahou is a coeducational college preparatory school in Honolulu. Through the years increasing numbers of non-missionary children have attended Punahou. Currently the 3,700 students (Kindergarten through grade 12) reflect Hawai`i's ethnic, cultural and socioeconomic population.

Some of the original members of our class of '52 who entered Punahou in 1939 left the school to attend public and private schools in the Islands and on the Mainland; others joined the class. By 1952 our number had increased and about 180 diplomas were given out at graduation. Eighty-six stories from those who attended Punahou in the class of 1952 are included herein.

Old Hala tree symbolizing site of Punahou School (JBB, 1950).

The lily pond was and is the focal point of the Punahou campus (JBB, 1949).

Punahou Campus in "Lower Mānoa" (JBB, 1950).

Before, During, and After.

—John B. Bowles

Before 1941 most of us in the Hawaiian Islands lived relatively tranquil lives. We spent lots of time at the beach playing in the water, often at Waikīkī but frequently at our own family beach homes.

Much of our time was spent at the beach (JBB, 1950).

"Boat Day" was one of the big events and ships came in from all over the world. We often made our own leis to give to visitors, or we bought them leis downtown. Of course, we often bought leis where the ships docked and watched young boys dive for coins thrown by the passengers.

"Boat Day" was a major event in the 1930s and 40s (JBB, 1950).

Streetcars and trolley buses took us almost everywhere in the city. The eight-storied Aloha Tower was the tallest building in Honolulu. Otherwise the skyline was relatively unimpeded.

Sugar cane and pineapples dominated the agricultural scene in the Islands in the '30s and '40s. Sometimes we watched sugar cane being hauled to the mill in small trains, and other times we stopped to see the workers picking the pineapples for the cannery.

Watercress grew near Pearl City as it does today, and taro for poi (the local staple) was grown in many places.

In the 30s and 40s the only "short cut" across the Ko`olau Mountains that separated Honolulu from Kāne`ohe was a long narrow winding road over the Pali (precipice). There were no tunnels and some crossed by foot.

Pali lookout (Tai Sing Loo, Bishop Museum).

Pali road (Elias Shura, Bishop Museum).

Pali from the air, looking toward Honolulu (Hawai`i State Archives, 1924).

This relaxed atmosphere began to change in the late 1930s, however. Many of us have recollections of the incidents prior to the December 7, 1941, attack that disrupted the tranquility of our children's world and warned us of what was to come. Such was the case in 1939 when I was 6-years old and my family was returning to Honolulu after a summer on the Mainland. During the voyage, on September 1, 1939, Germany invaded Poland. On September 3rd, Britain and France declared war on Germany. While we were on the high seas, our ship, the *Empress of Canada*, which was of Canadian/British registry, was blacked out, and we had to zigzag in order to avoid German submarines.

Honolulu waterfront from the air. Aloha Tower, in the lower left, was the tallest building (JBB, 1949).

By the late 1930s and early 1940s the increase in defense workers and military personnel in Hawai`i was in full swing. Perhaps the most visible sign of things to come for us was the presence of the three carriers (*Lexington*, *Enterprize* & *Saratoga*) anchored off of Diamond Head. Mock air battles were on the increase and many of our fathers and brothers had joined the reserves or the National Guard. Others became block wardens or increased their first-aid skills in response to the calls by local newspapers and radio stations to "Be Prepared;" and some families even dug bomb shelters. There was, of course, an increase in military personnel; our families often entertained the young men (many being sons of Mainland friends or relatives) who had "joined up" as the threat of a world war increased. A few families even left the Islands prior to December 7th.

The *Lexington* & *Saratoga* anchored off Waikīkī prior to December 7, 1941 (Hawai`i State Archives).

Other events also affected our families. In early November 1941, for instance, my father, Dr. Herbert Bowles, was called aboard the Japanese ship *Taiyo Maru* that had docked in Honolulu Harbor to tend to a sick American

Taiyo Maru was the last Japanese ship to dock in Honolulu before December 7th (H.E. Bowles, 1933).

woman. Unknown to him at the time, two Japanese agents were on board to gather final data for the impending Japanese fleet movement and the attack on Pearl Harbor. One was a purser. When my father questioned the second, who was posing as a physician, and found that the "doctor" knew nothing about the condition of the patient, he realized that something was amiss but didn't know what it was until he read about it years later.

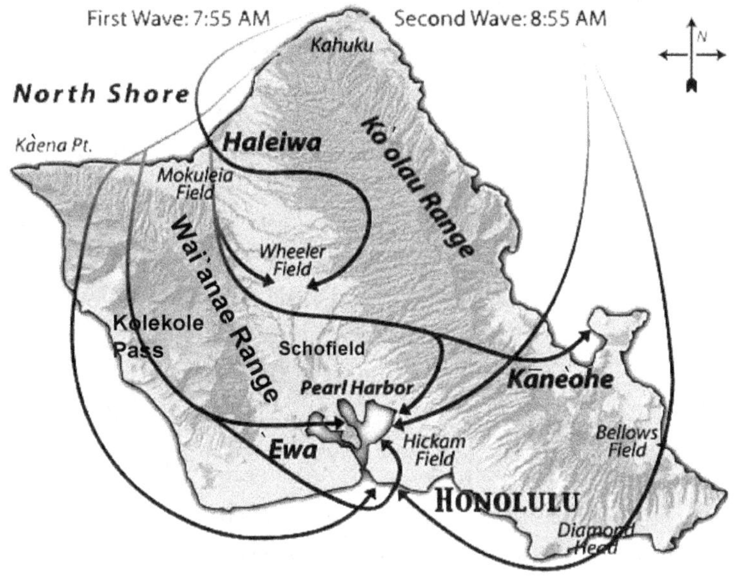

Approximate flight paths of attacking planes on December 7, 1941. (Drawn by J. Esquivel, 2003).

On December 7th, the first group of Japanese planes arrived over the North Shore of O`ahu about 7:55 AM and flew along the coastline toward Ka`ena Point (above). Some of the dive-bombers and the fighters split off at Haleiwa and hit Wheeler Field, then headed for either Pearl Harbor or crossed the Ko`olau Range to Kāne`ohe. The rest of the first wave crossed O`ahu near Mokuleia and headed along the Wai`anae Mountains toward Ewa and then to Pearl Harbor and nearby Hickam Field.

The second wave of attack planes came to O`ahu about 8:55 AM. Some of this group crossed the Ko`olau Mountains, near Kāne`ohe and headed for Pearl Harbor. Others hit Bellows Field, crossed the Ko`olau Mountains and swung westward over Diamond Head and Kaimukī to attack Hickam Field and Pearl Harbor. Long before mid-day, the Japanese planes were heading back to their carriers.

Most of us lived in the central and eastern parts of Honolulu (Mānoa Valley to Kaimukī) and probably had arisen by 8:00 AM or shortly thereafter. When we looked or went outside, we were greeted by billowing black smoke from the early Pearl Harbor strike and by some of the planes circling back for additional runs against the back drop of small black puffs from our anti-aircraft guns. Although some families undoubtedly listened regularly to the news on the radio, most did not; and of course we had no television. Many families eventually tuned in and heard Webley Edwards broadcasting news of the war. We also heard many rumors during and following the attack, including reports of saboteurs poisoning our water supplies and parachutists landing on the mountaintops.

The Pearl Harbor attack, of course, had an immediate impact on all our lives, for some real fear and for others a sense of bewilderment. Few of us were in the combat zones, but some of us had fathers or other family members who did experience the chaos of Pearl Harbor and vicinity. My father was called to Tripler "Army" Hospital. (An old rambling wooden structure located across from Ft. Shafter, it was officially called the 147th General throughout most of WWII.) That morning he parked at the entrance and found a confused Army doctor with no stethoscope wandering about the dead and wounded babbling something about having no way to tell whether they were alive or dead. "Open the shirt," my father said, "Put your head against the chest. If the heart is beating, you can hear it."

Tripler Hospital where some of our fathers spent December 7th and 8th (U.S. Army Museum of Hawai`i, 1934).

`Iolani Palace was headquarters for the military government of Hawai`i during martial law (Hawai`i State Archives).

"Oh, thank you, I never thought of that," was the reply.

In the hospital, there were wounded and dead along the corridors and everything was in confusion. My father's *Recollections of Pearl Harbor* reveals that he was asked to get to work right away in the operating room: to do what "we could for those patients we thought would live. We felt very badly leaving those too far-gone to do anything for. We had amputations, sucking wounds of the chest with lungs showing through, some had intestines hanging out. It was too gruesome to try to describe." Shortly after he began working, all the sterile gowns and gloves were used up, so "we worked stripped down to the waist." He went on to say, "About 3:00 AM of the 8th when we had taken care of the last case, we looked about us and saw a row of bullet holes about waist high right where we had been working. No one was hit."

Martial law, which was imposed immediately after the attack, authorized blackouts, curfews, regulation of food sales, gasoline rationing, mail and news censorship and it curtailed the rights of all Hawai`i residents. `Iolani Palace became the headquarters of the military government.

Under martial law, agents of the federal government began arresting suspects without having to establish any burden of proof. Many who were of Japanese descent had family whisked off by government agents suspicious of sabotage, especially if they were fisherman, priests, teachers, editors of Japanese language newspapers and even some holding responsible positions in the community. Many of the older Japanese continued to be detained and some were interned (imprisoned) on the mainland.

Many schools were closed and taken over as emergency hospitals. Punahou, on the other hand, was occupied by the Corps of Engineers just two hours after midnight of December 8th and remained so throughout the duration of the war. The campus was surrounded by barbed wire and was heavily guarded.

Punahou students resumed their studies in nearby homes and were later housed on the University of Hawai`i campus until the war was over. We reentered the Punahou campus with a symbolic walk together in the fall of 1945 when we started 6th grade in Rice Hall; I was in Mrs. Wriston's homeroom.

The Army Corps of Engineers occupied Punahou campus for the duration of the war (Punahou School Archive).

Punahou students frequently had "gas mask drills" when classes were held on the UH campus (Punahou School Archive).

Punahou was "reclaimed" in 1945 when we symbolically marched from the UH Campus to Rice Hall where we entered the 6th grade (JBB, 1952).

In the immediate aftermath of the December 7th attack on Pearl Harbor, most families expected either another attack or an occupying force. Rumors of parachutists or poisoning of our water supply, of course, continued. More bomb shelters were built and others fortified with food and necessities. We had regular air raid drills, and all were issued identification cards and gas masks. All paper money was stamped with "Hawai`i" in case of an invasion. This was used from 1942-1944. The few civilians with permission to drive at night had to have blackened headlights except for a tiny slit of light.

Of course, beaches were immediately closed off and strung with barbed wire. Everywhere there were signs to keep off the beaches, and we were constantly reminded to "Speak American." The Japanese language schools that existed in many neighborhoods were closed down; few were reopened until long after the war.

Many of us had airplane spotter guides and became quite good at instant recognition by silhouette. We also had playing cards with airplane silhouettes. Neighborhoods and schools had "Victory Gardens," and there were sewing circles where women and girls prepared clothing for wherever it was needed. Many men joined the services or enlisted in the local militia such as the Hawai`i Rifles. Because so many field workers shifted to defense jobs, many of the older school children helped out in the pineapple fields.

Once a year bases were opened and we had chances to climb into airplanes or board

Mrs. Wriston's 6th grade home room (Na Opio O Punahou 1946).

Barbed wire on the beach at Kawaihae, Hawai`i (Courtesy of E.M. Luhrs).

Hawai`i Rifles, a local militia formed in Hawi, Hawai`i (Courtesy of E.M. Luhrs).

Servicemen crowded into Honolulu Stadium (J.R. Reasoner, 1944).

Major league baseball players for the 7th Army Air Force team. Standing L-R: Sgt. Walter Judnich, formerly of the St. Louis Browns; Cpl. Mike McCormick, formerly of the Cincinnati Reds; & Sgt. Joseph P. DiMaggio, Jr. formerly of the New York Yankees. Kneeling are Sgt. Dario Lodigiani, formerly of the Chicago White Sox and Pfc. Gerald Priddy, formerly of the Washington Senators (Hawai`i State Archives).

some of the ships; Kolekole pass was opened for the day so we could drive over the middle of the Wai`anae Mountains.

Everywhere, of course, there were military camps and temporary structures set up. Whenever a military unit was on O`ahu for R&R or ships were in port, servicemen were everywhere, and downtown Honolulu got very crowded at times. There were even "dummy airfields" with plywood and canvas full-sized airplanes, intended to fool any future attack force.

We had great baseball in those days at Honolulu Stadium, including battles between the Navy team and the one from the 7th Army Air Force. Many big leaguers made appearances during the war years. The thrill of seeing Joe DiMaggio's 435-foot homerun that broke the Honolulu Stadium record is an indelible memory.

V-J day finally arrived on August 14, 1945. The signing of surrender on September 2nd triggered great celebrations in Honolulu and elsewhere. Little by little we returned to living without martial law. Nevertheless, the memories of those few moments when we were the ones under attack, when it was our lives that were disrupted by war, have lingered with us more than sixty years and hopefully made us more understanding and sensitive citizens of the world.

Note: The stories in this book are grouped according to where we lived on December 7, 1941. With the aid of the map (page 15) showing the approximate attack routes and the comments in the story, we hope the readers will be better able to understand what we saw and how we felt that Sunday morning. Accounts are accompanied by a high school graduation photograph and a short biography.

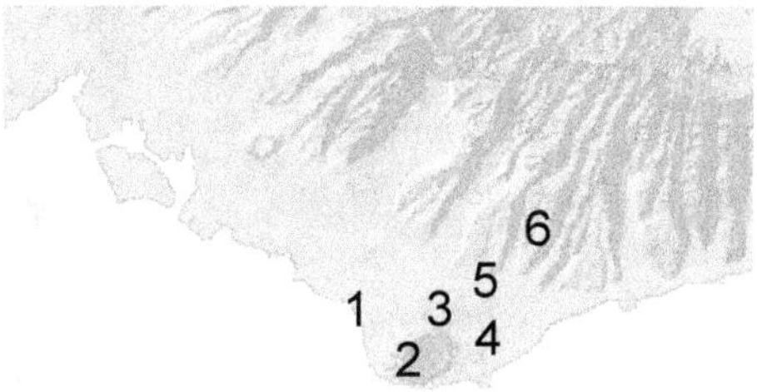

1. Waikīkī
2. Diamond Head
3. Kapahulu
4. Kāhala
5. Kaimukī
6. Maunalani Heights

Kaimukī

(To facilitate locating the observer we have arbitrarily divided Honolulu into two general regions: "Kaimukī" and "Mānoa.")

Jack Altman, Jr.—Kaimukī
John (Johnny) Bowles—Maunalani Heights
William (Bill) Bush—Maunalani Heights
Barbara (Bobbie) Carter Reed—Maunalani Heights
Clinton Ching—Kaimukī
Pauline Cordes Webster—Kapahulu
Faye Erwin Field—Diamond Head
Mariette Hiu Newcomb—Kaimukī
Harry Jefferson—Kāhala
Donald (Don) Joy—Kaimukī
Corinne Kong—Waikīkī
Lawrence Lee—Kaimukī
Carl (Linky) Lindquist—Maunalani Heights
& Rae Medley Lindquist (Mainland)
Richard H. (Dick) Ludewig—Kāhala
Rosalie Lyons Davis—Maunalani Heights
Wendell Marumoto—Kaimukī
Mike McCormack—Diamond Head
Jacqueline (Jacquie) Myatt Milikien—Maunalani Heights
Polly Pintler Digges—Kaimukī
Roberta (Bobbie) Purvis Murray—Diamond Head
Robert (Schoen) Shane—Waikīkī
Christopher (Kit) Smith—Kāhala

Recollections of Jack Altman, Jr.

Fresno State College; US Army, professional baseball player, business manager, part-time scout, and Humboldt State University administrator (thirty-six years) as well as a city councilman. Married 1962 to Beverly. Twins Jean and Jay (1965). Lived in Ferndale CA for thirty years. Now retired in Ashland, OR.

I was born in Queens Hospital, Honolulu. My father, Jack, Sr., grew up in Los Angeles and my mother, Jean, in Seattle. My parents first met in Honolulu after their arrival in the late 1920s. My father had come as a salesman to the military Post Exchange; my mother to attend a conference, but she never returned to Seattle. My brother Jim ('58) and sister Anajean ('54) also went to Punahou. My Punahou years: 1949-1952.

On December 7, 1941, we lived on Koko Head Avenue in Kaimukī. On that Sunday morning my father was on the Wai`alae Golf Course; my mother, my sister, my baby brother and I were home. We heard some explosions: my mother thought it was unusual for the military to be conducting target practice on Sunday. A little while later a telephone call informed her that the Japanese were attacking the Island.

I was playing in the garage with my cocker spaniel, Teddy, when my mother told me to stay inside because of the attack. I put on my toy helmet, got my toy gun and played soldier.

The story I recall from my father was that the golfers saw some planes flying over the course fairly low; they could see the rising sun emblems on the planes. Shortly after that someone came running and told them of the attack.

Early in 1942, we children convoyed with Mother to California on a British Cunard liner. Jacquie Myatt Milikien, who also lives now in Ashland, Oregon, tells me that she was on the same ship (see her story). My father joined us later in 1942, and we lived in Berkeley, California until returning to Honolulu in 1949.

Like several fathers, Jack's dad was playing golf on December 7, 1941, at the Wai`alae Golf Course (Hawai`i State Archives).

Recollections of John (Johnny) Bowles

I went to Earlham College (AB), the University of Washington (MS) and the University of Kansas (Ph.D.). Except for a short stint as assistant director of the Waikīkī Aquarium 1961-62, I taught biology for thirty years—Punahou 1959-61, William Penn College in Iowa 1963-67, and Central College in Iowa 1969-93. My research focused on small mammals and bats in Iowa and Yucatán, México. My wife Grace (Gay) and I have two sons and two daughters and five grandchildren. I retired in 1993 and we moved to Austin, Texas, so I could volunteer at Bat Conservation International. We now live in Greensboro, NC near our two daughters.

I was born in Karuizawa, Japan and came to Hawai`i on the* Taiyo Maru *from Tokyo in early 1936 with my parents and older sister. My father grew up in Japan but much of his education was in the US, with a medical internship in Hawai`i. His mother had gone to Japan in 1893 and his father in 1901; both were from Kansas.

My mother came from central New York and met my father in college in Indiana. They lived in Hawai`i in 1929-31, then moved to Japan for about five years. My grandparents remained in Japan until the fall of 1941 when they came to live next door to our home atop Maunalani Heights. My three siblings also went to Punahou—Helen ('47), Steve ('56), Ginny ('59).

Sunday, December 7, 1941, began early for my father (Herbert). He was an obstetrician at The Clinic (now Straub Clinic) but was on general duty that weekend. At about 2:00 a.m. of the 7th, he was called to Kapi`olani Hospital to deliver a baby. As was not uncommon, he saw U.S. troops with machine guns at various intersections, presumably watching for saboteurs. This morning, he was confronted by a soldier with a bayonet, and then told he could go on.

Shortly after he got home again, my father had a phone call from a woman in Kaimukī who was tired of being beaten up by her husband who had been "drunk for three weeks." When he had returned home from Kaimukī, it was time to get ready to head downtown to see his regular patients. On the way, he was to take Helen (whom we called "Honey") and me to Sunday school at the Church of the Crossroads. We had to go even though we rebelled at going on her birthday. Yes, that Sunday

We left Japan in early 1936 on the *Taiyo Maru* for Hawai`i because of the war buildup (H.E. Bowles, 1931).

was her twelfth birthday. My lucky younger siblings, Steve and Ginny, stayed home.

As we prepared to leave our home atop Maunalani Heights, we noticed Japanese planes flying in formation between Diamond Head and our house (see upper photo pg. 6). I vividly remember seeing the pilot and rear gunner in the closest plane of what I believe was a torpedo bomber ("Kate"). As we headed down the hill, we saw smoke billowing up from Pearl Harbor. At the top of Mikahala Way (part way down the hill), we asked a large Chinese man what was going on. "Sham-battle," I can still hear him say. (We didn't have a car radio in those days.) Along Harding Avenue, police kept trying to wave us off the road. After letting us off at the church, my father headed to Kapi`olani Hospital to begin his rounds, only to be told to head immediately to Tripler Hospital (near Fort Shafter). He was there until about 3:00 a.m. on the 8th when he returned home, much to our relief. He was driven home in an Army jeep.

Needless to say, our Sunday school was interrupted by the announcement that Pearl Harbor was under attack by Japanese planes. Along with the kids who lived nearby, Honey and I were herded up Mānoa Valley. On the way, in response to a droning sound and whistle overhead, my sister recalls that we were ordered to get facedown and flat. (I actually have no recollection of this incident.)

Eventually, we made our way to my aunt and uncle's house in Lower Mānoa. The only thing I recall during the next few hours was sneaking out into their yard and watching a dogfight overhead—we were all supposed to stay indoors. Late in the day, my grandfather appeared, having hitched a ride with a neighbor who had delivered meat to military bases that day for Armour Company. They drove us home and I'm sure our mother was much relieved!

I don't remember much of the rest of the day except that the Hind Clark Dairy deliveryman appeared with the ice cream for my sister's now-called-off birthday party and a comment that "life must go on." Of course, 8:00 p.m. curfew had been imposed and complete blackout was in effect that evening.

Some strong memories of the early war years:

➢Naturally school was called off, and we had to stay close to home. At that time, I attended the University of Hawai`i Teachers College Elementary School (TC). We shared bomb shelters with the Punahou kids on the University of Hawai`i front campus. I repeated 5th grade when I started at Punahou in Mrs. Wriston's homeroom.

➢We initially dug a small shelter under a mango tree in the garden but later joined a community shelter in a garage dug in the hillside and closed off by sandbags. The sound of the air raid alarm triggered a flurry of activity—first filling of the bathtub (in case of water poisoning) and then rushing to the community shelter.

This picture of Sarge Reasoner and the Bowles family was taken at their North Shore beach house and commemorates their friendship (J.R. Reasoner, 1944).

➢We always had to lug our gas masks around and made fancy knots with the strings on the cover.

➢Every year for several years we were fingerprinted and issued cards that had to be with us at all times. I still have mine from 1944.

➢A radar station was set up across the street from our house. I remember frequently walking through the camp unimpeded, playing football in the street with the soldiers and having two of them over for dinner every Thursday evening. A huge storage cave dug in the side of the mountain and a sunken bunker with slits in which to see out were left behind when the camp was closed down.

➢Right after the war began, beaches were blocked by barbed wire and riddled with machine gun nests; we could not go to our beach house at Sunset Beach on the North Shore for several months. One "nest" was set up at the base of a large ironwood tree in front of our neighbor and the crew came out every evening. When we were there, the soldiers posted guards to watch for their commanding officer and came over to play volleyball with us. We got to be good friends with the sergeant in charge, J. R. Reasoner. A couple of years ago, I made contact with him in New Jersey and he sent me some snapshots taken in 1944.

➢We frequently hitchhiked from our beach house to Niimi Store at the start of Pūpūkea Road near Waimea Bay. Occasionally, a convoy would come by and miraculously give us a ride—on occasion even in a tank or half-track.

➢Airplanes often flew along Sunset Beach; some dipped so low over the beach they were below eye-level as we watched from our yard.

➢On occasion, a Maunalani neighbor and I crawled through the barbed wire barrier on Waimānalo beach and watched the landing maneuvers. Sometimes we got to ride in a landing craft or one of the amphibious vehicles.

➢Neighborhood women and the group from the Quaker Meeting we attended formed "sewing circles" and prepared clothes to be sent wherever they were needed.

➢A dummy airfield was built across the highway from our Sunset Beach property. My brother and I often snuck over there. At least once we cut a hole in one of the wood and canvas B-25s, crawled inside and pretended to fly it.

During the war, Minnie Bowles joined a local sewing group to prepare clothing for anyone who needed it (JBB, early 1940s).

➢Because of our family connections with Japan and with local Japanese, we were well aware of the trauma that faced many families. My grandfather set out as soon as December 8th to visit as many Japanese families with interned members as he could. He and Grandmother devoted much of their time to helping families in the Japanese community in Hawai'i.

Looking back now, it is staggering to realize that we are among the youngest who can vividly recall at least some of the events of December 7th . As kids, we were lucky not to have been in the middle of the fighting. However, we were close enough to experience the horror and disruption of that day. Wars are tragedies for all concerned and we must never forget it.

Like many '52 classmates I attended Teacher's College Elementary School (JBB, 1992).

Recollections of William (Bill) Bush

My mother and her mother were both born in Hawai`i. There is no clear history of from where, or why my maternal great-grandmother came to Hawai`i. She was of Spanish ancestry. My mother's father was of Portuguese/Spanish and Scot/Irish ancestry. Again, there is no family record of why or when he came to the Islands.

On my dad's side, my grandparents left Kerriemuir, Scotland due to the harsh winters and poor economic climate and went in search of a better life. Grandpa Bush arrived in Hawai`i about 1911. In 1912, after finding work at one of the many sugar plantations employing Scots, he sent for his wife, my dad and his sister. The two oldest children stayed in Scotland with relatives for their K-12 schooling.

I married Sarah Ann Benjamin in 1955 and we adopted four children: Allan, Barbara, Katherine and James Donald. ("JD" was killed by a drunk driver in Brussels where he had been assigned to NATO headquarters.) I graduated from Oregon State University in 1957 and soon joined the Oregon State Parks' staff. In 1962 I became Chief Park Planner and later the Chief of Research and Long Range Planning for the Washington State Parks and Recreation Commission. I was appointed to the Lacey City Planning Commission in 1969 and the City Council in 1973 and was the first mayor under the newly approved Council/Manager form of government. I retired from politics in 1997. The City recognized my service and leadership by dedicating a park to me in 1999. I am a member and officer of St. Andrew's United Methodist Church. I am also an avid sail boater and motor home camper.

Before the war, we lived on Lurline Drive on Maunalani Heights. Our house was on one of the steep hillside lots with a sweeping view looking right down into Diamond Head and, off to the right, into Pearl Harbor. Sunday morning, December 7th found my family eating breakfast and getting ready to leave for church. The dining room window was on the Waikīkī (Diamond Head) side of the house, so we saw the Japanese planes flying in. What got our attention was the smoke from several small fires down by my grandmother's house and the high plumes of water sent up by what appeared to be bombs dropped in the ocean off Waikīkī. My dad was in the Army Reserve and was sure that something more was happening than had happened the previous day, so he turned on the radio. He was mobilized instantly and was instructed to report to his station. Soon huge plumes of smoke were rising from Pearl Harbor. We never got to church that day.

My aunt and uncle lived in Foster Gardens, right next to the mortuary, and I remember talk of the dead arriving by Army truckload. Fortunately, I didn't see any of that. Within a day or two, our basement was hung with blackout materials and a displaced military family had moved in. For a long time I had a bullet recovered from Hickam Field. I have no idea where I lost track of it. Because Dad had been mobilized, we soon learned that the rest of our family was to be evacuated to the Mainland. I remember the folks discussing where the family dependents should go and that the discussion soon expanded to other extended family members. Greeley, Colorado was chosen as the most secure site and we began making plans. Soon we had to pack everything we could take with us (several trunks and suitcases) and then we waited. We had to be ready to leave on several hours' notice, but for security purposes we had no idea of when that would be. Mom couldn't leave the house without someone minding the phone and sure enough, when she had gone to town and I had gone to get a haircut, the phone call came.

My Aunt Nora had to finish the last-minute packing and send the shipment off before Mom got home. The boat to which we were assigned was a luxury liner being sent to the Mainland to be converted to a military transport. Not too bad, you think. Well, it was overcrowded to the point where I bunked with a bunch of older boys (alone) in a stateroom while Mom and my two sisters (five and six years younger than I) were in a mass accommodation in a former lounge. We landed in San Francisco in mid-March, and after a night in a downtown hotel, we caught the train for Colorado. Mom had all she could do caring for my much younger sisters, so I pretty much had the run of the train. All were helpful and friendly when they learned why we were traveling.

One person on the train suggested to Mom that she would be much happier in Boulder than in Greeley and invited us to stay with her in Denver while Mom went forward and made a decision. Mom rented a big old three-story place on a huge lot with an alley behind it and a general practitioner doctor living next door. The only hitch was that the furnace burned anthracite (rock-hard) coal, which was delivered in one and two-man-sized chunks which required chopping and shoveling. An older boy was quickly found to take care of all this strange and physical stuff—ash, clinkers—all mysterious to us. It wasn't long before all but one of my aunts arrived with all their kids and after a short stay with us in our basement, found houses nearby to wait out the war years. We had my mom's mother and a girl-cousin of mine living permanently with us. Those were idyllic years: riding bikes all over the University of Colorado campus all summer, often sitting outside chemistry lab windows waiting for some apparatus to chip or partially break so the students would pass them out the window to a buddy and me, skiing and ice-skating in the winter and donuts and movies during the summer. In those days, Boulder was thirty-five miles from Denver and not on the main highway. It was a semi-closed community and a great and safe place to let a grade-schooler roam and I did.

We were on the boat returning home when President Roosevelt died, casting a gloom over the voyage. I set foot back in Hawai`i to severe culture shock.

The three-plus years away were critical in my growing up and self-awareness. I didn't speak or understand most of the Island colloquialisms; I didn't know how to play the games that Hawai`i kids played and was painfully shy and quickly bullied about it all. Because the year was partially over, I was enrolled in Lincoln Elementary (across from the Straub Clinic). In Boulder I had walked just four or five blocks to school. Now, suddenly I had to ride the crammed HRT (Honoulu Rapid Transit) buses (or trolleys) to McCully Street. It seemed to take hours to get home. Often bus after bus would pass us by because they would already be loaded. The next year, I repeated sixth grade and started at Punahou. By that time, Dad had moved us to Liloa Rise and once again I could walk to school. I never again really took to any sports, but after a rocky start at Punahou, I gradually settled in.

First streetcars, and later, the trolley buses (below) took us "to the end of the line," e.g. Waikīkī (Hawai`i State Archives) and Kaimukī (R.J. Baker, 1946, Bishop Museum).

Recollections of Barbara (Bobbie) Carter Reed

I was born in Honolulu in 1934. My father sailed to Hawai`i from San Francisco the day after he graduated from Stanford in 1931. He returned to California two years later to marry my mother, who taught at Punahou for almost thirty years. They lived happily in Hawai`i until my father's death in 1986.

I graduated from Stanford—in 1988 with my two sons—after "stopping out" to marry after my sophomore year back in 1954. It was a memorable experience, as was my marriage to Ron Reed in November, 2002. I have five children from my first marriage, and six grandchildren, one an adopted 6-year-old boy from Kazakhstan! Ron and I live in Kirkland, Washington where I am an Executive Secretary with the Bureau of Education & Research, the country's largest producer of seminars and educational products for teachers in grades one through twelve. Ron and I welcome any and all Punahou alums to visit us in the beautiful Pacific Northwest.

On Sunday morning December 7, 1941, I sat at the breakfast table with my mother, father, younger brother and sister, probably contemplating fresh pineapple and papaya, waffles with syrup or maybe French toast. Living with us was an "adopted" Japanese sixteen-year-old orphan named Shiko, who helped with meals and housekeeping chores. Shiko had been dating Bill, a sailor from Georgia based at Pearl Harbor, and on this Sunday morning she opened the door from the kitchen and said, "Excuse me, but Bill just called to say that the Japanese are bombing Pearl Harbor!"

Dad laughed and said, "Oh Shiko, Bill is just pulling your leg;" but then we listened, and we heard what was indeed the bombing of Pearl Harbor.

Sunday School was now out of the question, so I changed out of my good clothes and paid attention to what was happening. There were frantic phone calls; the radio was turned on, then off so that too much chaos would not upset the younger children. At seven, I was among the elderly and privy to much that was being planned. To distract us, Dad took us outside on the swing hung from the tall trees out front, but he gave that up when he saw a Japanese Zero make a ninety-degree turn over our yard and fly out over Diamond Head, apparently out of fuel.

Later the floors of our home were covered wall-to-wall with mattresses as neighborhoods were urged to consolidate for the sake of conserving electricity and sharing food provisions. We painted our windows black and turned off all but one or two of our lights at sundown so that no enemy planes would find us. Dad was later armed with a baseball bat and put in charge of protecting the reservoir at the top of our hill (Maunalani Heights) from the enemy that had supposedly landed and was poisoning the water systems. Eventually all of us except Dad were put onto the *SS Aquitania*, a converted hospital ship, to make a twenty-one-day zigzag trip to the mainland, where we stayed for almost the entire duration of the war.

I still have the letters Dad wrote to Mom while they were separated during those war years. My kids have read them—tearfully. This bit of history is thus very real to them. Dad's letters are a real gift that he couldn't have known would mean so much when he wrote them!

We returned to Hawai`i the same way we had left and when I was ten, the war ended as memorably as it had begun. We were spending a few days at Punalu`u and after listening for news on the radio all night, the entire family had gone hiking at Sacred Falls. On our return through the cane fields, we saw the workers hold up their fingers to signal "V for Victory!" In the days that followed it was great fun to catch the boxes of K-rations tossed by the soldiers as they were whisked to the ships that would take them home. Shiko eventually married Bill and they raised five daughters, the first one named after me!

Excerpt from a Punahou mom's diary... It was two o'clock on the 20th of February [1942] in Honolulu. I was resting after a particularly difficult day at school. The children were just rousing from their rests. I hoped they would be quietly congenial with one another for a while. But no, the phone. "Hello, Mrs. Carter? Are you ready to go to the mainland?" It had come, the call I had hoped I would never have to answer..."Take down the following information...Have your baggage for the hold on board this afternoon...you are allowed one bag apiece for the children and two for yourself...be on board tomorrow between 9 and 2. Say nothing to anyone about this as your life and the lives of others depend upon it." I sat down to breathe. What was this I was doing; why did I have to do it? Was I doing the right thing? I was leaving my husband and home to take our children to supposedly safer ports. I was doing it, directly because the Japanese had bombed Honolulu. Time will tell whether or not I was doing the right thing... in my heart I had known all along that the children were the ones to be considered, not Fred and me or our being together. The business of keeping our departure a secret was impossible...but I could not think of that now. The decision had been made. The whole city seemed to know a convoy was about to embark. Someone said, "one half of the city knew you were going, and the other was going too"...Was it worth it? Into the car and off to the pier...the wheels ground out the constant phrase of "damn the Japs, damn the Japs"...it was the first time that I had used the word "Jap." To me that expressed the worst...that day I thought the worst of them...I was not thinking of them as friends but as people who were bringing treachery and cruelty and frightful suffering to our very doors...now for the first time the 7th touched me...I didn't suffer pain from bombs, but now I was losing my husband, my home, my friends, for what? I was selfishly thinking only of what was happening to me. We joined the long lines of cars going onto the pier...got out and waited for Fred to park the car and come back...we waited... porters came and went but we stayed by the bags not letting them go yet, for when they went we went, too. A kindly voice said "You'd better go aboard, lady, they won't let him back." So there was to be no farewell. Perhaps better so.

Recollections of Clinton Ching

I had always been told by my parents that I was third generation from Canton, China, which suggests that my grandparents were born in China and emigrated to Hawai`i. Frankly, I know very little about my paternal grandparents. I believe Grandfather Ching lived in the Palama section of town and ran a little general merchandise store. I got to know my maternal grandparents slightly better, but they too died when I was very young. Grandfather Lum was a giant of a man and Grandmother Lum was an extremely tiny woman. Grandfather Lum ran a very successful store in Mānoa, and at one time was one of the major landowners in Mānoa Valley. In addition to raising rice and bananas, Grandfather Lum raised taro and manufactured poi. Much of the real property he acquired and owned during his lifetime is still held in the family corporation which carries the name Lum Yip Kee, and which is today run by my cousin, Tan Tek Lum—class of '53.

My father started his business career by fighting for his daily newspaper corner in the Kalihi-Pālama section of town. As a young man he found his way to Kansas State University and received his degree in agricultural chemistry. When he returned home he found a job with Pacific Chemical and Guano Company. Because of his pleasant personality and his ability to get along with almost everyone from the rice farmers on Kaua`i to the influential Dillingham family, he eventually gathered enough support in the Chinese community to help form the American Security Bank and he became its president. My mother came from a more sheltered and privileged background and was one of the early Asians to attend Punahou ('27). As a result of my mother's influence, all five of my brothers and my sister attended Punahou, thereby establishing some kind of local "Guinness record."

December 7, 1941, started like any other sunny day in Hawai`i. My brothers Norman and Franklin had risen early and the three of us were snacking on breakfast when we weren't fussing and fighting. I don't recall what my sister Jan was doing, but then she usually did her own thing. I remember going out to our front lawn with Franklin and goofing around outdoors. Since our house was on a little knoll in Kaimukī we had a sweeping view of Waikīkī, Honolulu Harbor, Pearl Harbor and beyond to Mākaha. About 8:00 a.m. there seemed to be a lot of noise and activity in the harbor area and the waters immediately outside of the harbor. We started to notice what looked like explosions and water spouts in and around the harbors. There was also an unusual number of aircraft in the skies. We soon

I graduated from Harvard College in 1956; then spent six months active duty at Ft. Sill, Oklahoma as an artillery second lieutenant; that was followed by three years at Stanford Law School. Most of my career was spent in the general practice of business, corporate and real estate law. Prior to retirement, my practice focused on foreign investments. I retired from Damon Key Leong Kupchak Hastert at the end of 1999. My wife Alice and I have three children and one grandchild.

realized that the noise was that of numerous large explosions. My brother and I thought that it was some kind of military practice exercise, but that was soon dispelled when my mother received a telephone call from one of our uncles that Pearl Harbor was under attack by enemy forces. Just about that time a group of fighter planes flew low over our house. My brother and I did not realize the significance of those planes until much later. Two more planes flew low over our house, no more than 100 to 150 feet above our roof. I remember looking up at the plane on the left as it headed towards the harbor and I could see the face of the pilot smiling down at me. I waved to him, and in no time he was flying past the Ala Wai Golf Course. I looked back towards the mountains to see if any other planes were headed our way, but my childish thoughts were sharply interrupted by my mother screaming for us to come into the house "immediately." She told us about the telephone call from Uncle, who told us to turn on our radio so we could get information about the situation.

Mother was especially stressed that morning because Dad had been on Kaua`i for the last few days and was scheduled to return to Honolulu on Sunday at mid-morning. She had not heard from him all morning, so the news of an enemy attack was particularly distressing. He was to come by inter-island freighter and would arrive via Honolulu Harbor. Aside from having to cope with three wild boys on her own, Mom was eight-and-a-half months pregnant with my fourth brother, Wallace, so it was not a particularly pleasant Sunday morning for her.

We boys, recognizing the seriousness of the situation, tried to behave ourselves and spoke in hushed voices. We turned on the radio and heard the announcer repeatedly say, "This is an emergency...we are under attack...get under cover immediately..." There was a genuine sense of urgency in his voice. The more he repeated his announcements the more excited he seemed to get. Not really understanding the command to "get under cover," my brothers and I sat under our living room table, which was about the size of two card tables. Many years later, I would realize how foolishly ineffectual our actions had been, but I was about seven years old and somehow could sense serious problems and dangers and, with my brothers, I made every effort to be a "good" boy.

By noon it seemed the attack had either let up or ceased. The big question for everyone was, "What's next?" Mom continued to busy herself with whatever mothers do in times of danger and crisis. I would peek out the front door to see if Dad had come home, but it was two o'clock in the afternoon before he came walking up the front lanai steps wearing his agricultural field leggings and an exhausted look on his face. Mom was greatly relieved, as were we kids. We gathered around Dad as he put down his dirty field bag and took off his leggings. He told us that the ship behind his had been strafed and bombed. He saw another ship bombed and he thought that it had sunk. For some reason his ship had not been attacked, for which we were all more than grateful.

The *Hawaiian Citizen* was one of the many ships that hauled goods to different ports in Hawai`i in the 1940s (JBB, 1947).

The weeks that followed were probably more stressful than the day of the attack. Rumors ran rampant throughout the city. There were stories of sabotage, enemy landings on the beaches, enemy spies and agents poisoning the city water supply, mysterious blinking lights at night, two-man submarines preparing to destroy military installations, and most troubling of all, the rumor that the enemy was preparing to invade the Islands. Each of us spent untold restless hours wrestling with moral and philosophical questions: "What will I do if faced by armed invaders? What can we do under those circumstances? How will I react to a cruel enemy? Will I be able to escape? Will I be able to protect my family?"

Because my father worked for the fertilizer company and it was considered an essential chemical wartime industry, he and his fellow workers were required to "guard" the fertilizer plant and facilities. They were given no arms or equipment for that task. The result was that most of the men took whatever arms and munitions they personally owned; those that did not own guns took baseball bats, machetes, slingshots and whatever other contrivances they thought would give them a measure of safety or defense. Dad would tell us he was actually more afraid of his fellow workers than he was of the enemy. It was a scary time, and the fright element escalated with the setting of the sun. Oftentimes, Dad would tell us they would hear noises at night and before anyone could ask, "Who's there?" a dozen gunshots would pierce the night. It was never clear what they were shooting at. Dad would say it was best to duck your head until everything quieted down. Of course, the next morning there were three or four dead cats around the perimeter of the plant.

While Dad was on patrol at the fertilizer company at night, our family stayed at Uncle H.P. Choy's house for the first three or four weeks following the attack. We would all crowd around the short wave radio until midnight each night listening to the police dispatches. The police had the unenviable task of tracking down every report of suspicious activity, especially those involving blinking lights. Block wardens made sure that no lights of any sort could be seen coming from any residence. Most automobiles were prohibited from traveling at night and those that did could be assumed to be on official business. Initially, all vehicles had to travel at night without lights of any sort.

Eventually, it became evident that there would be no further attacks. Of greater relief was the realization that our beloved Islands would not be invaded. But the threat always existed. Indeed, Dad was able to make arrangements for our family to leave the Islands and to locate to California if the situation called for it. Each American victory in the Pacific reduced the urgency of that contingency and after the Battle of the Coral Sea, our home in the middle of the Pacific Ocean seemed more secure. Yet, I will always remember the attack on Pearl Harbor on December 7, 1941, not only because of how it affected us in Hawai`i, but because it represents the only time American soil was under direct military attack, and because it forced us to face the horrible consequences of war on a civilian population.

In those years, bananas were grown in Upper Mānoa Valley (JBB, 1953).

Recollections of Pauline Cordes Webster

I graduated from the University of Oregon with a B.S. in Speech Correction. I earned my elementary teaching credential from Humboldt State University in California and spent thirty-two-and-a-half years as an educator in the State of California.

My paternal Grandfather was Gustave Cordes from Bremen, Germany. When he was fifteen, his parents put him on a ship as a cabin boy to keep him out of the wars. Two years later he landed in Honolulu. To him it was "paradise" and he jumped ship! At that time there was a tight-knit group of German nationals in Hawai`i who took care of their own. Under their guidance he became a policeman and eventually worked his way up to the rank of captain in the Honolulu police force before going into business for himself. At the age of thirty he married a Hawaiian lady, Mary Ann Ulili, who was from Maui. They had eight children–four girls and four boys. My father, Theodore Abraham Cordes, was the youngest boy.

When the Hawaiian Revolution started people took sides. Because he was from Germany, my grandfather sided with the Monarchy. He even joined their army. After they lost the "war," people who had supported the Monarchy thought it best to leave Honolulu for their own safety. Our family moved to the Nanakuli area, where they homesteaded a farm. There were very few people living in the area at the time. In fact my father remembered that until he was nine years old, there was only his family and a Japanese man who lived by the bay. There were no schools nearby and Father was sent as a boarding student to Kamehameha School when he was nine. At that time he spoke only German and Hawaiian. English was the only language allowed at school and Father quickly learned that language. He was 21 when he graduated from Kamehameha School in 1931 and apprenticed as a civil engineer–in those days you didn't have to go to college to be an engineer or a lawyer. He started with the City and County of Honolulu with the crew that surveyed the Ala Moana Park when it was a swamp and the Ala Moana Shopping area when it was scrub brush, kiawe *(mesquite) trees and coral. When Pearl Harbor was attacked on December 7, 1941, Father was a member of the U.S. Army Corps of Engineers.*

My maternal great-grandfather's last name was Ng. He came to Hawai`i from a little village in the province of Canton, China. He was employed as a cook for a Mr. Baldwin, who owned at least two sugar plantations. With Mr. Baldwin's help, my great-grandfather was eventually able to bring his wife to the Islands. They had five boys and two girls. Mr. Baldwin was a great believer in education. The two girls went to Maui Seminary for girls and became teachers. The boys went to Maui public schools, where the family name was changed. The American teachers found it difficult to pronounce Ng, so they named my grandfather Carl Ontai, which in Chinese means Carl, the oldest son. When his brother came along, they named him Albert Ontai and the name stuck. The boys eventually graduated from Kamehameha School, despite the fact that they had no Hawaiian blood. (I suspect the fact that there was a Mr. Baldwin on the school's board of trustees had something to do with it.)

Grandfather Carl married Ida Forsyth Metcalf. I have been told that her parents were both in King Kalakaua's court and were so busy moving from island to island with the king that my grandmother was raised by her maternal grandmother, Rebecca Forsyth.

My mother, Eva Metcalf Ontai, went to school at Sacred Heart Academy in Kaimukī and worked as a nurse for several years before marrying my father.

December 7, 1941: Mother was learning to drive. After church at St. Augustine's in Waikīkī, Dad let her practice driving back home to Kapahulu. Mother, Dad and I stopped at the store to buy milk; the Japanese owner was acting so different and strange. "We are being attacked," he said in a peculiar voice. He wouldn't say anymore or answer any questions, so unlike him.

We turned on the radio at home "This is the Real McCoy. This is the Real McCoy! If you work for the Federal Government, report immediately to your place of work." Because Dad worked for the US Corp of Engineers, he got ready to leave.

I was out on the street with the other kids watching the airplanes, we thought they were practicing; we could see ones with bulls eyes and ones with stars. We were jumping up and down and cheering on the "American" Planes—rooting for our guys in the practice game. They were weaving in and out, buzzing around. It was so pretty, big splashes in the Ocean, water rising up like geysers. All of a sudden there was a big explosion down the street toward the beach. We started to run down to see what was going on but stopped because of the noise and flames.

Dad had to go to his office, a Quonset at Hickam Field, and did not want to leave his wife and only child alone. He dropped us off with his older sister who lived on `Ālewa Heights. When we arrived, Dad's third sister was already there. Dad left three women and eleven children staring down at Pearl Harbor and Hickam—at planes, explosions, smoke and fire. The eldest of my ten cousins was a student at the University of Hawai`i and in ROTC. He was called immediately and sent to the Army, where he was made a lieutenant. He patrolled the streets with his buddies. They carried wooden practice rifles because there were no real guns. They hoped their wooden rifles would look real.

After two days, we ran out of food. That evening the eldest cousin came by the house. He took the second eldest, my fourteen-year-old cousin, into the night and broke into a store. For an interminable length of time, we ate bread and jam. No word from Dad, since after church on Sunday.

The gas tanks at the harbor burned brightly for a week; flames lit up the sky. Authorities enforced a total blackout, but we could read by the light of the fires. We still did not know where Dad was. We had heard nothing from or about him for a week. It was the longest week, but he came back.. Then we learned that he had gone to his office at Hickam Air Force Base, which was in a building attached to an airplane hanger. He said that his office had been bombed to rubble. Had this been a weekday, he probably would be dead. He was sent then to Fort Shafter. On his arrival there, he was told to take off his shirt instantly;

it was the same color as the shirts of the Japanese pilots. He was given a shirt of a different color.

He worked continuously until he had burned all the records; it took a week.

Dad was put in charge of base yard 5, the site of the present McKinley High School athletic field. This base yard supplied all the building materials for the Pacific Basin. As a perk, Dad had no rationing of gasoline, but where can you go on an island? Even worse, you could only drive at night with a narrow slit of light from the headlights, and all surrounding homes were blacked out. If any light showed, soldiers on patrol were authorized to shoot at it—which happened to our neighbor across the street.

All civilian and most military vehicles were required to have the headlights covered except for a small slit that allowed enough light for the driver to see the road. A small hood projected above the slit (Hawai`i State Archives).

Recollections of Faye Erwin Field

I went to Stanford, wonderful place, for two years then transferred to the Art Center School of Design and married my Stanford sweetheart. We have four children. After many adventures in Europe, we were in Los Angeles for a year, went on a job in Montana and then on to Spain, Virginia and Costa Rica. Finally, by my sixtieth birthday my marriage was no longer functioning and I decided I wanted to come back to the Islands. So here I am on Maui, still healthy, swimming in the ocean every day, and as happy as if I had good sense.

My father came to the Islands because there was no work for an artist in northern California in 1930. He got on a tramp steamer and came to Hawai'i hoping the depression hadn't hit the job market in the Islands. He did get a job in someone's print shop and eventually started working for Consolidated Amusement Company as artist in residence. He designed all the posters at the movie theaters (and painted all those movie stars in weird colors), working in a shop on Fort Street where Soot's father also worked. (Carl "Soot" Bredhoff's account appears in this book.) After I graduated from Punahou in 1952, he decided to work on his own and started painting on black velvet, something he had learned from his friend Edgar Leeteg, who lived in Tahiti.

My mother came over from Los Angeles about 1932, I think, and they met on the beach at Waikīkī. They married and I was born in Kapi'olani Maternity Hospital, the same place as my youngest daughter, Maile. My mother worked at the University of Hawai'i as a clinical psychologist for the Territory of Hawai'i until John Fox (Punahou's president 1944-1968) lured her in to the admissions office testing children for entrance to Punahou. Her office was in Pauahi Hall; she loved her job and stayed there until she retired.

On December 7, 1941, my family lived on the beach at Niu (between Diamond Head and Koko Head). My father was in Kāhala, I think, at someone's house, doing some artwork of some kind for a Red Cross benefit, probably painting signs of some sort. I remember that my mother phoned him repeatedly to come home because Webley Edwards had told us on the radio that the Japanese had bombed Pearl Harbor, and no one knew what was going to happen next. Further, the military was traveling all over the Island in their big trucks, setting up bases of some sort. My father said, "Aw, that's a bunch of baloney. Let me get my work done and don't bother me!" This action was repeated a number of times, and when whoever was with him told him he'd better quit and go home, he finally did. I don't recall what time it was, but I heard the adults saying later that his was one of the last civilian cars on the road. By the next day, machine gun "nests" were set up all around the perimeter of the island, one not too far from where we lived. Also, barbed wire was put up on the beach shortly after that: one row right at the edge of people's property, the next about halfway to the barrier reef and a third right at the edge of the reef where it dropped off and the deep water started. One of those machine gun nests is still visible about a mile from where I live on Maui, as well as bomb shelters where the plantation camps were located, not far from the Pu`unene Sugar Mill. My family stayed on O`ahu for the entire duration of the war.

Apparently, the military didn't figure out how to feed all the young soldiers that it sent out to guard the island where I lived; I think the neighbors helped. I know for sure that they supplied thermoses of coffee. Blackout was declared and all lights had to be turned off. People coped with this by putting black construction paper over windows so that light could not be seen from outside and thus we were able to carry on with our lives. My father, who was in his late 30s, went down to enlist as soon as possible and was told he was too old.

Pauahi Hall was one of the most distinctive buildings on the Punahou campus (JBB, 1952).

Visiting service men often brought their friends to our homes (J.R. Reasoner, 1944).

Recollections of Mariette Hiu Newcomb

I earned a BA in Music from Oberlin College, then a BA in Music Education from Oberlin Conservatory of Music in 1958. I married fellow student Tony Newcomb. After graduation, we lived and worked in Washington, D.C. raising four children, Hana, Lani, Anna, and Charles. We are now vegetable farmers in Virginia outside of Washington. Tony died in 1984. Our farm, Potomac Vegetable Farms, is certified organic and sells vegetables, cut flowers, herbs, and eggs through our roadside stand, farmers' markets, a subscription program and a few restaurants.

My mother's parents came to Hawai`i from Chungshan District of Kwangtung Province, China in late 1880s. Her grandfather recruited young men to work as contract laborers on Kaua`i. Her father came as a teenager and was placed by his father in the home of the plantation manager as a houseboy where he learned western ways. He became a valuable employee. A few years later, he was called back to China to marry my grandmother, who had bound feet and had been raised to lead a privileged life. Unlike other young brides, she refused to be left behind and accompanied her husband back to Hanalei, Kaua`i.

The plantation manager provided them with a house that straddled the Hanalei River down by the old iron bridge, which still exists. My grandfather became the person who took the plantation's rice on a barge to Honolulu. He also served as a liaison with the Chinese workers, writing letters and sending their money home to China for them. He and my grandmother, who raised six sons and six daughters, also served and sold lunches to cowboys who worked on ranches in nearby Princeville.

When California started raising rice and the market for locally grown rice declined, my grandfather moved his family to Honolulu and built a small grocery store on Liliha Street near King Street. It was at that store that I remember my grandfather AuHoy and where my earliest memories of aunts and uncles began. Less is known of my father's family who came from Macao in the late 1880's to Kona, Hawai`i. My grandfather, too asthmatic to work in the fields, worked as a tailor. I didn't know either of those grandparents.

My mother, Hana AuHoy, and father, Francis Hiu, met and married in Honolulu, built their house on Sierra Drive, less than a block up the hill from Wai`alae Avenue, Kaimukī. We had a great view of the city from our large diningroom window.

Early Sunday morning, December 7, 1941, our whole family drove downtown to drop off my father at his accounting office. We then stopped off at the Honolulu Advertiser building to see Santa Claus. (I don't understand why he was seeing children and hearing their Christmas wish lists at 8 am Sunday morning—was it an Advertiser promotional?) As we were waiting in line, we were told there was an explosion behind the building and to get out and get on home. My mother piled us five children into the car, and we raced home, wondering if those puffs of black smoke in the sky weren't the aerial dogfight practices we had often seen before.

From our dining room window, we could see the flames and huge clouds of black smoke in the direction of Pearl Harbor. We heard on the radio that we were being attacked and that some incendiary bombs had been dropped in the city. That night we were told to observe total blackout; we even had to put a blanket over the old cabinet radio to block out the lighted dial.

Recollections of Harry Jefferson

My arrival in Hawai`i was a planned and blessed event. On a dark winter's night in the early '30s, a very large stork swept down on Queen's Hospital and presented my mother with a twenty-two inch long, nine-and-a-half pound baby boy. She didn't get to choose.

My father, of German and English decent, was the son of a seafaring captain who decided Hawai`i was to be home about the time Robert Louis Stevenson and Mark Twain were visiting. Father was born five years prior to the last millennium. He was actually born William Henry Jefferson and not Harry Dayton Jefferson. The hospital mixed up the twins. He also sailed the "Seven Seas," and was a commander in the Matson fleet in his early 30s and settled working for James Dole, way back when, as an electrical engineer. He retired after forty-five years of picking pineapples.

My mother was an Irish lass. She was from the town of Waterford, Ireland, of the Power clan. I said she was an Irish lass except for the fact that Waterford's original settlers were French. She was a good and loving mother, a traditional '30s and '40s stay at home mom.

My parents were quite different. My father was very Prussian; actually a cross between the Kaiser and Johnny Bull. He spoke engineering. My mother had a great sense of humor. She shared the "Irish Tragedy." She is the only member of her family that survived all the famines.

For me, growing up in Hawai`i, compared to what I know now, was informal but structured. It was still that period of American life and culture where everyone knew each other and their place, and everyone went barefoot. Going to Punahou for twelve years did make an impression; it was my life. Most remembered are the teachers and classmates. The most impressive teacher: Mrs. Townsend. I had her for American history, science, physics and yes, Bible study. Sociologists say the best friends you will ever make are during the grammar and high school years. This is pronounced and grows through the Punahou experience.

As a youngster growing up in Hawai`i, I found the war to be a world away in places I had never seen. Places with names like England, France, Dunkirk, Germany, Poland, Russia, Manchuria, China, Indonesia and Japan. These were places on our school maps. During the early years, 1939-1941 The Eyes and Ears of the World *was our visual connection to the world and the war...only if you went to the movies. Who was this character that looked like Charlie Chaplin; they called him Hitler? Who was Mussolini, the guy with the big chin? Who was Tojo? He had thick glasses. We were soon to find out.*

The European and Asiatic wars were discussed and debated in living and dining rooms amongst the adults. We children just listened. The big question raised over and over was: when would the United States enter the war? We

After six hard years of study and fun I did end up with BA and BS degrees from UCLA. I served my country for eight years in the Submarine Force, active and reserve duty, and am Submarine Qualified. My income years were devoted to engineering, industrial and resort development. My favorite projects were Boeing, Mauna Kea Beach Hotel and the Lodge at Koele, Lana`i. Presently, I am a struggling inventor with twenty-eight patents and no market product to date. The best thing that has happened to me long-term is marrying my wife, Gay, and having three sons—Peter, Stephen and Timothy and a granddaughter, Malia.

had already saved the world once and that man Roosevelt was trying to get us into another war. Let "them" fight their own wars. We were insular, out in the middle of the Pacific…too far away to get hurt. Little did we know.

The irony was we knew through our parents that the war was coming. When and where? The military in Hawai`i had high stakes with Pearl Harbor, Hickam, Wheeler, and Kāne`ohe. The brass here knew there would be a strike at Hawai`i by the Japanese. After all they could not have been too far off as our Naval Intelligence had broken the Japanese secret codes. They were convinced the Japanese would strike the military bases and follow up with an invasion. When?

Hawai`i was America's gateway to the Pacific and the shared home of the Pacific Fleet, San Diego being the other. Hawai`i was also Japan's gateway to the United States through California, Oregon and Washington. They could almost walk to Alaska from Japan. In early 1941, Military action in Hawai`i was visibly on the increase. The top military advisers "suggested" that the civilian population be prepared. By the summer of 1941, our family, along with others, had stockpiled a storeroom with non-perishables. By November, we had a bomb shelter fully provisioned in the backyard of our Kāhala home. The military encouraged stockpiling. They needed the warehouse space, and further could not guarantee food shipments when the war came.

Thanksgiving came and went. Now what? The count down was on. Will it or will it not happen? We did not have long to wait.

Sunday morning, December 7, 1941, was a bright and sunny morning like any other Sunday morning. The family gathered at the breakfast nook about 7:30 for juice, fruit, eggs any style, bacon, toast, home made cinnamon rolls, and a large glass of Hind Clarke milk…you had to shake the bottle.

Within a few minutes a rumbling started, punctuated by muffled explosions. It was about 7:50. My father's immediate reaction was "the gas company is blowing up." He was an engineer for Hawaiian Pineapple Company (Dole) and had always feared their next door neighbor, the gas company, Gaspro, would explode and take the cannery with it. He left the breakfast nook to another room to make a phone call. He returned in a few minutes not looking well. He whispered something to my mother who immediately did not look well also. We finished our breakfast in near silence, none of us daring to ask the question.

Workers at the Dole cannery prepare pineapples for processing (Hawai`i State Archives).

That breakfast made such an impression on me that 60 years later I can still remember what the eggs looked like. I can still see my father sprinkling *Ajino-*

moto (a Japanese flavoring consisting mainly of monosodium glutamate) on his sunny side up eggs with the little ivory spoon that came in the can.

After breakfast my father immediately went to the big RCA radio in the living room. It had a green magic eye so you could tell when it was tuned properly. The green eye would fluctuate like a cat's eye but more quickly. It held your attention. It also had short wave, police and military bands/frequencies. He switched it on and soon the green eye glowed. He turned from station to station, band to band. First KGU, KGMB, the police, the military and short wave. He said I could go and play in the yard, but not to leave it. He had never said this before. I would have asked why, but from the tone of his voice, I knew not to ask.

Out I went just in time to see the 155-mm Long Tom cannons going down Kāhala Avenue. This was a normal Sunday event. Fort Ruger was about a mile away and was the home of the Army's heavy artillery. They would tow the cannons to Bellows with tractors, set them up and have target practice out into the Pacific. My early Sunday morning routine was to wave at the soldiers as they went by and they would wave back. This Sunday they did not wave back. The cannons had camouflage nets on them and the soldiers had rifles. They wore helmets and blue denim fatigue uniforms.

I ran into the house and said "Daddy, Daddy, something is wrong, the soldiers are not waving back." He looked away from the radio and stoically said, "Son, we are at war with the Japanese. They are bombing all our military bases." He was glued to the radio shifting bands to get new information. I listened for a while. It was a madhouse. No one knew what the hell was going on. There were police and military reports of paratroopers landing on the hills, only to be canceled when the reports came back that they were white bed sheets drying on clothes lines.

The governor of Hawai`i came on the radio literally crying and announced that Hawai`i was under attack and that Martial Law had been declared, that Constitutional Law was no longer the law of the land and to heed instructions from the military.

My father suggested that I play in the yard, but again said not to leave it. This time I understood why. Just then one of our B-17s, part of the squadron flying in from California, flew over our house headed to Maui or Hawai`i to land. Hickam had been destroyed and they had only enough fuel to make it to one of the neighbor Islands. It was flying at about 1,000 feet with two silver Japanese planes on its tail. They had big red circles on the wings. I could see the yellow flame bursts from the Japanese guns and the return fire of the B-17s' tail gunner. I could actually see the 50-caliber shell casings glistening in the morning sun as they fell slowly toward earth. In a few seconds one of the Japanese planes burst into flame and crashed out in the ocean, beyond the reef, so to say. The other turned 180 degrees and went back towards Pearl Harbor. I have always wanted to find that downed plane. That was the only actual combat action I saw of WWII.

Within hours of the morning attack, the military started to put out instructions to the public by radio, KGU and KGMB. Stay in your house...do not use your car...no lights on after dusk...do not try to call the Mainland...civil law is canceled, you are now under martial law...the Japanese may be preparing another attack and preparing to invade...listen to your radio for further instructions. Martial law lasted the duration of the Second World War.

During the morning, our Japanese mama-san, who lived on old Farmers Road, walked to our house about a mile away to ask that we forgive her ancestors and prayed that we would not hold the attack against her. She cried the whole time. My father and mother calmed her down and reassured her. My father walked her to her house, telling her not to leave home, to take care of her family and not to come to work till he called her. He feared that the patrols of Army and National Guardsmen, who were patrolling the Kāhala streets, would shoot stray civilians, especially if they were Japanese. Roy Yamaguchi, her son, worked for my father at Hawaiian Pine (Hawaiian Pineapple Company). Mrs. Yamaguchi's eldest son was killed during the war. Unfortunately, he was in the Japanese army.

The rest of the day we all stayed close to home. I guess I played soldier or aviator with my toy guns and planes. My father broke out his rifle and pearl-handled Colt 45 pistol, just in case. His weapons were real. We did eat lunch, but I don't remember what we had. I do remember dinner. It was prepared early, as there was a declared blackout. We had dinner at the dining room table using two flashlights with blue lenses pointed toward the ceiling. I guess you could call them wartime candles. Our dinner was a cold salad of king crab caught and canned in Japan. We went to bed early and prayed at the side of our beds for a better tomorrow.

Postscript: The fear within the military was that when the Japanese invaded, the local Japanese, who were the majority population in Hawai`i, would welcome them to the detriment of the other citizens.

Within hours of the attack known leaders within the Japanese, German and Italian communities were detained on Sand Island. Comparatively few were relocated to camps on the Mainland. At least one of our classmate's fathers was detained and released.

The rest of my war remembrances are of daily life.

Recollections of Don Joy

Following my graduation from Punahou, I obtained a BS degree in chemistry in 1958. I married my wife Joan in 1957. After graduating from OSU, I had a series of jobs as a chemist, supervisor, senior engineer, and senior safeguards physical scientist in a variety of nuclear labs in New Mexico, Idaho, New York, Illinois and Pennsylvania, then spent twenty-one years with the Nuclear Regulatory Commission as senior safeguards physical scientist in Maryland. Linda, Kathy and David were born in Idaho. Upon retiring, my wife and I moved to South Carolina (near Myrtle Beach). I still do occasional consulting work.

My father was raised in Wisconsin and moved to California after graduating from Beloit College. My mother grew up in Iowa and California. They met in Southern California and were married there. Following their honeymoon in Hawai`i, my father managed to land a job in Honolulu as a chemist with Pacific Chemical & Fertilizer Company. My parents packed up and relocated to the Islands in the mid-1920s. I have an older sister, and our family lived in Mānoa Valley until I was five-and-a-half-years old. Then we moved to Kaimukī.

I was a Punahou second-grader at the time of the December 7, 1941, attack. On that morning, I had gotten up around 7 a.m., before anyone else in the family. Knowing that it would be awhile before breakfast, I decided to walk over to a neighborhood playground in Kaimukī about six blocks from our house. It was probably the first time that I had ever left our immediate neighborhood without asking or telling one of my parents where I was going. At about 8 a.m., I headed home. There was very little automobile traffic and very few, if any, other persons walking along my route.

As I was leisurely walking homeward, I saw some small black puffs in the sky from anti-aircraft gunfire. I don't recall for sure, but I believe that I also heard guns firing off in the distance. In any event, I recognized the black cloud puffs as being the result of military guns. However, I just assumed that there was some kind of military maneuvers taking place. I also saw two planes flying overhead at a relatively low altitude heading in the general direction of Pearl Harbor. I don't know to this day whether they were Japanese planes that had already attacked the Kāne`ohe Naval Air Station, or the two American fighter planes that made it off the ground from Bellows Field.

When I was just a few houses from our home, one of our neighbors saw me walking and came out to tell me that we were at war and that the radio was telling everyone to stay off the streets. I hurried on home to find my parents and sister listening to the radio. They were aware that I was not home and had been wondering where I was. They seemed relieved to see me, but my parents were too concerned about the war news to bawl me out for leaving without informing them.

Following the Japanese attack on Pearl Harbor and other parts of O`ahu, all schools were closed, I believe, until after January 1st. The Punahou campus was immediately taken over by the Army Corps of Engineers, so it was even longer before all Punahou students were back in school. Many of the Punahou first and second graders attended class in private homes. In my case, I resumed my schooling in late January (or perhaps it was February) in a private home on the beach in Kāhala, which accommodated one first grade and one second grade class. My memory is somewhat fuzzy as to who else was in that Kāhala second grade class, but I do remember that classmates Lawrence Lee (see his account) and Diane Trease Elzey (1934-2002) were also there. I think that most, or all of the others in that Kāhala class left Punahou before our Senior Academy days. From grades three to five, I was at the Teacher's College complex at the University of Hawai`i campus, as were all Punahou students from grades three through twelve. I was back at the Punahou campus, from the sixth grade until completing my senior year. I can still remember walking, one day in late May 1945, with the entire Punahou student body as we marched from Teacher's College to Punahou in a symbolic reclaiming of our campus.

As for the first few weeks after the December 7,1941, attack, life was somewhat different, to say the least. Like everyone else in Hawai`i, we had to cover our windows with blackout paper. My father was a civil defense block warden and he had to make periodic patrols around our block at night to look for blackout violations. I can remember my mother boiling water for drinking and cooking purposes for several days because rumors had it that the water supply had been poisoned. I also remember that everyone was required to be fingerprinted and was issued an identification card. And then, of course, there were the gas masks that all school children had to have with them when attending school for at least the first year of the war. I'm not sure when it was no longer mandatory to carry your gas mask.

Many families, schools and other groups had large "Victory Gardens" during the War (JBB, 1952).

Recollections of Corinne Kong

After college, I worked a year in Hartford, Connecticut and then returned home. I took a job at Pan American World Airways and stayed for twenty-nine and half years. Pan Am literally gave me the world as a playground and the opportunity for unlimited travel. I am now retired and a happy contented homebody.

My paternal grandparents arrived in Hawai`i around 1860 as Christian missionaries, accompanied by three of their four daughters. They had been trained at a Swiss Basel mission not far from Hong Kong to read and write Hakka *in Romanized script instead of Chinese characters. They were brought to Kohala under the auspices of the Hawaiian Board of Missions to organize the Chinese Congregational Church in Makapala, Kohala, and to help Christianize the Chinese plantation workers. This was brought about in large part by Frank Damon, whose wife was legendary among the local Chinese largely because she spoke* Hakka *not only fluently, but also beautifully. My grandparents remained in Makapala for several years, where my uncle and father were born, and then moved to Honolulu where they operated a "mom and pop" store on the corner of Kina`u and Pi`ikoi and later on Beretania Street near Pi`ikoi.*

My maternal grandfather left China at age fifteen and arrived in San Francisco after spending thirty-two days on a wood steamer with side-wheels. He unabashedly came to America because of its gold and wealth. He stayed in San Francisco for ten years, working first as a dishwasher and then as a houseboy, before moving to Portland and starting his own business. He became a highly successful merchant but went bankrupt in 1916-17, losing a vast fortune. He then relocated to Seattle where he ultimately regained his stature but only after again suffering several reversals. During an interview on August 22, 1924, for a published social document he commented: "...then English agent for big English hop company swindle me out of lots of money. This cause me to go bankrupt. He make lots of money out of me, but he come back from England on Titanic. *You know what happened to* Titanic. *This God's way to show me that he no good."*

My maternal grandmother was born in a silver mining camp somewhere along the California-Nevada state line in 1872. She was brought up in a San Francisco convent when she got separated from her parents or was kidnapped at the dock upon their departure back to China. My grandfather returned to San Francisco in 1893, seeking a bride. They married shortly thereafter and left for Portland.

On Sundays, my mother usually took my three-year-old sister and me to Sunday school while she attended church; or, if she had shopping to do, she would drop us off and come back for us. This Sunday, December 7th, she needed to shop. When we got to the church on Queen Emma Street around 7:30 a.m., we noticed that the doors were still locked and no one was about; but feeling certain that someone would be along shortly, she dropped us off and headed for Chinatown. In those days it was perfectly safe to do so. My sister Barbara and I waited on the front landing of the church for what seemed a very long time. I soon noticed activity in the street: people rushing around, speaking very animatedly, and in what seemed an ominous manner. I noticed black poofs in the sky and planes that did not seem friendly. In fact, they were shooting at each other. Sensing something was not right, I put my sister in the corner of the porch and stood in front of her, protecting her from I knew not what. Finally, my twelve-year-old cousin appeared…she had run over from St. Andrew's Cathedral and was very excited: she had heard there was a war! I remember asking her what a war was. Then she dashed off as quickly as she had arrived. Barbara and I continued to stand in the corner until my mother was able to make her way back to the church. She had got caught in the congestion resulting from a bomb being dropped in front of the Governor's Mansion. She was further distraught to hear that my cousin, who lived with us, had run off instead of staying with my sister and me. After awhile, my mother decided my cousin had found another ride home, so we left. The drive home was uneventful.

In those days we lived on the Ala Wai Canal near Lewers Street. Kūhio Avenue was still a dirt road with *kiawe* (mesquite) growing on both sides of the road. By the time we arrived home, all doctors had been called to report to the Mabel Smythe Auditorium for assignment. From there they were dispatched to various posts. My father was sent to Tripler Hospital where he remained for three days caring for the wounded and working around the clock. Years later he related that aside from the horrendous casualties, the most distressing part of the ordeal was the lack of medical supplies and how painful it was rationing what was in stock amongst the needy.

Blackout that first night was quite adventuresome yet boring as we camped out downstairs on the floor. We huddled in the dark around the radio, waiting for news, until we all drifted into slumber. Soon we would get used to that routine and even looked forward to listening to our favorite radio programs (*Lux Radio Theater*, *The Shadow* and *The Iron Door*, to name a few).

Days later, my mother found a piece of shrapnel (about seven inches long), which had lodged itself inside a window at the top of our stairs on the second floor. She called the authorities who came to pick it up; they later said we were the only ones in the neighborhood who had reported such an occurrence and they never returned our "souvenir."

After the initial attack, many requirements were imposed: blackouts, curfew, Civil Defense teams, food and gas rations, Territory of Hawai`i identification cards with our fingerprints (identification bracelets were optional), gas masks (heavy, cumbersome, hot and smelly), Victory Gardens (see note to right), air raid drills and bomb shelters. Since we lived across the street from the Ala Wai Canal, our shelter was dank and watery and the stench made me prefer risking my life on the outside.

I went with my mother to the Red Cross to help fold bandages. I was the youngest person to earn a veil and pin, which were awarded after working a required 100 hours…I still have them. It was also during the war that my mother taught me to knit. We would knit squares for blankets (and later socks) for the Red Cross; more experienced knitters made sweaters. In other relief work, we separated and saved tin foil from cigarette and gum wrappers to make huge, heavy balls and we saved rubber bands and the rubber string from inside golf balls. My father was the Block Captain for the Civil Defense. Life was busy!

Living in Waikīkī at the time meant we could no longer go to the beach and that was pretty sad since we were used to walking down Lewers Street to swim, play and climb the *hau* trees. To our dismay, there were huge coils of barbed wire all along the coastline. Not only was it restrictive, it was UGLY!!

Classmate Nani Robertson (1934-1991) and I had been playing "chase" in the **Victory Garden** across the street on Wilder…laughing, running and acting silly while everyone else was tending their radishes and carrots. Suddenly our teacher, Mr. Brown Watanabe (such an intimidating name!) loomed in front of us and sternly reprimanded us. Part of our punishment was to write, "I will not run in the garden" 500 times, which I dutifully performed that evening. To this day I do not run in any garden!

I think many of us grew up fast during those war years. I know I was constantly reminded that as the eldest child I would be responsible for my younger sisters should anything happen to my parents (which really wasn't true—we had lots of relatives.) At any rate, with all the suffering around the world, we were thankful our family was together and safe. Life was not unkind to us and God had taken care of us.

Recollections of Lawrence Lee

My dad came from China with a swim team and decided to stay. My mother, who was born in Honolulu, met and married my dad while attending Claremont College in California. They came back to Honolulu to raise a family of three boys and three girls and earned a living owning two shoe stores. My dad used to drive to his customers' homes to have them try on shoes and sell them the shoes they liked.

I went to the University of Hawai`i and Missouri Valley College in Marshall, Missouri, then on to dental school in Washington, DC. After a stint in the Air Force and internship at Brook Army Medical Center, San Antonio. I entered the Air Force and spent time in Washington, Japan, Thailand and Hawai`i, then on to Washington, DC, Germany and the former Soviet Union. I retired after twenty-seven active years. My wife and I have two daughters, a grandson and a granddaughter.

On December 7th, I was at Sunday school and out on the playground when I heard planes flying low overhead. Then I heard loud noises. When I got back home, my father was putting black paper on all the windows. He had already taken down the radio antenna. He had heard we were at war and a blackout was ordered. I don't remember much more about the war but remember my sister knitting "watch caps" for the sailors who had to patrol the far north seas. Also, when we were attending school on the UH campus, some of us were involved in "Victory Gardens."

Pineapple fields (top) in central O`ahu (JBB, 1952). Pineapples (bottom) ready to be harvested (JBB, 1952).

Recollections of Carl (Linky) Lindquist & Rae Dean Medley Lindquist

After Rae and I were married, I worked for a time as an aircraft mechanic, beginning a business career in 1958 when I was named Sales Manager for the Sen Steel Furniture Company. In 1959 I joined Trade Publishing Company, where I held a number of positions, eventually becoming the firm's president and majority stockholder. I left Trade in 1983 and established my own communications consulting business, and in 1984 was appointed General Manager of the Hotel Hana-Maui.

Rae first worked at Hawaiian Telephone Company, later joining me at Trade Publishing, where she was named Research Manager. She began her real estate career in 1967, joining classmate Mike McCormack as a sales person. She was later appointed to the position of Manager of the firm's Kailua office, and served in other executive capacities

Linky's Story:

My dad, Hank Lindquist, was a refrigeration and air conditioning engineer with the Union Ice Company in Los Angeles, where I was born. In 1936, he was "loaned" to Von Hamm Young Company, ostensibly for six weeks, to come to Hawai`i to oversee the installation of the first commercial refrigeration equipment in Chinatown. (It seems that while Von Hamm had sold the equipment, they didn't have anyone who knew how to put it in.) He sailed out of San Pedro on an Australian ship called the Aorangi, *and after several months sent my mother some money and told her to sell the furniture and get on the boat with my sister and me because, "this is it!" My mother was quite young, and the prospect of traveling to Hawai`i (which must have seemed like halfway around the world) with a four-year-old and a two-year-old was daunting to say the least, so she talked her kid brother Don, into going along to help baby sit. To make a long story short, he never went back to the Mainland either, first marrying a Hawaiian woman from Punalu`u, and later, after divorcing, marrying classmate Bob Nelson's mother, my Aunt Margaret. Being a working class haole (Caucasian) in Chinatown gave my dad a certain distinction, and up until just a few years ago I could still run into people in that area who remembered him by the nickname of "Ammonia Man."*

As I was growing up in the Kaimukī/Wilhelmina Rise area (Maunalani Heights), Sunday mornings always meant a trip to the bakery before church, and that's where my dad, sister and I were going on the morning of December 7th. My dad was the one who first noticed the huge billows of black smoke rising above Pearl Harbor, and at just about the same moment a couple of Japanese planes flew over our heads, so low that we could see the pilot's faces and the white scarves they were wearing. Hank was by then the manager of the air conditioning and refrigeration department of Von Hamm Young, and one of the projects they were involved in had to do with repairing the air conditioners on two submarines at Pearl Harbor. We raced home, picked up my mother and drove up to Alex and Yolanda McAngus' house on Wilhelmina Rise, where my dad deposited us while he took off for Pearl. It would be three days before we would see or hear from him, and my mother later told us that she thought sure he had been killed. I remember all of us kids taking shelter under the McAngus' pool table, and listening to the repetitive drone of Webley Edward's voice saying over and over, "We are under enemy attack, take cover, take cover. This is the real thing, we are under enemy attack, take cover, take cover." My mother also recalled hearing instructions not to resist if we were approached by enemy troops. For a seven-year-old, a good part of the whole episode seemed like an adventure, but even today, whenever they test the air raid sirens, my clearest memory is one of seeing my mother being very, very afraid.

Rae's Story:

At the outbreak of the second world war, my family and I lived in Fresno, California. Wanting to do his part for the war effort, my dad, Ray Medley volunteered as a civilian defense worker and was sent to Hawai`i early in 1942. He spent the duration of the war in the Islands, and as did many others, fell in love with Hawai`i, moving the family to Honolulu permanently on October 2, 1946.

Known then as "Rae Deane" I first attended Stevenson School, then transferred to Punahou at the beginning of my Sophomore year. It was there that I met Carl "Linky" Lindquist, who would later become my husband. We went together through high school, but following graduation, I enrolled at Fresno State, and after a brief stint at the University of Hawai`i, Carl joined the Air Force. Communication between us was sporadic, finally stopping altogether until Carl ended his Air Force career and returned to the islands in early 1957. The romance was rekindled. We were married in November of that year and had three children, Lynne, (deceased), Lars and Lacey, and have four grandchildren.

before leaving to become Education Director of the Hawai`i Association of Realtors in 1980. When we moved to Hana, Rae resumed her real estate career, becoming Principal Broker of Hana Land Company. I left the hotel in 1983, joining Rae in the firm we still own and operate, Hana Coast Realty. We also have a partnership in the Hana Coast Gallery, Hana's only art gallery.

Our love affair with Hana began on a camping trip to Maui with classmate Emmet "Temme" Cheeley's family in 1967. We bought a condominium there in 1970, then sold it to buy a home at Hamoa. We sold that to buy oceanfront property at Ula`ino, where we now reside. We have both been very active in the Hana community, and were involved with the establishment of Hale Hulu Mamo, Hana's first senior center. I was recently appointed to the Governor's Maui Advisory Committee. (both d. 2009)

Recollections of Richard H. (Dick) Ludewig

My father first came to Hawai`i in 1921 or 1922...shortly after graduating from U. of California, Berkeley. With a friend, he spent a few weeks in the Islands. He liked what he saw. He returned home to Richmond, CA. Then in 1924, he returned to Hawai`i to make it his home. So the lure of the Islands brought him there. On my mother's side of the family, we are native Hawaiian. She was born and reared in Hanalei, on Kaua`i. Through her mother's side of her family, she traced her lineage back to the matriarch of her family, Kawe Ka`u. Her father, Wm. E. H. Deverill, arrived in Hawai`i from England during the last quarter of the 1800s with his brother, Alfred. Legend has it they arrived bearing gifts from Victoria, for the child of Kamehameha III, I believe. They were destined to the Orient and on around the world. They got as far as Hawai`i. He married Sarah Benson Fredenberg of Kaua`i, and together, they took up residence in Hanalei, where they had six (6) children—one of whom was my mother, Annie Deverill. She and my father, Otto Ludewig, were married late in the 1920s–1929, I believe. I was born in August 1934, my sister in June 1938, and my brother in December 1941.

December 7, 1941, started as did most Sunday mornings in the Ludewig household. My sister and I got up early with our dad. It was customary for him to prepare Sunday morning breakfast—a treat to which I always looked forward.

The only one missing this morning was Mom, and she was at Kapi`olani Maternity Hospital, recovering after having given birth to my brother on December 5th. I recall the phone ringing on the lanai (porch) and Dad answering it. Then, I recall getting into the car with him and my sister, and driving from our Kāhala home, around Diamond Head and through Waikīkī, to his "office" in the Alexander Young Hotel building. The previous Friday afternoon, Dad had another office—W. A. Ramsey, Ltd. This Sunday morning, Dad went to the office of the U.S. Naval Reserve, where he was an Intelligence Officer. The following Monday, Dad was activated into the regular Navy, and offices at the Alexander Young Hotel would become his...and W. A. Ramsey would have to wait some three and a half years for his return. Something happened while we were there, and then we went home. And, that, dear friend, is all I remember about December 7, 1941. I was seven and a half years old at the time.

As I said before, my mother was in the hospital recovering after having given birth to my brother. A family legend, authenticated on many occasions by my mother, goes like this: A stray projectile or two—shells or bombs—found their way into Makiki, a neighborhood bordering on the area in which Kapi`olani Maternity Hospital was located. Mom told us that the explosions gave indication that something was amiss.

She went on to say that when she asked about the incident, the answers she got were vague and ill-defined. She became edgy. Soon, wounded began to arrive at this hospital, as they did at every hospital in the city. Mom became aware of this, and then became aware of the attack. As she told it, she got out of bed, went into the nursery, gathered up my brother and headed for the door. She was nabbed enroute and asked where she was going. She told the staff that she had two children and a husband at home, and that home was where she belonged. She didn't make it. She was firmly returned to her bed, and my brother returned to his crib in the nursery.

Later that day, as Mom told it, she again started toward the door, this time without my brother. She was at the last door out when again, she was nabbed and returned to her bed. Mom says she was given a serious shot of something that knocked her out for two days. Knowing my mother, and the determined woman that she was, I get amusing visions of what the scene must have been —a determined woman with newborn child heading for the door, vowing to go home to her waiting family "where she belonged!" Apparently, when she was stopped the first time with my brother in her arms, one of the nurses was so shocked that she fainted. A nurse, fainted dead away, sprawled on the floor of the hospital. Through the rest of her life, Mom told this story with great gusto and amusement

As did everyone else in Hawai`i at the time, I have a vague recollection of blackout curtains being installed throughout the house. I have an equally vague recollection of the sounding of warning sirens and blackout alerts. Very thrilling to a youngster. Also, I recall that very shortly after the attack, my parents had a bomb shelter dug in our back yard. It became a favorite play place and fort for my sister and me. It remained there throughout the War and was finally filled in after our return from California in 1945.

Immediately after the start of WWII, U.S. Naval Intelligence believed that there was a very good chance that the Japanese would reach the Hawaiian Islands. Naval officers stationed in Hawai`i were given the option of evacuating their families to the continental U.S (the Mainland), or keeping them in the Hawaiian Islands. My dad and mother decided it would be best if Mom took the three children to a temporary residence on the mainland, pending the end of the war.

It was during our ocean crossing to California that an amusing incident took place—again, one that became a family legend. In the spring of 1942—I believe it was in May—we sailed from Honolulu aboard the *Lusitania*, once a French luxury liner and now converted to troop carrier. Our destination was

San Pedro, California. We sailed unescorted, since the ship was considered very fast, and capable of running alone. However, throughout the voyage, she executed a regular course of zigs and zags—evasive maneuvers. Our cabin, in better days, had accommodated 2-3 passengers. It had been converted to accommodate troops in tightly stacked pipe berths. Fortunately, we did have our own bath. My brother, then only five months old, had his pram, in which he slept. Being only five months old, he was still being fed baby formula. In our cabin, my mother would regularly prepare his formula and stand the bottles upon a small table to cool before she would put them away in a cooler. And now, to the story.

One afternoon, while my brother slept in his pram, my mother prepared the supply of formula, and then stood the bottles in place on the table to cool. Shortly, the captain decided it was time to go from ZIG to ZAG. To complete the maneuver, the ship listed heavily to one side. And so began the early stages of road-racing afloat. My brother, in his pram, launched and accelerated across the deck. Enroute, the pram wheels hit an obstacle. It upended, depositing my brother, the mattress, a lump of blankets and a supply of diapers in a pile on the deck. At about the same time, over went the small table with its cargo of baby bottles filled with formula. What a mess!

Following the initial shock, Mom said that all ended well. Not all the bottles, or my brother, broke. A replacement supply of bottles appeared from somewhere on the ship. The voyage continued and ended well. And the story had life. It became family legend.

After our arrival in California, we took up residence in Palo Alto from late spring 1942 to late August 1945.

Sugar cane was grown in the same general area of central O`ahu as were pineapples (left). When the canes were mature the harvesting began with burning, sending white clouds of smoke into the skies (right, both photos JBB, 1952).

Recollections of Rosalie Lyons Davis
(1935-2001)

As told by her brother, Merlyn, on February 3, 2001:

I was ten years old and Rosalie was six. We had gone to the 8:00 a.m. Mass at St. Patrick's. I had often taken her to church. Services got out around 8:45 a.m. and we were on the morning bus. The bus would often get to the top of the hill (Maunalani Heights) ahead of schedule and wait. At that point some of the neighbors came out and told us that we were being attacked by Japan. This was the first we (Rosalie and I) knew of the events. Our parents were anxiously waiting for us. The bus pulled over a block above our house. From here the view to Pearl Harbor was unobstructed and we could see the fires and the largest cloud of smoke we kids had ever seen. We didn't know enough to be overly scared, but immediately knew that things were BAD.

This was the bus that had the Maunalani Heights run in 1941. It was driven by Mr. McGrew (H.E. Bowles, 1940).

Recollections of Wendell Marumoto

My schooling included Hanahau`oli (through 6 grades), Punahou, and the University of Chicago (BA '55 and JD '58). After law school, I practiced for a year in San Francisco, where a regular hangout was the Hungry I, at which the Kingston Trio then made their "home" (see Bob Shane's recollection). While there, I married Barbara, the mother of my children, who all attended Punahou. Barbara and I divorced, and I have been married to Dee for 23 years.

My paternal grandfather came to Hawai`i on November 14, 1888, aboard the* Takasago Maru, *the sixth of 26 boatloads of Japanese immigrants who totaled 29,069 between February 8, 1885, and June 15, 1894, most of whom were contract laborers for sugar plantations. As a contract laborer, he was given #5,140 and assigned to Pā`auhau Plantation, on the Hāmākua coast, where he worked for 6 years at $15/mo, subject to monthly deductions of $2.60 for 26 months to repay travel expenses, and $3.75 as compulsory savings towards his return passage, deposited with the Japanese consulate.

In 1895, Grandfather left Pā`auhau and went to work for a Japanese general store in Chinatown, Honolulu. He returned to Japan in 1899 to get married. While there, the Chinatown fire occurred January 21, 1900, and his employer asked him to return as quickly as possible to help rebuild the business. He did so, and the store was rebuilt in Kaka`ako, where my father was born in 1906. In 1907, someone from my grandfather's village in Japan was returning there and asked my grandfather if he would buy his store in Captain Cook, in South Kona, Hawai`i, for $700. My grandfather had such a sum saved, which was substantial for those days, considering plantation wages to be less than $200/yr. Although he had never been to Kona, he bought the store, sight unseen, and moved his family there. He became a successful storekeeper and his store is where I was raised for my first five years. Later I spent my summer vacations there until graduation from Punahou.

I have no information on when my maternal grandfather came to Hawai`i, but it would have been in the very early 1900s. He came as a merchant and established a hat store on Nu`uanu Ave., just makai *(toward the ocean) of Pauahi St. His family lived above the store, the rear of which abutted the back of the Hawai`i Theater. A hat store has been an anomaly for many years, but until we graduated, there were two on Nu`uanu within a block of each other, so there must have been a brisk business in them. In fact, when I worked for a law firm in San Francisco right after graduating from law school in 1958, I wore a felt hat to work daily, as did almost everyone.*

Chinatown is one of the older sections of Honolulu (JBB, 1954).

I have fond memories of pre-Pearl Harbor downtown Honolulu, of which my grandfather's store was a part. That block of Nu`uanu has not changed much in those sixty years, although its surrounding neighborhood has. On the *mauka* (towards the mountains) side of Pauahi St. between

Nu`uanu and Smith, there was a public bathhouse that I frequented when I spent an occasional night with my grandparents. A block *mauka* on the mauka-Diamond Head corner of Nu`uanu and Beretania was the long-standing S. M. Iida Store, which recently celebrated its hundredth anniversary at its signature location in Ala Moana Shopping Center. A lot of my childhood was spent in that neighborhood, which included the Princess Theater and several Japanese "department stores." One image of pre-Pearl Harbor downtown that Pearl Harbor erased forever was that Japanese ladies of my grandmother's generation wore kimonos in town. One of the first security edicts issued on December 7th was banning the wearing of such clothing in public. The military was concerned that spies for Japan could use the long sleeves that were a part of kimonos to transport documents!

Just *mauka* of Beretania on Nu`uanu, stood the mortuary operated by the father of Raymond "Rayno" Akana (Punahou '46). With a mother who was Hawai`i's first Territorial woman senator, and being the only high schooler to break 10 seconds for the 100-yard dash on the old Punahou dirt track, "Rayno" had many stories to tell. But the one most fascinating to me of pre-Pearl Harbor Honolulu is his father "stockpiling" caskets containing bodies of deceased Chinese, awaiting shipment to their homeland for burial!

Back to my early life. I was sent to live with my paternal grandfather and aunt, who ran a general store in Captain Cook, in South Kona, for almost all of my first five years. This had two results that I don't believe any other member of '52 experienced. First, I did not use a flushing toilet until I returned to Honolulu. Upland Kona had no public water system until the late 1950s, and everyone's water source was a private catchment system, so flushing toilets were an avoided luxury. Second, I was not acquainted with decent English for some time. Kona was a coffee-farming community. The vast majority of its members were first-generation Japanese, with a few Hawaiians and Filipinos tossed in. When I returned to Honolulu, my primary language was Japanese, enhanced with a few Hawaiian and Filipino phrases in addition to some Pidgin English (a slang made up of words and syntax from the various island cultures).

That early Kona connection led to my spending all summer vacations until graduation at my grandfather's store in Kona, giving me well-appreciated rural "roots." It also led to a particularly memorable experience. The 1950 Mauna Loa volcanic eruption, which has been called "the largest and most spectacular eruption since written records have been kept." That's the one that started at Moku`aweoweo Crater on June 1 and from the time it overflowed, took only four hours to reach the sea. Considering that it covered a linear distance of thirty miles or so, that was a pretty good pace. It eventually sent three separate tongues of flows into the sea from around Ho`okena to Miloli`i, and lasted for 23 days. As usual, I went to Kona the day summer vacation started, and that evening drove to where the northern-most tongue crossed the highway. What we could see at night was a slowly moving mass of molten lava about 10 to 15 feet high, that lit up the immediate surroundings and had the viscosity of molten steel being poured into casts at steel mills. It emanated incredible heat, so that you couldn't get much closer than fifty feet to it.

A day or two later, we went on a fishing boat that was giving rides to people to see the lava entering the sea near Miloli`i. That was an unforgettable sight. There was so much steam generated by the lava pouring into the sea, that we knew where we were headed as soon as we left Kealakekua Bay. We got a little less than a mile from shore, but that was plenty close enough. By that time, we were surrounded by dead fish floating on the water's surface, killed by the boiling heat where the lava was entering the sea.

The next year, when I went there again, the around-the-island highway was still not open. Heat from the lava flow had not fully dissipated. Although bulldozers had cut a path where it crossed the highway, prominent signs advised against driving through the lava crossings because of the heat. Mother Nature is simply awesome!

For all of us in the Class of 1952, December 7, 1941, changed our lives. The effort engendered to win "the war to save democracy," brought about incredible advances in all areas of science and technology—communication, transportation, medicine, etc. Advances that would have been barely imaginable in peacetime were accomplished with incredible speed, essentially shrinking the world. Those who witnessed some of the military action that began just before 8 a.m. that fateful morning, must have indelible memories of scenes not generally available in days before TV news. Unfortunately, I was not one of them.

We lived "on the wrong side of the hill" to see any of that action. Our home was on the slopes of Kaimukī that gave us a gorgeous view over Kāhala beach, all the way to Koko Head, framed by Diamond Head on the right and Wilhelmina Rise (Maunalani Heights), Kāhala Heights, and Wai`alae-Iki on the left. No part of that had any military significance for the Japanese attack force, so it continued its peaceful existence, leaving my only memory of December 7th as the grave concerns of my parents listening to Webley Edwards reporting on KGMB radio, "This is no drill, it's the real McCoy!" I remember my mother's concern for the safety of her parents, who lived downtown on Nu`uanu

Ave. She had no way to telephone them to find out if they were okay. We also spent a good part of the day papering our windows with newspapers for the blackout.

The most direct impact that the Pearl Harbor attack had on me was that it removed a very good friend and Hanahau`oli classmate from my young life. He was the son of the Japanese consul-general, so was restricted to the consulate grounds until a diplomatic exchange was effected later.

Ewa Mill (left) and Kahuku Mill (right) were two of the many mills where sugar cane was washed and processed (both photos JBB, 1952).

Recollections of Mike McCormack

I earned a BA in Science and Commerce, then went into the real estate business and owned my own company for many years. I have three children and eight grandchildren.

My paternal grandfather, William McCormack, emigrated from Atholne, Ireland, after serving some time in the British Army, where he was assigned to the Royal Guard in London. Because of Irish tensions, he mustered out and came to New York, where his sister had already settled in Albany. Not having any other experience or skills, he eventually joined the American Army in the contingent known as Teddy Roosevelt's Roughriders, since he was a cavalryman. His assigned tour of duty came during the Spanish-American War in the late 1800s and he got shipped out of the East to the fight in the Philippines! On his journey, which took him around Cape Horn, he sailed to the Hawaiian Islands to stop for provisions, a rest and to train at Camp McKinley at the foot of Diamond Head, now Kapi`olani Park. He eventually left and went on to the Philippines where he did a tour of duty before returning to Hawai`i.

While there, somehow he and some friends learned that the Honolulu Police Department was looking for trained cavalrymen to fulfill the need for police on horseback. Turns out they shipped back to San Francisco, mustered out of the Army from the Presidio and sailed back to Hawai`i to join the police force. My grandfather served the force well for a number of years. He had a large family from which I descend on my Irish side.

My mother's family emigrated from Portugal when groups of families came from the Azores to work in the burgeoning sugarcane industry. My maternal grandmother came with her parents and was raised on the island of Kaua`i. Eventually they wound up in Honolulu, where my mother was educated and became a schoolteacher with the education department. She and my dad married and produced my sister Pat and me.

Counting my children born and raised in Hawai`i and now theirs, we have fifth-generation Island heritage. I have no Hawaiian or Oriental background but of course I feel just as Hawaiian as the rest of the Island kids born and raised in my generation. How things have changed with the rally for the Native Hawaiians and their new-found powers. For me, it somehow feels unequal now, and that is one of the reasons I live in California. I do like it a lot here, though I miss my family and friends who remain in Hawai`i. Three of my four kids also live in California, quite near me, so I do have the immediate gang around.

I remember well how my sister Pat and I had gone to early mass at St. Augustine Church on Kalākaua Avenue in Waikīkī. When we came out of mass and got in the car to drive home, my father pulled up along the beach-side area (*makai*) and from there we could quite vividly see the plumes of black smoke billowing skyward from Pearl Harbor. The Navy had been conducting maneuvers the previous weeks, but my father knew something was very different. Of course I was fascinated with the unfolding events as we raced home to get ready for some kind of attack.

After we got home (across from Jefferson Elementary School at the foot of Diamond Head), Dad prepared the house for the expected bombing by blackening windows and setting up a fortress of mattresses for us to sleep under during such an attack. After that he headed off to City Hall, where he was called to work to help in the days that followed. Meanwhile, curiosity got the best of me and my neighborhood friends. Later that morning I distinctly remember two of us climbing on the garage roof at the Hu`ehu`e residence and witnessing with rapt fascination the airplane duel of American and Japanese fighter planes over the Diamond Head crater. They were so close to us at one point, we could distinguish the pilot in the open cockpit of the Japanese plane wearing goggles like the ones we all saw later in the movie *Tora Tora Tora!* As the chase continued, the Japanese plane flew *mauka* (towards the mountains) and possibly dropped a bomb as it flew away.

On that first very scary night, we had to keep all the lights off and sleep under the mattresses set up as our little bomb shelter. We had no idea what it would have meant had we been attacked or invaded by the Japanese Army. You can imagine the images and fear. Well, of course it never happened, but how could we ever forget the changes to our lives thereafter? Gas masks, ID cards and concertina barbed wire rolled out on all our beaches. We even moved to the Mainland in 1944 because of my mother's fear of an eventual occupation. That was a fun experience—for a year or so. In fact, it was that curious transfer there and back that resulted in my going to Punahou.

When we returned, all the Catholic schools from St. Louis to Maryknoll were filled with students. As a public school teacher, my mother knew better than to put me in that system. Lucky for me, Punahou had space and took me. I entered sixth grade and started the best school days anyone could ever ask for. I remember well the lily pond and my classroom with Mrs. Wriston, my first Punahou teacher, and all the wonderful friends and classmates that molded my life from those war days on.

Recollections of Jacqueline (Jacquie) Myatt Milikien

Jacquie received her BS and MS from Sacramento State. She recently retired after many years as a laboratory technician and educator.

Sunday, December 7, 1941, began as most Sundays in the Myatt household. Mom and I got up early to see Dad off to his usual round of golf at the Wai`alae Country Club. He usually would get home around lunchtime after a round of cribbage with his buddies at the "19th Hole" following the game.

I remember looking out over the city from the front balcony of our home on Wilhelmina Rise (Maunalani Heights), just about a block from the home of Clara Inter, also known as Hilo Hattie. Smoke was billowing up around the Wai`anae Mountains. Mother came out and said "My goodness, that smoke looks much too black to be a cane fire." Just then, my aunt, uncle and cousin, who had moved to Hawai`i from New Zealand two years earlier, drove up the driveway. They had been on their way to a day at the beach and a picnic when live shells began whizzing across the road in front of them. Their car radio was full of excited voices that were broadcasting the first news of the attack.

Billows of black smoke, rather than the usual white smoke from the sugar cane burning, alerted families that something different was happening on December 7th (unknown photographer)

We went inside and turned on the big floor model Philco radio in the living room. Just about then we heard airplanes overhead and ran out in front just in time to see the results of the few bombs which fell on Honolulu. Smoke and sirens filled the air as the Kaimukī Fire Department responded down below Maunalani Heights. Soon Dad arrived home and told about being on the fourth tee when planes flew overhead. He saw the rising sun on the wings. When his Japanese caddy saw them, he dropped the bag of golf clubs and ran away.

As the day wore on, we suddenly realized that our little Japanese maid, who had been with us almost two years, was missing. Her parents lived on Maui and we loved her dearly. She taught me many Japanese words and phrases. My dad went down to the basement to get something and heard a noise. There, crouching behind a pile of lumber, was Mitsuke. She was terrified that we would turn her over to the police because she was Japanese.

That night we sat in the living room in the darkness in front of the big Philco radio, straining to hear every word in spite of the static and crackles. A complete blackout was in force. The next morning we heard more planes overhead. My parents said afterwards that they had not been really afraid until then. Were the planes American or Japanese?

The next exciting event was watching, with binoculars, the sinking of a tiny two-man Japanese submarine just off Waikīkī.

The next couple of months were a blur of blue cellophane on flashlights, curfews, blackouts (with the wardens who would knock on your door if they saw any light), rationing and trips to the bomb shelter. There was a run on the grocery stores, and a great fear of running out of toilet paper, which was used very sparingly.

Jacquie Myatt Milikien going into a family bomb shelter (J.M. Milikien, 1941).

The end of February, 1942, found the three of us and an aunt, uncle and cousin boarding the *HMS Aquitania*, which was part of a large convoy headed for San Francisco. The *Lurline* was also there. There was no *Aloha Oe* played as we left the pier, but a few flower leis scattered about.

Troop ships like this one carried civilians and service men between Honolulu and the mainland. The ships were all painted camouflage gray (H.E. Bowles, 1946).

We all had to wear "Mae West" lifejackets during the day and keep them on our bunks at night. Males and females were in separate quarters, even though they might be family. The bunks were stacked four-high and we bathed in tepid seawater. The *HMS Aquitania* was a British luxury liner with four smokestacks that had been converted into a troop ship. I guess we were the envy of the convoy because it was the only ship with the bar open. The ships were so close together that our passengers would go up on deck and wave their cocktail glasses at the poor dry Americans. We had our meals in the lovely dining room with crystal chandeliers and engraved silverware. Breakfast was usually powdered eggs, or very thin oatmeal and powdered milk, our first experience with that, and not very tasty.

We zigzagged across the Pacific with our destroyer escort and I had my birthday on board. There was a lot of excitement when two of the destroyers started dropping depth charges somewhere off the Farralon Islands near San Francisco. We finally steamed under the Golden Gate Bridge into San Francisco Bay. I had never seen so many tall buildings. Then we noticed that all of the other ships were docking but for some reason we were still anchored out in the Bay. The reason became apparent when a very British voice came over the loudspeaker, "Ladies and Gentlemen, no passengers will be allowed to disembark until all of the silverware is returned." Pretty soon there was a long queue on deck and I could hear the clinking of the silverware, engraved with *HMS Aquitania*, being dropped into boxes.

All of us refugees from Hawai`i were housed in the Mark Hopkins Hotel until we could find housing. My father returned to his job in Hawai`i, my Uncle Dean joined the British Navy and after the war went home to New Zealand where he served as Minister of Defense for many years. My mother and aunt found jobs as typists at Fort Mason and in true English fashion, my cousin Dean, Jr., and I were sent to a boarding school in Los Gatos until the end of the war.

Throughout the war years, Aloha Tower was the tallest building in downtown Honolulu (JBB, 1953).

Recollections of Polly Pintler Digges

We live on the eastern shore of Maryland about forty-five minutes from Annapolis. Nice. As to status, I am a Christian, a wife, a mother, and a grandmother. My husband Bill and I have a small Internet business dealing mostly in antiques.

I believe my family arrived in Hawai`i in 1939 or 1940, as I had just started kindergarten or first grade in Opportunity, Washington, where I was born in 1934. At age three I contracted rheumatic fever, which we now know is caused by the Strep virus, from my grandmother. Pale and wan, I spent a year in my bed with only A Child's Garden of Verses *and little toy soldiers of my brother's for playmates. ("What is that lovely poem about the counterpane?") The doctors informed my parents that I would not be able to live long if they remained in the Spokane area.*

About that time my father, who had an adventurous spirit anyway, was invited by his friend to accompany him to the Islands and see what he thought about the climate for his family. He loved the Islands and sent for us within a year. That's about it. Not very exciting, but I guess I owe my life to it.

Our home had been on seven valley acres with a cherry tree to climb, a milk cow to squirt each other's mouths with milk, a crabapple tree to munch from, an irrigation ditch to play in, a barn to lay behind and eat fresh peas from the garden rows and our own little world in which to look at sky-pictures. We played with our cousins in the root cellar and told ghost stories in the attic. In other words, our home was idyllic from my child's perspective. The only good thing, to my brother and me, about selling and going to Hawai`i was being with Dad again.

And it was good while it lasted, meaning, until World War II. Then, almost at the war's end, he wrote from Okinawa, instructing Mom (Cora Mae) to pack us up and return to the Mainland. We had a glorious year as returned heroes (to us) and enjoyed our reunion with our childhood friends and relatives (especially six cousins our ages). Then darned if I didn't get a recurrence of that disease in Spirit Lake, Idaho (a great swimming lake)! So, we packed up and went back to Hawai`i.

I must have been a wild thing because I remember running barefoot, pigtails flying, up to the corner to a girlfriend's playhouse, at that hour on that Sunday morning, scaring my parents badly. As the bombs were falling they were searching high and low for me as they had not found me at the church. I was found by them at our neighbor's playhouse where I was playing dress-up. They finally got their girl to safety under their double bed!

We lived in Kaimukī at the time, about ten miles or so from the area being bombed. I was attending Kapi`olani School. My father, Ted, was in Civil Defense along with his closest friend,

Paul Mayer. Paul careened up to the duplex in a jeep, Dad vaulted in and they were off to Pearl Harbor! We stood on the little entrance stoop watching the bombs fall until Mom collected herself and sent us back under the bed for an indeterminate time.

I remember a story Dad told us. As the jeep he and Paul were in headed toward Pearl Harbor they saw a little boy actually outside playing with his red wagon. Paul was driving so Dad jumped out and hauled the wee fellow up to the nearest house and literally threw him in the door. As they left they actually saw a bomb hit the red wagon. Since neither he nor Paul were injured, there must have been some distance between houses. I can't even remember for sure if Dad returned home that night, but have the feeling it was a day or two later.

That is what I remember. Little though it is, I still remember it starkly, along with the blackouts and the searchlights. Strangely, our close friend, Makoto Little, of Japanese ancestry, was never interned, or imprisoned. She was married to a haole (Caucasian), though. Their son, Patrick, was in the grade after us at Punahou. Remember coupon books? Well, I can see that I shouldn't get started.

Some trees, like the kiawe that grows everywhere it is dry, were important to the war effort—the long yellow seeds pods were collected and fed to cattle (JBB, 1962).

Recollections of Roberta (Bobbie) Purvis Murray

My paternal great-grandfather was Duncan McBryde, who arrived in Hawai`i around 1850 from Scotland. My paternal grandfather, Robert William Theodore Purvis, arrived in 1877 from Bruges, Belgium. His family originated from Scotland and had a shipping and trading company in Padang, Sumatra, where he was born. He married Mary Elizabeth McBryde and managed the McBryde Sugar Co. in Koloa, Kaua`i. My father, Robert McBryde Purvis, was born in Līhu`e, Kaua`i and settled in Honolulu.

I did not actually graduate from Punahou with our class. In the fall of 1949 I was sent to Miss Porter's School in Farmington, Connecticut. After graduation, I went to Vassar College in Poughkeepsie, New York, graduating with a New York State Teacher's Certificate. I met my husband, who is from New Jersey and went to Princeton University, while I was in college. After serving our stint in the Army (Germany) we settled on Long Island. I taught school for twenty-seven years; raised a daughter (married and living in Lake Forest, Illinois with two small children) and a son (a bachelor living in New York City) and served as Mayor of the Village of Mill Rock for ten years. I retired in 1999.

Our house was on Diamond Head with a panoramic view of Honolulu and Pearl Harbor beyond. On the morning of December 7th, while I was having breakfast with my mother and father, we watched as smoke rose from the vicinity of Pearl Harbor. At first, we thought it was sugar cane burning in the fields, but the smoke kept getting blacker and more acrid. Shortly thereafter, my father's police reserve partner drove up and announced that Pearl Harbor was being bombed by the Japanese. My father immediately put on his police uniform, and together they drove off. We didn't see Dad again for several days.

Quite frankly, I felt the whole day was extremely exciting. I sat on the wall and watched the proceedings unfold. I could see the clouds of smoke, hear the explosions and see black specks, which were the planes. It was controlled chaos for the next few days as the adults put wartime living conditions into place. My most vivid memories of those first few days were: trying so hard not to turn on a light due to the strict blackout regulations, filling every available container with water for fear of poisoning, hearing the deafening sound of anti-aircraft guns being deployed from within Diamond Head crater, being shuffled into our makeshift bomb shelter, which was a converted drainage pipe, at all hours of day and night, bumping into the sandbags that guarded the entrance as they were set up like a labyrinth—I could never remember which way to turn—and smelling the tar paper that covered all the windows and doors. You can see what has really stayed with me the most over the years are the sights, the sounds and the smells of December 7th.

All in all it was a scary yet exciting time in my life. What is most important is that we improvised, made the best of every situation and survived. To this day, I can walk through my house without a light on and never bump into a thing.

Aerial view of Diamond Head looking toward the mountains (*mauka*) (JBB, 1950).

Taro was grown in many places on O`ahu during the 1940s (above). The "root" was dug and ground into poi (right), a staple of the Hawaiian diet (both photos JBB, 1952).

Recollections of Robert (Schoen) Shane

The fifth company of missionaries, which included nine reverends, one doctor and one printer sailed from New Bedford, MA, November 26, 1831 arrived at Honolulu, Hawai`i May 17, 1832 (after 172 days on the whale ship "Averick"). Among those on board was the Reverend Harvey Rexford Hitchcock. He was on my father's mother's side of the family. My grandfather on my father's side was Bertram Frederick Schoen, who came to Hilo, Hawai`i in the 1880s from California. BF was a shopkeeper who originally started a saddlery supplying the ranches on the Big Island.

My brother and I were awakened by the sound of airplanes on December 7, 1941. We were living in an apartment on the water at the end of Beachwalk Avenue. We went out to the beach to see what was going on just in time to see a Japanese plane flying about fifty feet over the water directly in front of us; it was heading from Diamond Head towards Ft. De Russey. Shortly thereafter, we were called in by my parents and told that the Japanese were bombing Pearl Harbor. My recollection from that point on was very vague; however, I distinctly remember spending from about ten o'clock in the morning through the next day at Al and Marie Hasting's house on Maunalani Heights, where in the evening of December 7th, we could see the entire area of Pearl Harbor in flames. My father worked all day and all night as an ambulance driver with his 1939 Plymouth delivery truck. My parents thought it best we go to the highlands for fear of a Japanese land invasion. That's about all I can tell you. My brother reminded me just the other day that we heard a loud explosion around 9:00 a.m. December 7th on Lewers Road which turned out to be a spent aircraft shell (our own), but which delayed our going to the highlands for fear that it was a shell from invading forces.

I met Nick Reynolds at Menlo College in my accounting class during my junior year. We hit it off, and I introduced him to Dave Guard who was at Stanford a mile away. The three of us started playing at beer gardens and frat parties just for fun.

We started The Kingston Trio in 1957, and while playing at the opening of the Surf Room at the Royal Hawaiian in 1958, were told by Capitol Records to cut short our engagement at the Royal Hawaiian and come back to the Mainland, because *Tom Dooley* had just become "Number One" in the country. We made six albums between 1959 and 1961, all of which became gold. We toured an average of nine months out of the year for the first four years and have never toured less than twenty-six weeks a year since. In 1961, Dave

Guard was replaced by John Stewart and we cut fifteen albums with John. The Trio officially disbanded in 1967. However, from 1968-1976, I toured with two other guys as "The New Kingston Trio."

In 1976 I became sole owner of the name "The Kingston Trio," and we changed our name back from "The New" to The Kingston Trio again. Nick rejoined us in 1988, and after eleven more years, just retired for the second time about a year-and-a-half-ago. The current configuration of The Kingston Trio consists of me, George Grove and Bobby Haworth. We are still touring an average of twenty-eight weeks a year. Our music has been passed on from generation to generation, which, thank God, keeps our concert halls filled. I have been lead singer of The Kingston Trio for forty-three years and intend to do it until I can't sing anymore.

Note: The Kingston Trio received the first Grammy ever given for Best Country and Western Presentation of the Year in 1958 and in 1959. When the category was added for Folk, they received the first Grammy for Best Folk Presentation of the Year.

Recollections of Christopher "Kit" Smith

My career was spent entirely in journalism—as a financial reporter/writer— for, in order: *The San Diego Union, Business Week magazine* (Los Angeles Bureau) and *The Honolulu Advertiser.* I was employed by The *Honolulu Advertiser* twenty-four years, retiring in 1995.

My grandfather, who died when my dad was twelve years old, had come to Hawai`i as the booking agent for a traveling bicycle act, The Great Maltby. The bicycle act folded—or at least that's our assumption—but my grandfather stayed. In Honolulu he met and married my grandmother, Alice Wall, the youngest of seven children. She came here as a toddler, learning to walk on a sailing ship from California. Her father, Charles J. Wall, had been commissioned by King Kalākaua to serve as the second of three architects for `Iolani Palace.

Soon after the attack, my dad, Dudley W. Smith, got a call at our Kāhala home to report to his work place downtown. He was at that time superintendent of rail operations for the O`ahu Railway & Land Co. (OR&L), and rail transportation was considered "strategic."

My response to this excitement—or at least the only one I can recall—was to sit down with crayons and draw pictures of Japanese planes being shot down.

My older brother Dick and I were barred from running down to the beach to see what we could see. I expect we would have seen nothing from our low-lying vantage point, with Diamond Head lying between Pearl Harbor and us. Later in the day, I remember listening with my mother and Dick to the radio and catching, as best a seven-year-old can, the import and sober nature of the news. The advice I remember most was to boil water for drinking.

My mom must have been very worried about my dad, but being a stiff-upper-lip New Englander, born and reared in Connecticut, she didn't betray it. When he did arrive home—I'm not sure of the hour but it was before our bedtime—he was carrying a pistol that had been issued to him! That impressed me. I'm not sure how long he kept it or whether he carried it at all. I don't remember observing any blackout that first night, although we likely did. But by the second night I was sure we were observing the blackout, taping heavy, light blocking paper over the two

The freight train operated by OR & L made daily runs from Honolulu to Kahuku (Kent Cochrane, Bishop Museum, Waimea Bay, 1945).

windows in an upstairs bedroom. That became our evening gathering place as a family. I remember my dad reading the *Christmas Story* to me in that room one evening; Christmas day, of course, fell just eighteen days after Pearl Harbor.

Pearl Harbor recollections include:

➢My Punahou classes—I was in the second grade—being switched for a while to a large beachfront home toward Diamond Head, relative to our 4603 Kāhala Avenue home. That was caused, of course, by the Army takeover of the Punahou campus.

➢Being issued gas masks, which we had to carry everywhere.

➢Getting an ID card, with blood type noted on it. That made an indelible impression on my now sometimes-faulty memory. I have Type A blood.

➢Being shepherded to the basement of Lili`uokalani Elementary School in Kaimukī one day for shelter. I don't recall air raid sirens sounding but they must have. I don't know what caused the false alarm.

➢Getting gas rationing stickers for our cars—"A," "B" or "C" were they? (I'm not sure.) I think my dad must have gotten an A sticker, if that's what allowed the most generous fill-ups, because of his "strategic" job.

I have no compelling anecdotes to record of great irony, or suspense related to Pearl Harbor. But like all Hawai`i residents—and I'm sure more strongly by our elders—I did get a sense that the events that day would be somehow life-changing for all of us in various, dramatic, often troubling ways.

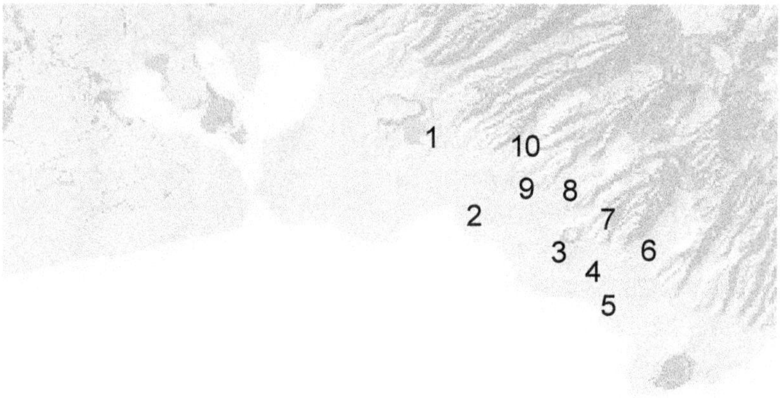

1. Fort Shafter
2. Kalihi
3. Punch Bowl
4. Makiki
5. McCully
6. Mānoa
7. Tantalus
8. Nu`uanu
9. `Ālewa
10. Pu`unui

Mānoa

Diane Ackerman Goetzinger—Makiki
Alice Belt Faust—Mānoa
Gordon (Demi) Black—Tantalus
Barbara Blom Ward—Punch Bowl
Carl (Soot) Bredhoff—Mānoa
Ron Brunk—Mānoa
Ellen M. Colburn—McCully
Charley Cooke—Mānoa
Virginia Crippen Claire—Fort Shafter
Bob Deatrick—Makiki
John Dunstan—Mānoa
Bonnie Edgar Lindquist—Fort Shafter
Alice Flanders Guild—Nu`uanu
Fred Hundhammer, Jr.—Mānoa
Malcolm Ing—McCully
Roland Jackson—Punch Bowl
Edward W.L. (Eddie) Kam—Pu`unui
Ann Kirsch Latham—Mānoa
Adrienne Madden—Nu`uanu
Diane McLean Stowell—Mānoa
Peggy Moir Vollmann—Mānoa
Barbara Moody Hudman—`Ālewa
Rita Paris Cowell—Nu`uanu
Beryl Peters—McCully
Don Smith—Kalihi
Robert (Bobby) Vieira—Nu`uanu
Joan Wood Fleming—Mānoa
Jackie Young—`Ālewa

Recollections of Diane Ackerman Goetzinger

After graduating from Punahou School in 1952, I went to the mainland to see how the other half lived. I married John Goetzinger in 1958, and had two children, Kurt and Shelley. I am also the grandmother of five. I have reached retirement age but am still working. I was a slow starter and went to college after my children left home to follow their dreams. I graduated from Sonoma State University in 1987 and found a job working in a senior residence in charge of social services. There are 200 people here at Silvercrest and I feel I still have a lot to give. (d. 2005)

My great-grandfather, Felix Correiro, was born and raised in Sao Miguel, Azores and he married Juaquina Quintanilla. They had eleven children. The oldest was my grandmother, Maria do Rosario Correiro. Family rumor has it that Great-Grandfather left the Azores and took his family to Hawai`i because he didn't want Maria to marry Antonio Jacintho Rodrigues, but Antonio followed Maria to Hawai`i where they were married, probably without the blessing of the family. They married on December 22, 1888. Maria was nineteen and Antonio was twenty-four. Antonio was a carpenter, a master mechanic and foreman of the carpenter shop at The O`ahu Sugar Company plantation in Waipahu. He was a first-class engineer who built top rate water flues in long, deep gulches, as well as large redwood water tanks, bridges, houses, etc. He also designed and built strong cane cars for the plantation. Antonio and Maria had eleven children. My mother, Sophia Rodrigues, was one of them.

My father's parents came from Unterwälden, Switzerland. Their families migrated to Philadelphia and that is where my father's parents met. They married and made their home in Mt. Angel, Oregon. Joseph Ackerman and Otilla Selm Ackerman had twelve children, my father, Gale Joseph Ackerman being one of the youngest.

Gale Ackerman along with his brother Leo decided to visit the Hawaiian Islands. There Gale Ackerman met Sophie Rodrigues. They fell in love and got married on September 24, 1928. My father secured a job with Piggly Wiggly Food Stores. My brother Gale and I are their only children. We lived in a house on Liholiho Street in the Makiki area of Honolulu, and that is where we were when the Japanese bombed Pearl Harbor on December 7th .

Sunday, December 7, 1941, was a beautiful day. My brother and I arose early so we could get in some playing before we had to go to church. It was a very usual Sunday morning, the sound of airplanes overhead did not distract us, this was very commonplace. But soon my mother was running out on the porch, screaming for us to get into the house. She told us that the Japanese had bombed Pearl Harbor and we were to wake the young navy man who lived in the cottage behind our house. All military men on leave were to get dressed in uniform and go down to the main highway where they would be picked up and taken to their stations. The man didn't believe us, so we told him to turn on his radio. Within minutes, he was a white streak, running down our driveway to the highway.

Then we were put to the task of filling large containers with water. We even filled the bathtub. There was fear that our water supply would be contaminated. Ten of our relatives and friends started streaming in from Pearl Harbor, and all I remember is running up and down steps, bringing coffee and food to the huddled mass of people grouped in our basement. We felt that was the safest place to be. The people wouldn't stop crying and some told stories of the Japanese planes diving so low that they could see the pilots. The day seemed endless, both scary and exciting.

In the days that followed there were many things to do. We dug an air raid shelter in our back yard and stocked it with survival things like a radio, flashlight, food and water. They dug shelters at the school I attended. All the people in the area, adults and children alike, had to go to Roosevelt High School and be fingerprinted. We were issued identification cards, tags and gas masks. We were instructed to have these items on us at all times. I still have my ID card and tags.

A curfew was imposed, and we all had to be indoors by nightfall. My father became an air raid warden and had an area to patrol. We blacked out the one bathroom, and from that day on it was considered the "reading room." At night when my dad was on patrol, the rest of the family sat on the porch and watched and listened, for what I don't know.

Helen Bowles Nicholson was one of the Punahou students who helped pick pineapples during the war years because of the shortage of workers.(H.E. Bowles, early 1940s).

When things settled down, Dad took us to see the craters left by the few bombs that were dropped in Honolulu. We were required to get certain shots like typhoid and smallpox and had to wear shoes when going to the movies. Soon there were at least ten tanks deployed on our street, and the soldiers were bivouacked in a nearby park. We would go down to the park and take the men comic books and cookies. On occasion we would bring a soldier home for dinner. It was called "doing your patriotic duty."

My mother became a schoolteacher because there was a shortage of teachers. She didn't have a credential. She taught at the intermediate level and often took her class to the pineapple fields to harvest the "pine." Meanwhile, our elementary school class made slippers out of heavy cardboard, cotton and cloth for the wounded at Tripler Hospital.

President Franklin Roosevelt came to Hawai`i when I was a student at Lincoln Elementary. We were notified that the President would be coming by our school so all the children lined the street to get a glimpse of him. He was riding in an open car and as he rode by, he waved at us all. This was the first president I had ever seen in person. Everyone was so excited.

There must have been some rationing too, but I don't remember seeing a ration book. We were lucky though, because my father was a grocer. Because we lived on an island, some things were hard to get. When he did bring home cases of fresh fruit, we shared them with our neighbors. I remember that we had our share of Spam and powdered eggs. We bought saving stamps and when a book was full, we bought a bond. Everyone—man, woman and child—had a patriotic obligation to work for the common good and to bring our boys and gals home safely and quickly. It was a time when you were proud to be an American.

There were the sad times too. I was just eight years old on that fateful day. My mother had a good friend visiting from Idaho. Her friend's son, Ray, was stationed at Hickam field. I was madly in love with him. (You know how little girls get crushes.) He was so nice, very tall and slim, with red hair and freckles. He had a car with a rumble seat and took us, my brother and me, on rides and to the movies. I remember asking him to wait 'til I grew up, because I wanted to marry him. He was just a precious person. Well, the reality of the war came home to me when I found out he was killed December 7th.

Diane's friend Ray was killed on December 7th at Hickam Field (Courtesy of D.A. Goetzinger).

We had another wonderful soldier friend, Frankie, who was an Italian boy from the New York area. He loved to come to our house to cook and be with the family. He was like a big brother to me. He had a beautiful voice and would sing all the time. My favorite song was *Poinciana*. I still remember all the words.

Frankie was also the boxing champ in his division and won a medal in 1943 that he gave me. I still have it. Frankie managed to go through the war in the Pacific without a scratch. He was bothered by the thought that he had to kill women and children. The enemy would booby trap the women and children and send them out under a white flag. So it was kill or be killed. He was under orders to do just that. After the war, Frankie went back to his family, but could not live with what he had done and killed himself. I was privileged to know at least two very special, wonderful human beings and I will never forget them.

When the war was finally over our lives had changed in many ways. My parents divorced. I feel the war taught us to be survivors and we could get through anything as long as we worked together.

Frankie, who was from New York, survived December 7th, but took his own life after the war (Courtesy of D.A. Goetzinger).

Recollections Of Alice Belt Faust

My maternal grandfather had come around the Horn from Germany on a sailing ship in 1900 to work for Hackfelds, a German merchant. (During World War I, the name was changed to the more patriotic American Factors.) My mother, Dorothy, was born in Honolulu and attended Punahou. My father, Robert, came to Hawai`i in 1931 from Oregon, when the Great Depression made jobs scarce for civil engineers on the Mainland. He was county engineer for Kaua`i until he was called into the navy in 1941 and posted at Pearl Harbor. After the Pearl Harbor attack, my mother, sister and I lived in Oregon and Virginia. We returned to Hawai`i in 1945. Robert Belt founded the engineering firm Belt, Collins, and Associates.

December 7, 1941, is one of those dates that prompt total recall; you remember where you were and what you were doing when you heard that the Japanese had attacked Pearl Harbor. My memory is one of fear and horror as a war began without warning just a few miles from our family's home.

I was living with my parents and little sister in Honolulu. I had spent my first seven years on Kaua`i, a second-generation islander who knew only the idyllic life at Poipu Beach, but in the summer of 1941, Daddy was called up from the Navy Reserves to active duty at Pearl Harbor, so we moved to a small house in Mānoa near the University of Hawai`i.

That Sunday morning when I awoke there was an unfamiliar sound—the noise of loud explosions somewhere. My parents were curious but not yet alarmed by the blasts. Daddy speculated that it might be an explosion at a warehouse or even at one of his Navy projects. Then one of Daddy's fellow officers called from Pearl Harbor and told him that they were being bombed and needed him to report right away. He turned and gave us the news. Stunned, my mother turned on the radio to hear KGMB announcer Webley Edwards say that the Japanese were attacking Pearl Harbor, adding anxiously, "This is no drill! This is the real McCoy." For decades to come, every retelling of December 7th would include those exact words. He urged us, "Oh keep calm," but he sounded pretty excited. We ran outside, looked up and saw planes in the sky. The blasts continued loud and near.

In 1952 I went to the University of Oregon (it was familiar and I had good memories of my years there) where I eventually met my husband. We were married after my graduation. Then, I taught art while he went to law school in Eugene. After that we settled in Portland because our college friends and Jack's family were there. The Pearl Harbor attack and events that followed affected the whole course of my life! Instead of producing a third *kama`aina* (native born) generation, I raised webfoots. Our three children have lived and traveled elsewhere, yet all live in Portland with their families now.

Another officer summoned from his home picked up my dad in his car, and they drove off to war. Before that, Mama had cooked up a big breakfast of bacon and eggs and made Daddy two sandwiches, which she packed up in my little lunch pail. As he left, Daddy suggested that we go to stay with our friends the Tattersons, who lived further up the valley on Ferdinand Street. I felt afraid as we drove the deserted streets to merge with the other household. Like my dad, Tat Tatterson had reported to Pearl Harbor, so now there were two young mothers and five small children. It was common that morning for families to double up. The togetherness lessened the fear. We crowded around the radio as the bombing continued.

On the radio, Web Edwards told us to fill bathtubs and containers with water in case the supply was cut off. That possibility made us thirsty, so we children drank a lot of water. Soon after, a truck with a bullhorn came through the neighborhood warning us not to drink the water as the supply had been poisoned! Frantic, our mothers set about to induce vomiting and were successful with all but me. This, like most of the rumors that swept through the city, proved to be untrue. Other false rumors were that paratroopers were dropping into Waikīkī and that local Japanese were cooperating with the raiders.

All over town, families tried to prepare for the worst. They packed suitcases with valuables and staples, ready to flee the enemy, although no one knew where to go. Some neighbors rigged up hoses and ladders for fire fighting. One neighbor buried the family silver in the back yard.

Bombs and errant anti-aircraft shells hit Honolulu neighborhoods. My mother's friend, Alice White, for whom I was named, died instantly when shell fragments ripped into her house. She became the first American civilian killed in World War II. Her husband had gone out to walk the dog and thus escaped death. Like the destruction of the Whites' house, most of the damage to civilian Honolulu was caused by our own anti-aircraft, attempting to shoot down enemy planes.

The radio stations went off the air at about noon; the silence was as alarming as the news flashes had been. Everyone wondered if the invasion had begun. My mother and Mrs. Tatterson compulsively started a load of laundry in the old wringer washer. It wasn't until the next day that they remembered the laundry, which was still grinding away. Meanwhile, the day wore on, and the explosions finally stopped. We waited anxiously without any idea of what had happened to our fathers, or the Navy that was there to protect us.

Daddy and Mr. Tatterson returned from Pearl Harbor after dark. My dad described his commute to war. As they drove that morning, they somehow got between two ammunition trucks. There were planes flying low over them, so close they could see the pilots' faces. Some of them strafed the stream of traffic. Drivers panicked and abandoned their cars, jumping into others, which compounded the problem. Daddy would never say much about what he saw or did on the base that day, but since he worked among oil storage tanks, he surely must have wondered if he would live through it.

I recently asked my parents if they were scared when night came, and they said, "We were scared all the time!" But as night fell, people felt even jumpier.

We strictly obeyed the blackout orders and taped heavy paper to the windows. Rooms formerly cooled by trade winds became stuffy. We children were bedded down for the night on the floor, but nobody slept much. The next morning we heard the roar of many airplanes. Dashing to the back porch we saw big American bombers, with stars painted on their sides, arriving from the mainland. It was a comforting sight.

Within a few days citizens began digging air raid shelters, following directions given in the newspapers. In the weeks to follow, we had many air raid alerts, generally at night. I remember being aroused and carried sleepily into the sandbag-lined pit, which had filled with winter rain and insects.

Martial law was declared right after the attack. The Army Engineers movd onto Punahou's campus, cutting down the historic cactus and evicting the students. School resumed soon in private homes. My second grade class met on Kakela Drive. I believe it was Dr. Gottshalk's house. We braced ourselves for another attack, or an invasion which never came.

In March, my mother, sister and I were evacuated to the Mainland as decreed for military dependents. After December 7th, the Navy evacuated most dependents. We were shipped to Corvallis, Oregon, chosen because relatives lived there and it was safe. We traveled in a convoy of stripped-down former luxury ships with destroyer escorts. Our ship was the *SS Lurline*. The convoy followed a zigzag course, and passengers were required to wear heavy, cork, life vests all the time. We didn't know when we'd see our fathers, husbands, or Hawai`i again. When we returned after the war, I re-entered Punahou in Miss Nim's sixth grade homeroom.

Now, we take our children and grandchildren back to Hawai`i to see the *Arizona*, still visible just beneath the surface of the water. *There is little else to remind us of that Sunday morning when bombs fell from the sky and children awakened to learn that their world was no longer secure.*

Both wetland taro (left), and dryland taro (right), were plowed by water buffaloes. Much more wet land taro was grown on O`ahu than today (both photos JBB, 1953).

Recollections of Gordon H. "Demi" Black

My ancestoral story begins in 1820 when Hiram and Sybil Bingham came to Hawai`i as newlyweds from New England leading the first missionary company to the Islands. Twenty-one years later he founded Punahou School on lands donated by Governor Boki. My maternal grandmother was the Binghams` granddaughter.

After graduating from Punahou and Wellesley College (1902), my grandmother worked as a secretary in Minneapolis where she met and married my grandfather. He had come to this country as a boy of 13 when his father came over from Wales as a stone mason contractor to do the decorative stone work on the state capital.

My mother graduated from Punahou ('26) then attended the University of Washington where she graduated with a degree in music. She returned to Honolulu, taught music at Punahou and played violin with the Honolulu symphony until I came along in 1934.

My father was born in Pennsylvania Dutch country in 1901. When he was about ten years old his family made a series of incremental moves westward, including stops in North Dakota and Montana, and finally settled in Kirkland, Washington. My father was used to hard work from the time he was only six years old. During WWI, he worked in the shipyards while going to high school. He was acutely conscious of how hard people had to work in those days and saw how the proper use of machines could alleviate much of the back-breaking drudgery so common to the lot of the working man. He wanted to play a part in that revolution and enrolled at the University of Washington as an engineering student. Dad worked his way through college, including time to play football for one year, and graduated with a degree in mechanical engineering. After graduation, he worked for a year, then attended Harvard Business School where he graduated Phi Beta Kappa and was hired by Hawaiian Pineapple Co. A year after being hired, the depression hit Hawai`i and he was laid off. Not being one to be idle, he went to work in the insurance business. About this time he met my mother at a UW alumni dinner. Shortly after that he started his own agency for New York Life. He remained in the insurance and financial planning business for the rest of his life, including several years as the Deputy Insurance Commissioner for Hawai`i.

On Sunday morning, December 7, 1941, we were preparing to go to town for Sunday school when the phone rang. It was a neighbor, John Warinner (father of Keoni Warinner, '52). He said that we should turn on the radio as there was important news being broadcasted. (At that time it wasn't hard to get the right station—you either had KGU or KGMB.) Well, we soon

Since Punahou, I attended Oregon State for three years then returned to Honolulu to work. I've had many varied work experiences, but never a "career." My main interest has always been "what makes people tick" including the integration of spiritual laws and values along with psychology. My employment has included burglar alarm technician, armored car service, airplane refueler, oil refinery worker, construction, U.S. Fish & Wildlife Service, drill rig worker, U.S. Forest Service, truck driver, psychological aide for developmentally disabled, security guard and probably some others which I don't remember. All the while I've continued to study people, psychology, economics and spiritual development. Incidentally, my martial arts training (Judo & Aikido) meshes perfectly with all the other "life studies." Of course, the more

heard the excited voice of Webley Edwards advising everyone to stay calm and to keep off the streets—Pearl Harbor was under attack by Japanese aircraft. He kept repeating that this was not a drill, it was for real.

Pearl Harbor from Tantalus with superimposed black smoke, ack-ack and Japanese planes to simulate what Demi Black saw the morning of December 7th (JBB, 1949).

Our house was way up Round Top Drive overlooking Diamond Head so we were on the wrong side of the mountain to see Pearl Harbor. We all piled in the car and drove around to the Pauoa side of Tantalus where we had a grandstand view of Pearl Harbor. What a sight! There was so much smoke coming up from the burning ships and buildings that the Wai`anae Mountains were obscured. The air was filled with puffs of black smoke from the anti-aircraft guns, and planes were swirling all over.

We soon got a really close look at some of those planes. Groups of four to six planes had formed up after their attack and were flying away to the south. Some, flying at about three to five hundred feet, passed directly over us. We could plainly see the black engine cowlings, the big red "meatball" insignia on the wings and the long plexiglas cockpits with the aviators inside looking down at us. The ships were apparently watching the departing groups of planes also—they were shooting at them with their five-inch guns! The sound of the shells swooshing overhead was something that has been indelibly impressed in my memory. (While there was some damage in Honolulu attributed to bombs, I believe most was actually caused by our own shells landing.) After a while, things calmed down, so we went home.

one learns the more one knows he "knows not."

I lived in Kahana Valley for many years in a house without electricity. While the facilities may have been crude, the setting was beautiful. I was afforded the opportunity to learn a great deal about myself and the people who lived in the village out at the highway. After my house burned down and I lost most of my material possessions, I had to live in town (Kane`ohe) for a couple of years. It turns out I'm not a city person!

Then at age 46 a major life change—I got married! To a part Hawaiian gal with custody of three of her four kids: a girl (9) and two boys (11 & 13). We then moved to a small town in Grant County out in Eastern Oregon where the major industries are ranching and logging. Grant County is larger than some eastern states, yet only has 8,000 residents. It's over 130 miles to any town of over 15,000. I love it. Very friendly people.

After seven years of relatively uneventful marriage, my wife ran off with another man. I continued to be the father to the

Late that afternoon, about suppertime, a neighbor came to our door with a request; he and his wife had planned a party that evening to which several people had been invited. Obviously nobody was going to show up and there was all this food—would we care to come and help them eat some of it? We, of course, accepted. The man's name was S. Kawachi—we had been taught to address him as Kawachi-san—so we "celebrated" the Japanese attack on Pearl Harbor that evening by gorging ourselves on delicious Japanese food with our Japanese neighbors. Treachery was never on our minds.

Our lives changed radically after the attack. There was a total blackout imposed. Everyone hung blankets over windows and used lighting sparingly in their houses. Driving after dark was forbidden. For several days we weren't sure whether or not we were going to be invaded. Rumors were rampant. Bomb shelters were built everywhere. We were all issued gas masks, which we were required to have with us at all times. Gasoline and tires were rationed. For the rest of the school year my brother and I were home-schooled and then we entered Punahou in September on the University of Hawai`i campus!

Someday I'll be one of the few remaining witnesses to the historic event that transpired that Sunday morning, December 7, 1941.

two youngest and am still very close with my daughter and her two daughters who live in Roseburg, Oregon which is a seven hour drive from me, but we nevertheless see each other often.

Presently I'm comfortably retired (not by city standards perhaps) and keep busy with outdoor activities, volunteer services, teaching self-defense to survivors of domestic violence, serving on the County Sheriff's "Posse" and spend time with a beautiful lady who shares a love of the outdoors and spiritual values with me.

Watercress was grown in the vicinity of Pearl Harbor in the 1940s, much as it is today (JBB, 1953).

Recollections of Barbara Blom Ward

My great-grandmother (on my father's side) originated from Northern Germany. Her family migrated to Australia when she was a child. Part of the family stayed in Melbourne and the rest continued to the Islands. Lahaina, Maui was the first stop and then they moved to Honolulu. My grandmother on my father's side was raised in Honolulu and at age seventeen married a Swede off one of the whaling ships. He was twenty-seven. My father and his older sister, Alvina Blom, however, were born in Honolulu. After graduating from Punahou, my dad, Irving Albin Blom, went to the University of Hawai`i for one year and then on to USC to dental school. He had intended to apply to practice in Honolulu and to marry my mom after graduation. However, because the Territory screened all dental applicants and required them to serve as high school dentists for two years, they could not be married at that time. So Dad came back to the Islands and was sent to Lahaina, Maui, to be the Lahaina High School dentist for two years. My mother taught school in San Bernadino, California, during this time. At the end of two years, Dad went back to Los Angeles and married my mom and brought her back to the Islands. Hence, my sister and I were born and raised in Honolulu. When I visited the family plot in Nu`uanu Cemetery, I discovered that my sister and I are the fifth generation of Bloms raised in the Islands.

I graduated from the University of Arizona with an elementary teaching degree. I married Neil Ward, an Air Force pilot, in December of 1956. After Neil got out of the service we headed for Washington, D.C. for medical school, then on to Salt Lake City, Utah for internship and four years of residency in Otolaryngology (ear, nose and throat). We settled in Phoenix, Arizona and raised three children. I taught school for six years in the various states that we lived in while my husband was in school. We have been very fortunate to be able to travel to many foreign ports.

My parents had just built their dream house above Roosevelt High School in December of 1940. The city and county had paved the roadway just up the hill from our house. Since ours was the last house on the hillside, we had a view all the way from Waikīkī to Pearl Harbor. When the attack started on Pearl Harbor, my Dad woke us up and we gathered on the sun deck to "watch the Navy practice." My parents thought that the U.S. was practicing, until the smoke started rising from the battleships. Then black blotches from the anti-aircraft guns appeared in the sky.

I remember watching one ship getting out of Pearl Harbor and trying to sail south out to sea. Most of the ships headed east towards California, but this one was headed in the direction of the Philippines/Australia. It did get past the bombs that were being dropped—as far as we could see. The rest of the day was a blur of being very scared and not being allowed to go outside for fear of Japanese snipers that had been reported landing. The radio said that our water reservoirs would probably be poisoned by the snipers, so we were to boil all our drinking water. The radio also called for anyone with any medical knowledge to please report to the nearest high school to help with the wounded that would be brought there, so my dad went down the hillside to report to Roosevelt High School. We didn't see him for three days.

When he did come home, his clothes were covered in blood, and his stories relating to those three days taught us what the strange word 'war' meant. It was a time in my life I will never forget, and yet I find it hard to talk about.

The Punahou campus was taken over by the military, so my sister and I went to school (when it did resume) in a private home up in Mānoa Valley. Many people opened their homes to school Punahou students. I happened to be assigned to the Atherton home, which is now the home of the president of the University of Hawai`i. Each morning, my sister and I would walk down the hill to Roosevelt High School and wait for a certain bus to pick us up. We would wave a blue and yellow flag as each bus passed, and the Punahou bus would stop and pick us up and take us to the various homes in Mānoa.

We had a Japanese maid living with us when the war broke out. Her parents lived in Japan and she broke out in tears when she realized that Japan had attacked us. She knew her parents were PRO-AMERICAN and feared that they would be thrown into a concentration camp in Japan for being traitors. She was just as frightened of the Japanese soldiers as we were.

I think that the biggest part of the whole attack and the days that followed was FEAR.

When I saw my father after he returned from Roosevelt High School crying and covered with blood, I think I grew up quickly in just a few days. By "growing up" I mean that all of a sudden I was no longer living in my world of "play and make-believe" where all that existed (in my mind) was the neighborhood gang. Suddenly I was awakened to the real events and to other people's feelings. I was beginning to lose the childish feelings of self and to realize there was something very somber outside of my home and family.

I still have the letter that my mother had started writing to her parents on December 7th and finished at the end of January. Each day she would add tidbits of news heard over the radio. It's very interesting to read it now that so many years have passed.

In February of 1942, a stray plane flew over Tantalus and dropped a bomb. Our window glass and some arcadia doors cracked from the ground shaking. It was never in the news because martial law censored what was reported over the air and in the papers. My sister and I hiked up the hill to the site. It was surrounded by military police, but we were able to gather some shrapnel from the bomb.

Three months after the bombing of Pearl Harbor, my sister and I left the Islands to live with my mother's parents in Los Angeles. I took the bomb shrapnel with me, but I lost it some time during our stay. My mother decided (at the last minute) that since they were not evacuating any men off the Islands, she wanted to be with my father if he were going to be put in a concentration camp. Everyone thought that the Japanese would come back and take over the Islands.

My sister and I lived in Los Angeles for one-and-a-half years before it was all clear to come back to the Islands. Upon returning, we attended Punahou School in Quonset huts that had been hurriedly put up on the University of Hawai`i campus.

The *Matsonia* was used to transport both civilian and military personnel during the War. It was still “camouflage” gray in 1947 this photos was taken by JBB.

Normally all the Matson ships were white as shown in this photo of the *Lurline* (JBB, 1954).

Recollections of Carl "Soot" Bredhoff

The Bredhoff family came to Honolulu in the early 1900's, my dad, Carl Bredhoff, in 1912. He and his dad had a film supply company and also owned the American Theater in Honolulu. It was sold to a Mr. Young, who showed Chinese films there for many years. It was torn down in the 70s, I think. Dad eventually went to work for Consolidated Amusement Co. and ran the film exchange until he retired.

My mother, Elizabeth Thurston, was born in Honolulu. Her mother was of Hawaiian—Chinese ancestry and born in Hilo, but was raised by the Meek family in Honolulu. Her father was born in Nova Scotia, went to sea at an early age and ended up in Honolulu, where he became the fire chief of Honolulu (1901-1928). The Honolulu Fire Department's training facility near the airport is named for him. My mother's great grandfather came from China and lived in Hilo. He was a "sugar master" who was brought in to show the sugar growers how to process cane into sugar.

It was a peaceful Sunday morning at 2550 Malama Place up in Mānoa Valley. Malama Place was just *mauka* (toward the mountains) of the Mid-Pacific Institute campus, a dead-end street that curves around and up a slight incline off Parker Place. Both sides of Malama Place are lined with homes that were built in the 1930s. My mother and I were home and my dad was at work at the Consolidated Amusement Company film exchange, a little *mauka* of the fire station and a stone's throw *mauka* and across the street from the Princess Theater. (The film exchange and the Princess Theater are long gone.) My thoughts that morning were probably on breakfast and the Shriner's football game that my dad and I had attended on Saturday. From the 'shady side' (Southwest) of the old Honolulu Stadium I can still see the huge American, Hawaiian and Shriner's flags flying between the light towers on the "sunny side," with beautiful green Mānoa Valley in the background.

I was next door in Grandmother Bredhoff's yard when the boy who lived behind us ran over to tell us that the Japanese were bombing Pearl Harbor and other military installations. The boy's father, an officer in the Army, had called home from Schofield (see map on page 15). My dad eventually returned home from work. He gave me a piece of shrapnel that he had found on the sidewalk on his way to get his car. He said it had

After Punahou, I graduated from Colorado State University (Colorado A&M in those days). I worked at Kualoa Ranch on O`ahu and Hawaiian Ranch Co. in Ka`u on Hawai`i (C. Brewer). The Hawaiian Ranch Co. was made up of Keauhou, Kapapala and Ka`alualu ranches and also Na`alehu Dairy. The ranch pasturelands stretched from South Point to The Volcano. Then I went to Maui to manage Kaupo Ranch for fifteen years and then to Kahuku Ranch in Ka'u for seventeen years. I retired in 2000 and moved back to Wailea, Maui where I live with my wife, Judith. Our daughter, Sarah, lives in Honolulu.

Note—My dear friend Cordie Wysard ('53), who grew up across the street in Mānoa, originated the nickname "Soot." According to Cordie we once painted ourselves with a mixture of ashes and water from the fireplace.

still been hot and was probably from our anti-aircraft shells. Dad said that the soldier who returned the film cans from Schofield plunked them down, glanced at the film cans he was supposed to take and said, "No movies tonight;" and hurried out. The rest of the day seemed to fly by. For a just-turned-seven-year-old, the sudden, surprising impact of this "day of infamy" was not something I could fully comprehend right away, but it did not take long. That evening I remember sitting with my dad on our little second-story balcony looking out over the blacked out island.

Other capsule memories of the war:

- Blackouts—windows and doors plainly covered or artistically decorated and covered.
- Wardens patrolling the neighborhood streets and knocking on your door if any light shone out!
- Headlights painted and covered so only a slit of light guided you down the street at night.
- Bomb shelters—some you could live in. We never used ours when the sirens blared—too wet and too many mosquitoes.
- School at the neighbor's house.
- Identification cards.
- Gas masks carried everywhere.
- Vaccinations.
- Parents and neighbors sitting on the Malama Place curb in the evening to "talk story" (Pidgin English for "chat").
- Barbed wire along the coastline, beaches and around strategic buildings.
- Military Police (MP) & Shore Patrol (SP) patrolling and the military presence everywhere
- Dad and the neighbors in BMTC (Businessmen's Training Corps)—they guarded some of those strategic buildings such as the Hawaiian Electric building.
- Slogans—"A slip of the lip can sink a ship."
- Learning the silhouettes of enemy aircraft.
- Selling eggs from our chickens to neighbors.
- Picking up and bagging kiawe (a thorny hardwood tree with long tan-colored beans, similar to mesquite) beans for Dairyman's cows.
- The military coming up our street in the evening and spraying for mosquitoes (DDT?).
- Gasoline and other rationing.
- Locally made booze—Five Island's Gin comes to mind.

➢My dad's homemade beer exploding in the garage.
➢Victory gardens at home and Mr. Brown Watanabe's across from the University of Hawai`i campus.
➢Walking to school through the Mid-Pacific and University of Hawai`i campuses with the Wysards (Punahou school mates), Diane McLean ('52) and Fred Peterson ('53).
➢Blue cellophane paper over the front of our flashlights.
➢Collecting pots and pans and grease for the war effort.
➢Grey Ladies, USO, etc.
➢War bonds.
➢Following the war on the maps of both the Pacific and European theaters and learning the names of many foreign places.
➢D-Day.
➢Midway, so decisive.
➢The songs and music inspired by the war.

... on and on and on. Never forget Pearl Harbor!

Shortly after the attack on Pearl Harbor, many of us purchased aircraft spotter guides (left) and became quite skillful at identifying planes by outline. We also had playing cards with airplanes (right).

Recollections of Ron Brunk

In early August, 1926, my parents were married and set out for Hawai`i. My father had signed a two-year contract to teach at McKinley High School. Dad taught those first two years at McKinley and my mother attended the University of Hawai`i. The second two years Dad taught in Hilo and my mother, having completed two years at the University, taught at Mountain View near Hilo. After that, for a total of forty years, my dad taught at McKinley and my mother finished at the University of Hawai`i and taught at Washington Intermediate School. I came into the world at Kapi`olani Maternity Hospital in 1934. I was the only baby in the hospital and, as was customary in those days, we were there more than a week! Since most of our class was born in 1934 and we had 180 or so, I wonder why there was not at least one other baby at the only maternity hospital in Honolulu during that week?

I went to Earlham College, then Iowa State University for my master's degree in agronomy. I worked in agriculture development in Vietnam (1958) and Poland (1959-60), then agriculture extension in Eldora, Iowa. At church in this community I met my wife-to-be and bought a corn, bean and hog farm in 1963, which I now run with son Steven. We have three children and six grandchildren.

On December 7, 1941, I was visiting my aunt's house on Pensacola Street, as was my cousin, who was in the Coast Guard. We were eating breakfast and the radio was playing music when just before 8:00 a.m. we heard the announcement telling of the attack on Pearl Harbor. I remember those moments well, especially my cousin running out the door (as he put on his shirt) to catch a ride to his base. My uncle at that time drove a panel truck for Young's Laundry. He was soon called out by radio, along with his fellow drivers, to come with their trucks to serve as ambulance drivers. We couldn't hear much except for explosions such as that caused by the bomb or shell that fell on the front steps of the main entrance to McKinley High School.

After what must have been a couple of hours during which the radio reported no further attacks, my aunt and I walked the two or three miles to my home past Punahou School and up Mānoa Road. An interesting note is that my father was "moonlighting" on Saturday and Sunday at a construction job. He and some other carpenters were up one of the valleys working on a large building away from houses, people or any telephones. They could not see Pearl Harbor, but they thought all those planes in the distance were part of an extremely large practice maneuver. At noon when they quit for lunch, one of the workers listening to his car radio first heard the news of the attack. They were close enough to see planes in the distance and hear explosions, but they were some of the last Americans to know what was happening. It does show in a way how little communication there was that first day. How the rumors spread! A parachutist had landed; the Japanese were landing on such and such a beach; submarines had been sighted here and there.

In the following days and months of blackout I remember we could not drive with our lights on and later only with our headlights covered with blue cellophane. We could only walk to neighbors' homes in the evening and sit in the dark on porches and visit. It was so hot and stuffy in the room blacked out with tar paper on the windows. Those were the days when we only had screens on the windows and relied on a breeze coming in to keep us cool. We had black tar paper on one room and the kitchen and the neighborhood warden checked to see if any light could be seen from outside.

I don't remember how long it was before school took up again. I was attending TC (Teacher's College Elementary School–University of Hawai`i) along with a number of others of our Punahou class of '52. When we eventually returned, we had trenches to go into during our daily air raid drill. We had to put our gas masks on during those drills. At first they were homemade gas masks, but soon we had regular issues. I believe we carried them with us by a shoulder strap. I think by the time school had begun again we had been fingerprinted and vaccinated and had our identification cards. Our long-time next-door neighbor, who had a fishing boat and had been born in Japan, was taken away to detention camp in the States.

Sampans (fishing boats) similar to this one, were used by Ron Brunk's Japanese neighbor (JBB, 1953).

Unfortunately, at the end of August my mother and I evacuated to California. I remember that ten-day trip in a large convoy of ships. Every morning before dawn we had to be on deck in our life jackets. I think it was at dawn that the enemy submarines were expected to attack. I came back to Honolulu a little over a year later, after the Japanese aircraft carriers had been destroyed. I traveled in an Army hospital ship with sixty other young boys in a single ward. That trip too was in a convoy and took ten days. We took a longer route away from the usual shipping lanes. While in California, I attended school in third grade and started fourth grade. I don't remember much about that school except there were forty or more of us in a class and I didn't learn anything that I know of. I remember how great it was to start fourth grade at Punahou, then on the University of Hawai`i campus when I returned and how much I liked Mrs. Wriston's class and all the interesting things we did in the fourth and fifth grades. I walked the mile to and from school each day and it was uphill both ways. Demi Black (his recollection appears in this book) will remember our walk home together each day. We moved back to the Punahou campus for sixth grade (1945) and after seven years on campus we all graduated.

Recollections of Ellen M. Colburn

Two Colburn brothers, Marcus and John, came to Hawai`i in the early 1800s on a whaling ship from Massachusetts where the first two Colburn brothers had settled in Dracut from England in 1635. Marcus and John stayed in Honolulu, with my great grandfather, Marcus Rexford Colburn, becoming a member of the first Honolulu Fire Department and my great granduncle, John Colburn, ending his career as the Minister of the Interior for Queen Lili`uokalani. My grandmother, Alice Neville, was a true hapa-haole, *(part English and part Hawaiian). Another ancestor, my namesake, Joseph Maughan, from Gosport, England, was Honolulu's first Harbormaster.*

My mother's ancestors, the Rose and Dutro families, came to Maui from Portugal also in the early 1800s. I have Hawaiian ancestors on that side of the family as well, from whom my mother learned to speak and write Hawaiian fluently. Most influential was Mary Pā of Wainiha, Kaua`i, who married Antone Dutro, a childless uncle who adopted my mother from his brother, Joaquin, in the Hawaiian tradition of "hanai," where a child was a precious gift within the extended family.

My father, Frederick Whitney Colburn, met his sweet Wailuku "Maui Girl" in Honolulu when they were teenagers. He dedicated his career to Hawaiian Electric Company where he rose from lineman to the position of Superintendent of Maintenance of all electric facilities that provided power for Honolulu and the island of O`ahu. He and my oldest brother, Frederick, Jr., who was HECO's Chief Load Dispatcher for O`ahu, were very busy on that fateful day.

December 7th. I had spent the night with my oldest brother's family in a little cottage on Pensacola Street across from McKinley High School's football field. When we heard loud booms on that quiet December 7th morning and went out to investigate, I remember seeing black "flowers" exploding against the blue sky in the *makai* (seaward) direction. Before long my father arrived to whisk me home to McCully Street. My parents seemed agitated but I didn't know why.

Then we heard a very loud whistling sound and my mother took me by the hand as we ran out to the driveway and looked up. As the whistling grew louder, we saw something coming right down toward us. Seconds later, the whole roof of a house only two doors away went up in a giant pillow of bright orange flames. We thought it was a bomb. It may have been an antiaircraft shell. Whatever it was, it shook everything and scared

I graduated in Humanities and Comparative Literature from Scripps College in Claremont CA, then completed a Master's Degree at Columbia University. I later earned an inter-disciplinary Ph.D. in Education and Bioethics at the Union Institute in Cincinnati, OH. My work experience ranged from teaching children in New York, California and Washington to teaching adults in exotic places and the U.S. I served as an Education Officer at Siriba College in Maseno, Kenya for several years where my Swahili took me safely "up country" and where I took flying lessons in a Cessna in order to see the more remote parts of East Africa. After returning to Hawai`i in 1978, I consulted for schools in Micronesia and Australia, and in Honolulu I served as a fulltime consultant to the Queen Lili`uokalani Children's Center before becoming chief administrator of Antioch Univer-

us. I later learned that it killed my friend, a young Japanese mother and her new baby.

I don't remember exactly what happened next except that my father took our garden hose, climbed a tall ladder, and started watering down the roof. Then he came in and said he would take me to Lunalilo School where it would be safer to be away from the approaching fire.

My next vivid memory is of my father once again coming to pick me up from the school. When told that I was safe there, he said that the school's roof was on fire, probably from burning embers from the McCully fire. Since my father was a Hawaiian Electric superintendent, he took me to the HECO substation on Pumehana Street only a block from the school, its thick walls providing a sense of quiet and safety.

In the meantime, since the fire was heading straight for our house with its very tall hibiscus hedge, the American Legion sent members to remove all of our furniture, right down to the oven with its cooking turkey. Photos document our strewn possessions, including the baby grand piano, as they sat on the sidewalk across the street. Archival movies have a clip of our Algaroba Street entrance and the frantic "civilian" activity of those moments. It was shown on the national newsreel in theaters around the country. And even today, sixty years later, the same clip is rolled out during December 7th commemorative events.

We turned out to be very lucky that day, not only to avoid the direct hit, but because the "wind shifted," as I would hear my parents recall for many years after that. The fire then burned toward King Street instead of Algaroba Street, leveling those commercial buildings. I would later skate on the concrete floors of those burned out buildings where, one day, a newspaper photographer gave me a nickel to pose for a picture with a burned teddy bear.

We spent the next few days on Wilhelmina Rise (Maunalani Heights) with my Auntie Alma and Uncle Tom Cockett until it was safe to return home to a refurnished house. For a long time after that, I had nightmares about fires. I had just "turned six" only two-and-a-half months before.

sity's undergraduate and graduate programs. In 1987 I joined the doctoral faculty of my alma mater, Union Institute, where I still enjoy a fulltime professorship. My most interesting and rewarding community service was a six-year term as a member of Hawai`i's Judicial Selection Commission where we screened and selected finalists for judges at all levels from District and Family Courts to the Supreme Court. I was elected Vice-chair after two years as the only female on the commission of 4 attorneys and 5 laypersons. Because of the timing of my staggered term, since 1995 I enjoyed the unique role of having been involved in the selection of Hawai`i's entire 5-member Supreme Court, which includes one woman and is the most diverse in the country. I cherish with great pride the signed photo of the five Justices which is in a prominent place in my office. I intend to keep active as a fulltime professor with "the Union" as long as I enjoy good health and the regular travel that is expected in my position.

Recollections of Charley Cooke

*As a member of four different Missionary families, Cooke, Rice, Wilcox and Lyman, my brother and I represent a cross section of many that came to Hawai`i for various reasons. The Cookes were originally hired by the Crown to teach the children of the* ali`i *(royalty). Many in the various families were engaged in agriculture on the islands of Kaua`i, Maui and Hawai`i, with others working in ranching on Moloka`i, and banking and retailing on O`ahu. Many of us today are still involved with these various fields of endeavor.*

After high school graduation, I went off to college, then into the service for two years, then a three-month trip to Africa to do game control work, then back to college. I was married in 1957. I worked two years for Bank of Hawai'i, twelve years for Honolulu Sporting Goods and twenty-nine years in real estate. I have four children, two boys and two girls, three of whom are living on the mainland and one on Maui, and seven grandchildren. We were hanai (foster parents) to two boys of Samoan descent and raised them as our own. One of the boys graduated from the University of Oregon with a Master's and the other from the University of Hawai`i. Both played football at St. Louis and then received full collegiate scholarships. I still live in Honolulu on the old family property.

On December 7th I was just eight years old when war erupted in Hawai`i on that now famous Sunday morning. Reliving that Sunday, I can clearly remember a number of things.

My dad, mother, brother and I left our home in Mānoa around 8:00 a.m. and were headed to our beach home on the North Shore at La`ie. We were driving down Punahou Street opposite the track and football field when Dad commented on all of the activity at Pearl Harbor (we did not have the proliferation of concrete buildings to block our view in that era). I can remember him saying that it certainly looked like a real war was on. About that time a military sedan passed us at a very high rate of speed, which brought forth an additional comment—"look at that darn fool and how fast he is driving." My parents then realized something was not right.

Dad turned on the radio, and we heard Webley Edwards announce that civilians were to get off the road as we were under attack by the Japanese. He kept repeating this message over and over. By the time we decided to follow the instructions to seek refuge in a safe place, we were in Nu`uanu Valley near my great uncle's home (Teddy Cooke). As we drove into the yard we heard a loud screeching sound followed by a tremendous explosion across Nu`uanu Avenue. We later learned that one of our own anti-aircraft shells had demolished a home when it failed to explode until it hit the house.

Uncle Teddy instructed my dad to go out to the garage and fill as many kerosene lanterns as he could find, as he thought the Japanese would bomb the Hawaiian Electric plant in downtown Honolulu. Dad and I had set out for the garage some fifty yards from the main house when two Zero fighter planes flew over us. We could see the red "meatball" insignia on the underside of the wings of the aircraft. Dad picked me up and threw me through the open garage door so that we would not be seen by the pilots. We learned later that the planes were headed for Kāne`ohe Air Station to bomb and strafe the Navy seaplane (PBY) base.

Late in the afternoon we were driven home to Mānoa and spent the next few days living at our grandparents' home (next door to our house) as it was considered to be a safety zone in the area. Dad took our 1940 Ford "woody" (Banana wagon in those days) and went to help the Red Cross. We did not see him for a week. The "woody" was taken over by the Government (martial law), as was his thirty-two-foot fishing boat. The boat was used throughout the war to patrol Honolulu Harbor.

So many things happened after the 7th. We had to carry gas masks with us at all times, had bomb shelters dug in the front yard and had to have an identification card with finger prints on us at all times. Gas was rationed and if you were lucky, you were issued a sticker with a "C" on it. This sticker was placed on the inside of your windshield and allowed you a larger ration of gas each month versus the "A" and "B" stickers. Much to the concern of many adults in the civilian community, booze was limited and sugar was rationed along with many other items.

As a sub-teen it was an exciting time for me. Playing war with my friends, being able to identify most of the airplanes we saw, and being taken into Pearl Harbor to see some of the big ships were such a treat. Memory begins to fade regarding most of the war years as we were put on a routine schedule and, with martial law in effect, we were limited as to what we could do and where we could go.

We had no supermarkets in those days, but we did have "neighborhood" grocery wagons like the one pictured here (1930s postcard).

Recollections of Virginia Crippen Claire

After a year at Oregon State College, I was married for twenty years and raised four daughters. Following our divorce, I was a waitress and bartended for six years while I attended Red Rocks Community College and graduated from Regis in 1987 with a cum laude degree in Mathematics. Since then, I have taught a variety of study skills and administered various tests in the Denver area. Four years ago I bought my own town home, and today I live with my two little black dogs in Thornton, CO.

My father was a civil service welder for the Army in California. One day, in late 1941, he passed by the "Job Openings" bulletin board and noticed an announcement for a welder at Fort Shafter in Honolulu, Hawai`i. He thought Hawai`i might be an exotic place to work and live, so after talking it over with my mother, he applied for and was awarded the job. The three of us moved to the Islands. We lived in upper Kalihi Valley until the end of November, 1941, when Army housing became available. During those years, civilian employees and their families could live on the base. We moved to Fort Shafter on December 1st, just before that fateful day.

My eighth birthday was on December 6th. During the morning of my birthday, I asked my mother if I could have a birthday party. She was still knee deep in boxes, so she told me that if I could be patient, she would have coke and ice cream for all of the kids on Sunday afternoon. That seemed like a good idea to me so I readily agreed. By that evening the house was in pretty good order and my mother fixed a nice dinner for my father and me. Sunday morning, December 7th, after breakfast, the kids that lived near me and I were all playing outside in the quadrangle between the civilian housing. Some airplanes flew overhead and the pilots dipped their airplanes' wings in order to wave at us as we played. The airplanes looked funny to us because they had big red circles on the sides, and the pilots wore leather helmets, but what did we know, we were just kids, so we waved back. After several of these planes went over, some of the parents came out to see what was happening because they could not understand why the planes were flying so low. They were familiar with airplanes flying overhead due to training missions, but these planes seemed to be flying too low.

One of the women, Kitty Brown, went inside to turn on her radio to see if anything was on the news about these low-flying planes. She came bursting out the front door yelling that it was war, that those were Japanese planes, and for all of us to get inside quickly. Within just a few minutes, Army personnel came to all our doors, telling the men to report to work and the women and children to prepare for Army trucks to come pick them up. About twenty minutes later, the trucks arrived and the women and children were taken to a hillside, given Army blankets and told that when we heard planes we were to cover ourselves with the blankets and lie on the ground. While we were on the hillside, we could hear the bombing and the strafing of the ships at Pearl Harbor. During those hours on the hillside, children became restless and started chasing each other all over the place. At one point, as I was running from a playmate, I stumbled over a rock and fell flat on my face. It was at that exact time that some heavy shelling took place. My mother went into hysterics, certain that I had been shot dead. Another mother ran over and picked me up, skinned knees and all, and returned me to my mother, with the assurance that I was not seriously injured. Needless to say, that ended the children's play on the hillside.

Luckily, after just a short while, the Army trucks returned and took us all back home. We were told to pack up enough stuff for twenty-four hours. An hour later, the trucks returned and took us to nearby Red Hill where some ammunition storage caves were being dug. The cave my mother and I were in was huge. The Red Cross was there. Holes had been dug in the ground and planks were laid across the holes. These were rural latrines. The Red Cross gave all of us peanut butter and jelly sandwiches and mugs of milk. As I was consuming my dinner, my mother reminded me that this was my birthday cake and ice cream, and that I was a mighty lucky little girl to be getting this treat. After eating, we were given blankets and pillows and told we would have to sleep on the ground that night.

The next morning we were taken back home and told to pack enough stuff for three days because we would be returned to the cave. We were gone from our cave for three hours. When we were taken back, we were astounded. Monstrous wooden doors, closing the cave from the outside, had been erected. When the trucks drove into the cave, more astonishment awaited us. The Seabees had been very busy while we were gone. Along with the outside doors, the Seabees had put in place a complete kitchen, a hospital, a clinic, washrooms with running water, real latrine and cubicles for each individual family with cots for us to sleep on that night. There were stacks of empty boxes where we could put our personal belongings and rocks where we could hang our clothes. There was a big community area where people could gather and talk or play cards or listen to the radio or whatever. I really don't have much memory of the next three days. I just know those days were OK.

When we were finally taken home, we were asked, if at all possible, to please go to the Mainland until the war was over. My mother and I went to Southern California, leaving my father in the Islands. We stayed there for a little over two years before returning to Honolulu. Before we left for California, I had been a student in the second grade, along with '52 classmates Bonnie Edgar, Donald Smith and Fritz Abplanalp, at Kapālama School in Kalihi Valley. When my mother and I returned to the Islands, I went back to Kapālama because we now lived in lower Kalihi Valley across the street from Kalākaua Junior High, and there, at Kapālama, were Bonnie, Donald and Fritz.

At this point, I might add that if my parents and I had not moved to Fort Shafter, I probably would not be here writing to you. You see, the house we had lived in had been completely riddled with shrapnel from one of the American shells that landed in the street directly in front of our house. The people who moved into the house after we moved out were Catholic and were at church. We are not Catholic, and we would have been at home. Everything in the house had shrapnel holes: the furniture, the refrigerator, the stove, and the walls, all the clothes in all the closets, everything. That same American shell killed two of the girls I had played with on many, many occasions. One lived directly across the street and the other, along with her father, lived down the street a few houses. They had been in their garage washing their car.

Fruits and vegetables could be purchased from truck farmers along the highways (JBB, 1952).

Recollections of Bob Deatrick

(1934-2002)

My father was manager of the Brunners store in Sacramento. His family members were originally ranchers in Orange County. Brunners sold furniture and appliances and is still in existence. The Fukunaka family hired my dad to manage their Easy Appliance store on King and Fort streets.

Bob received his BS from UCLA and was Vice President of Human Resources for Ernest & Julio Gallo Winery in Modesto, CA for many years. He and his wife, Betty Lou, had three children (two sons and a daughter) and a grandson.

In 1941, prior to December 7th, I was living with my parents on Makiki Street and attending First Christian Church School on Kewalo Street. On this particular morning, I was walking down Makiki Street when I reached Wilder Avenue. Crossing the street, I noticed my teacher waiting for me at the corner of Wilder and Kewalo streets. I started to run toward her, but when I passed a large house surrounded by a high wooden fence, a gate suddenly opened and a large police dog attacked me. It bit my left leg (the tooth scar still shows). The ensuing commotion brought several men out of the house, all speaking Japanese. My teacher arrived and they carried me inside the house. They cleansed my wound while the teacher was yelling for someone to call an ambulance. I stopped bleeding after they applied some dressing, and soon I was able to stand up. They filled my pockets with all kinds of goodies, and I agreed I was able to continue to school. My teacher reluctantly agreed. A few weeks later two men visited our home. They identified themselves as FBI agents. They questioned me about what I saw inside the fence and the house that day. They wanted to know if I had noticed any radio equipment. I replied in the negative. The house was the Japanese Consulate.

Another story on December 7, 1941—our home was close to the concrete-lined Makiki drainage ditch. When things calmed down, several men obtained 2x4s and laid a floor in the ditch under the Makiki Street overpass. They later obtained sand bags and fortified the entrance. We spent five nights in the air raid shelter with half of the insects of O`ahu. With everyone else, we listened to the rumors circulating around Honolulu. When it was safe to move out of the shelter, the ditch became the favorite play area for the younger kids during the day (and the favorite play area for the teenagers at night).

Recollections of John Dunstan

I retired six years ago as a physicist. I am now semi-retired in that three days a week I play cowboy at a supermarket, rounding up shopping carts. I live in Hiram, Maine, a small community of 1,100 people stretching over a hundred square miles. Quiet and peaceful.

I was born in York, Maine in 1932. Early in 1933, my father accepted the position of associate pastor at Central Union Church in Honolulu. We left New York by ship and traveled through the Panama Canal to Los Angeles. I nearly gave my parents heart failure while we were passing through the Panama Canal. We had an outside cabin. My parents were on deck enjoying the trip. They had left the cabin door open so they would hear me in case I cried. I slipped out of the crib and went to sleep under the dresser. When my parents checked and found my crib empty, they turned the ship upside-down looking for me. They found me still asleep under the dresser after several anxious hours. I learned to walk during the trip to Honolulu. In 1937 my father accepted a position at the University of Hawai`i to teach religion.

On the morning Pearl Harbor was bombed, we turned on the radio to listen to the news, but heard only static for about fifteen minutes. Then we heard an announcement to the effect that all were to remain at home, off the streets, and to keep calm. At about nine o'clock, Dad, my sister Jane ('51) and I went to church. We walked from Seaview Rise, along Vancouver Drive, through the (Punahou) school grounds, across Wilder Avenue and on the back road to church. We knew what had happened when we started down the hill to the back gate at school. Black smoke was rising from Pearl Harbor. Sugar cane burns with white smoke. The return trip home was just as eventful.

Many families of Punahou classmates attend Central Union Church on Beretania St in Honolulu (photo courtesy of S.W. Tinker, early 1960s).

Before the war, say 1940-1941, we used to have baseball games on Rocky Hill behind the Punahou campus. The hill was used as a pasture by one of the local farmers. We would find the freshest cow-pie for home base. Needless to say no one stole home. When Army guards were first placed on the campus, after the attack, no one explained to them about the cows. The poor farmer lost most of his cows that first night. The cows did not stop when challenged with, "Halt! Who goes there?"

I walked to school on Monday, December 8th and went the same route we used on Sunday. When I approached the back gate, I was met by an armed guard saying, "You can't go to school here any more." This was the beginning of a long Christmas vacation and a hectic time for the Dunstan family. My mother and my aunt, both teachers in junior academy, had to salvage what they could of books and equipment that the Corps of Engineers had thrown out of the classrooms onto the lawn. Remember the USED cars and trucks around town? They were stationed at Punahou. After the salvage work, the next job was to find places to hold classes and time bus rides so that no one was on the streets after dark. Towards the end of January we were issued gas masks. I was one of the fortunate students who did not have to travel far to class. Mine was held next door in the School of Religion. Mrs. Gibson was my teacher.

On December 7, 1941, there were about 33 kids almost my age, in the neighborhood, mostly from navy families. By the end of January, it seemed only my sister and I were left.

In late 1942, my sister and I were rudely awakened between 2:30 and 3:00 in the morning by three bomb blasts. We found ourselves under our beds. Duck and cover training worked well. My father, on his next trip to the States to recruit missionaries, found out what had happened. The crew that had dropped the bombs was on my father's plane. It seems that this crew strayed from the rest of the flight coming from California. They did not know the password. The rest of the flight, on crossing Waikīkī Beach, was challenged and gave the correct password. They were permitted to proceed to Hickam Field. About a half hour later, the stray approached and was challenged. Because the crew didn't know the password, they were held up. A trigger-happy gunner on the beach fired a burst at them. The pilot ordered the bomb bay doors open and the bombs were dropped. The loaded bombs were to have been used against any subs that the crew might have sighted on the trip from the West Coast.

Each graduating class painted its year on Rocky Hill, an outcrop in the back of the Punahou campus (courtesy of J. Dunstan, 1951).

By 1942 my father had taken the position of General Secretary for the Hawaiian Board of Missionaries. As islands in the Pacific were taken from the enemy, my father was one of three men who helped the navy re-establish the mission field in the Northern Pacific area. The work that Dad was doing was felt to be so essential to the war effort that he and the two other ministers were given priority status such that only General McArthur, Admiral Nimitz and

Admiral Halsey could bump them from air transport to and from the Coast. The upper brass often resented that.

Every trip my father made to the States required an exchange of bills. Going to the States, Hawaiian money had to be exchanged for American money. If Dad had tried to use the Hawaiian money on the Coast he would have faced arrest as an insurgent.

Jane and John Dunstan try out the gas masks issued to them by the Civil Defense shortly after the attack (courtesy of J.Dunstan).

I remember that when President Roosevelt came to Honolulu, his people were upset that his special open car had been left behind in San Francisco. They hunted in vain through every car dealership in the Territory for a Cadillac convertible for the President to use. Finally, the Department of Motor Vehicles searched its files and found one that was duly commandeered. I doubt the President ever learned who owned the car or whether the people were cheering him or the car. The car he was riding in was the pink Cadillac convertible that belonged to the owner/hostess of the largest brothel in Honolulu!

Early in 1943 I took on a paper route that I kept until the war was over. I remember that, in addition to my gas mask and ID card, I had to carry my permit to be out during blackout. I lost that card when my parents moved to the States.

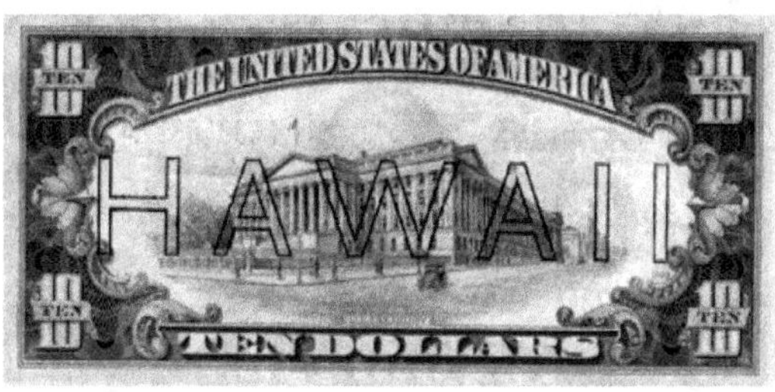

All bills used in the Islands from 1942-1944 were stamped with "Hawai`i" in case of invasion.

Recollections of Bonnie Edgar Lindquist

After Ken Lindquist, a handsome Naval Lieutenant J.G., saved me from spinsterhood in 1954, we moved first to California, then Nebraska, then to Chicago for thirty-seven years, and finally (we hope) to Carbondale, Illinois. We have four sons, four daughters-in-law and seven grandchildren. I retired from a Park Ridge Nursing Home as a Music Therapist in 1995 and we moved here in December of that year. We love Southern Illinois, and invite you to fish the lakes, hike the hills, and kick back and enjoy the beauty.

Bert Edgar, my dad, left Glasgow, Scotland, in the mid-1920s on his way to this small group of islands anchored in the Pacific called Hawai`i. Why Scotland to Hawai`i? His sister, Jean Edgar Muirhead, had come to Honolulu as the bride of John Muirhead after World War I. When Dad graduated from the University of Edinburgh, his sister wrote from Honolulu to tell him of the good opportunities for foresters in the Hawaiian Islands. Dad traveled across Canada in a cattle car, left Vancouver on the "Ariana" and arrived in the Hawaiian Islands in 1926 or 1927. In 1928 Bert was living in the Bachelor Quarters on Waipahu Plantation and working as a luna (foreman) on Waipahu Sugar Plantation.

One Sunday morning, this redhead Bert spied a petite, raven-haired Canadian nurse by the name of Ethel May Pinnegar watching tennis on the courts, which by chance, were situated between the nurse and bachelor quarters. Ethel had come to Honolulu instead of going to Grenfell settlement in Greenland because her doctor in Buffalo, New York, had warned her not to go to such a cold climate. Oh yes, there was the story of the petite nurse standing over the redhead who was recovering from an appendectomy, brandishing a hammer and threatening dire consequences if a wedding was not in the near future. The real story is that Ethel returned to New York to fulfill a commitment to a colleague to work a year in Wellsville, New York. The lovelorn Bert cabled his proposal and Ethel returned to Honolulu via the Panama Canal and San Francisco. Within the week of April 19, 1933, she became Mrs. Bert Edgar. In 1936 we left Waipahu Sugar Plantation for Moanalua Gardens on the Damon Estate. Here we were, at the intersection of Pu`uloa and Moanalua roads just down the hill from Fort Shafter on December 7th, 1941.

Dad had gone out early in the morning to play tennis. I was helping (?) Mom bathe my six-week-old baby sister, Margaret. Mom and I heard the booms and checked for rain; there was none. We checked the calendar for Chinese New Year—wrong date for that! When Dad returned, he explained that he was lucky to be home. He said that the Japanese were bombing O`ahu and that he had been stopped three times by Military Police. He repeated three times that his wife, just recovering from Cesarean delivery, was home with the baby daughter and a seven-year-old. I can see my Dad's face as he told us the story of his journey home.

Soon after Dad got home, the long line of lorries began and was to continue throughout the day of December 7th. These lorries carried wounded Military Personnel from Pearl Harbor to Fort Shafter's Tripler Hospital, a small wooden structure on the Diamond Head side (south) of our home in Moanalua Valley. We watched this endless line of lorries from our front yard. Later on that morning a group of women in chenille bathrobes wandered through our lawn. We never could find out where they came from or where they were going. During the afternoon, Military Police visited Japanese workers' homes on the Damon Estate and confiscated short wave radio sets, telescopes and binoculars.

On the afternoon of December 7th, Dad found some old scratchy heavy carpet and nailed it to all of our windows (as I remember). No light leaked from those windows, but neither did any air leak in or out. To this day I remember the palpable fear my parents had of another Japanese air attack or invasion that night, or the next day. Dad worked fast on that carpeting to prepare for the blackout that was to begin at dusk the evening of December 7th. If memory serves me correctly (and sometimes it fails completely), I spent a restless night. Mom went to work a few nights later; she had no choice in the matter. She drove up on the University of Hawai`i campus to a MASH unit at 11:00 p.m. every night following the highway line through pinholes of light from her mostly blackened headlights. She said later that it was the hardest assignment she ever had. An oriental man had driven up to the gate of a military installation and did not understand the command, "Halt." When he accelerated, the sentry shot him in the abdomen, and he was a sick man when he arrived at the MASH unit at the University of Hawai`i.

In 1942 civilians were given a choice to move to the Mainland or remain in the Islands. Mother said, "The girls and I will stay here with Daddy." (My parents remain on the Islands they both so loved, buried in a Masonic Plot across the way from the graves of my auntie Jean and Uncle Jack Muirhead.)

One of the classic old buildings in downtown Honolulu during the war years was the Aala Pawn Shop building (JBB, 1962).

Recollections of Alice Flanders Guild

I graduated from Punahou School in 1952 and Colorado Woman's College in Denver in 1954. Later that year, I married Robert W. Guild of Honolulu. We have four children. After careers in advertising, shopping center management and historic preservation, I retired as Executive Director of `Iolani Palace in 2002. Currently, we split our time between Honolulu and the Big Island of Hawai`i where we have a small ranch outside of Waimea. Our children all reside in Hawai`i.

My mother, Muriel Macfarlane Flanders, was part Hawaiian on both sides of her family. Her paternal great grandfather, Judge Herman Wideman came from Bremen, Germany and settled on Kaua`i, where he established Grove Farm Plantation. His wife, Kaūmana, was from a chiefly Kaua`i family. One of their daughters, Emelia, married Frederick Macfarlane who arrived from New Zealand with his family in the second half of the 19th century.

My mother's maternal grandfather, James Campbell, arrived in Hawai`i from Scotland, settling on Maui, where he was a partner in Pioneer Mill in Lahaina. There he married Abigail Maipinepine and eventually moved his family to Honolulu. My grandmother, Alice Kamokila Campbell, was one of four surviving daughters. After marrying and divorcing F. Walter Macfarlane, she went on to become a colorful political figure and a proponent of Hawaiian Culture.

My father, Walter E. Flanders Jr., was the son of a Detroit automobile manufacturer who has been credited with the invention of mass production for Henry Ford. In the early 1900's, his mother, Hazel, divorced her high-spirited husband and brought her three children to California. My parents met and married in San Francisco, where I was born. Traveling to Hawai`i in July 1934, at two weeks of age, I was the youngest child (not born at sea) to cross the Pacific.

On Old Pali Road (Nu`uanu), Sunday morning, December 7, 1941, Naka-san was feeding baby Judy in the kitchen, and Mary and I were enjoying a rare family breakfast with our parents. My father had recently opened a branch of his haberdashery, Flanders Store for Men, on the arcade fronting the original Outrigger Canoe Club. Sunday was a busy shopping day with many locals and tourists in Waikīkī, so Daddy had given up his usual tennis game at the Kailua Racquet Club to man the Kalākaua Avenue store. As he was getting into the car, there was a drone from planes directly overhead and, at the same time, loud booms could be heard in the distance. My father reassured us that it was probably army maneuvers and he headed off to the store.

View from the Pali looking northward. Kaneohe is toward the right (1930s postcard).

We learned of the attack on Pearl Harbor when Mother called her pal, Ma`ili Yardley, to see if she wanted to play tennis. When Ma`ili's mother answered, she told her to get off the phone, we were being bombed! While Mother was rushing around trying to find a radio that worked, the Hite twins came racing in to say that Japanese troops had parachuted into Nu`uanu valley and had poisoned the reservoirs. This proved to be false information but, because the twins' father was the Lieutenant Governor, it had to be taken seriously. Reports were coming in that people had been killed in downtown Honolulu, giving credence to the rumor that the Japanese had indeed landed.

Today, the old Pali road is closed in favor of tunnels (JBB, 2002).

Today, we understand the term "friendly fire." At that time, it was inconceivable that our own anti-aircraft guns could be shelling the city. Everyone went to bed in his or her clothes that night. My guess is that very few adults actually fell asleep.

It wasn't until the next day that we learned from President Roosevelt's radio speech that we had not been invaded. My mother's recollection is that the city was in chaos and people were hoarding food and supplies. School was suspended indefinitely and people were evacuated from their shoreline homes. Over the next few days, friends and relatives and their household help moved into our Nu`uanu Valley home. After dark, everyone congregated in the blacked-out dining room, where the smell of cigarette smoke and whiskey kept us kids at bay. Once it was determined that the Japanese were not lurking off shore, our houseguests went home and life settled into a constant state of unsettlement. In order to adhere to stringent blackout requirements, evenings were spent in a small, windowless, interior pantry. We ate early meals by flashlight and were all in bed by dark. Almost every night I could hear my parents talking late into the night, and I knew that they were not in agreement on something very important. We soon found out that, over Mother's objections, Daddy had decided that we would be evacuated to the safety of his mother's home in Menlo Park, California.

During the second week of January, our mother and we three children were bundled off at 11:00 p.m. to a freighter docked at Aloha Tower in Honolulu Harbor. Our uncle, Walter "Mac," then a Territorial senator, had pulled strings to get us into a convoy to the mainland. Only passengers were allowed on board, so, fully expecting to be at sea by morning, we bid a tearful goodbye to Daddy and Uncle Mac.

When we awakened, we were still tied to the dock and remained there for the next three days. We were not allowed to disembark and visitors could not come aboard. Those hot, humid days were spent walking the decks and waving to relatives who regularly came by to see if we were still in port. The ship was filled with elderly people, mostly women, outnumbering the crew five to one. Lifeboat drills were held several times a day, including the wee hours of the night. Everyone was required to wear large, rigid life vests at all times and, since Judy's was much too big, Mom had to carry it while dragging her on a "leash." The only other children that we saw were Louis ('52) and Mariette Gaspar ('54) who were traveling with an elderly nanny. Our mother often looked after them, too, since the whole ordeal was overwhelming for the old lady.

After the second day in port, my mother decided she was incapable of making the trip alone. We children were filthy from the grimy decks and there was no hot water in the cabin sink, only in the communal shower shared by three other cabins of six people each. Meals were nearly impossible, with two sittings of thirty minutes each in which to get three children fed. The food, mostly canned, was terrible. She asked the purser to contact her brother to get us off the ship. Walter "Mac" called both the civil and military governors but the answer was no. We had seen the where the ship's guns were located and they could take no chances of "leaks."

On the fourth night we sailed out of the harbor, with no lights showing, to join the convoy of ghost ships headed for California. On the first day at sea, the captain called Mother into his office and told her that since there were only rope railings on our deck, she must hold the children's hands whenever we left the cabin. With only two hands and often five children in tow, venturing on deck was a scary ordeal. The captain had put the fear of God into my mother when he told her that the convoy would be zigzagging across the Pacific to avoid detection by the Japanese and that there would be no stopping or going back for anyone who fell overboard.

We shared a tiny cabin with an older woman who, I found out later, had a drinking problem. She would often stagger around at night, locking herself in the bathroom for hours. She must have run out of liquor after the first few days because she spent the rest of the trip in her bunk, insisting that the room remain dark at all times. We couldn't play or read in the small, dark room, there was no lounge or common room and the decks were filthy and slippery. An old gypsy couple had brought their belongings on board in an orange crate. Whenever they came on deck they hauled the crate with them and used it as a deck chair. Everyone was so envious because, with the exception of the mess hall, which was kept locked between meals, there wasn't a single available chair on the entire ship.

Our poor mother had her hands full with a frightened and bored trio of little girls, ages one, four and seven. For ten days we zigzagged across the Pacific, responding day and night to lifeboat drills, never knowing if it was the real thing. With no available play area, we walked the decks all day, holding on to the rope "railings." Luckily for all of us, a young steward took a shine to our mother and brought her meals on a tray, taking Judy's dirty diapers along with him to the ship's laundry. This was strictly against the rules, but without his help, I think my mother might have thrown herself overboard or perhaps, one or all of us! Everyone was on deck cheering as we sailed under the Golden Gate Bridge and into the safety of San Francisco Bay. The captains and crews of those convoy ships deserve special recognition for the thankless job they performed. Although Japanese submarines were often sighted, every American convoy made it safely between Hawai`i and California.

Note: I received help for this recollection from an interview with my mother, Muriel Macfarlane Flanders.

February 26, 1942

MEMORANDUM FOR ALL PERSONNEL ON BOARD.

Subject: Security of information.

1. The following is quoted for information and compliance:

"THE OFFICERS, CREW AND ALL PASSENGERS EMBARKED FROM WAR ZONES SHOULD BE VERY CAUTIOUS AND CAREFUL NOT TO DISCUSS OR FURNISH INFORMATION ON OBSERVATIONS IN OR NEAR COMBAT AREAS. THIS, OF COURSE, INCLUDES GIVING ANY INFORMATION RELATIVE TO DAMAGE SUFFERED BY ANY NAVAL OR MERCHANT SHIP. ALSO NO INFORMATION OF ANY KIND SHOULD BE GIVEN CONCERNING THE FOLLOWING; CASUALITIES OF THE PERSONNEL OF ARMED FORCES, DEFENSE WEAPONS, PLANT PRODUCTION CAPACITIES, FACILITIES FOR THE REPAIR OF NAVAL CRAFT AT NAVAL SHORE STATIONS, COMPOSITION OF AND SIZE OF CONVOYS, INFORMATION RELATIVE TO THE ESCORT OF SAID CONVOYS, SHIPS SEEN ENROUTE OR ANY CONCENTRATION OR MOVEMENTS OF MERCHANT OR NAVAL SHIPS".

C. A. Goebel,
Commander, U.S. Navy,
Executive Officer.

(Letter above courtesy of Ellen Luhrs, [transcribed from original]).

Recollections of Fred Hundhammer, Jr.

Fred received his BS from the University of California (Berkeley) and was an investment banker in California, then president and owner of a communications company in New York. He and his wife, Joan, have two children and two grandchildren. Fred and Joan now live on board their boat in Florida.

I was born on September 27, 1934, in Honolulu, the eldest son of Fred and Dinah Hundhammer. Fred, Sr. came to Honolulu in 1932 as an automobile salesman for Von Hamm Young and sold Packard automobiles. Dinah Dunn, my mother, was the youngest of thirteen children, a 1926 graduate of Kamehameha Schools and a 1930 graduate of University of Hawai`i. Her father, my grandfather, Francis S. Dunn, emigrated to the Kingdom of Hawai`i in 1857 from Edinburgh, Scotland, as an engineer of the Sugar Plantation Owners to build sugar mills. In his lifetime, he built and worked on forty-two mills throughout the Kingdom. I have three siblings, brothers: John (deceased December 1998); Tom, Makawao, Maui; and a sister, Demetra, Hilo, Hawai`i.

Although I entered Punahou in kindergarten, I left in the first grade and attended Central School, across from the Academy of Arts. I know Bob Deatrick (whose story appears in this book) was in my class because he is in a picture taken at my seventh birthday party. We had just started the second grade and it was 1941. We lived in a large, white two-story colonial home in Woodlawn above the Chinese cemetery in Upper Mānoa. I remember we had many of the trappings of 1941; we had two Japanese maids and a full-time gardener. We always had new cars. My Dad was a used car dealer (Hawaiian Auto Exchange offices on King Street across from the Honolulu Advertiser and later across from Kau Kau Corner—a landmark drive-in restaurant located at the corner of Kapi`olani and Kalākaua avenues). But for this story, it is the King Street office and car lot that matters. Dad took all the trade-ins from Von Hamm Young and Schuman Carriage. I should mention that Jimmy Pell's grandfather was the manager of Von Hamm Young and, of course, Scotty Schuman (Manu's father) owned Schuman Carriage (Both Jimmy and Manu were '52 classmates). Schuman was the Cadillac and Buick dealer, so we always had the latest Cadillac four-door.

So let's get to the story. December 7, 1941, was truly a "day which will live in infamy!" I now identify the day with the beginning of my childhood memory. Before that date everything I know about had been told to me by my parents, or I have photos to prove I was there. But not so with December 7th...that day I remember vividly without any assistance from my parents.

The first thing I remember was that we did not have to go to Sunday school. My father had some reason to go into the office that Sunday morning and my mother was going to drive him there, and then pick him up later. That left my brother,

John, and me at home alone with one of our Japanese maids. (The other maid did not show up for work.) John was six at the time. All we ever did was play soldiers. War was everywhere in the newspapers, which I had just learned to read, and all over the movie and radio news. War in Europe and China was talked about in our household as we had relatives in Germany and Britain. To us kids, war was fun. We had a big fort in our back yard and a tree house fort from which to shoot at planes.

Well, on that Sunday morning, excused from Sunday school, we were playing soldiers and were up in the tree house shooting with our various toy weapons at all the planes which, we thought, were "practicing." Target practice was very common in the skies over Honolulu in those days. At least two, maybe three, Zeros flew right above our special tree house on their way to their Pearl Harbor targets. We could have shot them down with the proper equipment, but remember it was 1941 and we kids only had toy weapons in those days.

About the time the last plane flew over our tree house, my father came driving into the driveway at what seemed to us a very dangerous high speed. He got out of his car screaming at us "crazy kids" for being outside, and in the tree house yet! He kept asking for Mother who was not yet home. It seemed to me she just drove him to work a few minutes before. She arrived home about twenty minutes later, not the least bit disturbed, but very confused about Dad being there as she had just dropped him at his King Street office.

Now my father is shaken up and starts to tell us all we are being attacked and INVADED by the Japanese. Our maid was very upset too, apologizing for her race. Our other maid, who did not show up that morning, had sent three sons back to Japan the year before to fight against China. Now, they were there in Japan and members of the Japanese armed forces.

Dad had been in his office about ten minutes, when a bomb fell across the street in front of the Honolulu Advertiser building. That bomb turned out to be a stray and a mistake. The Japanese did not drop bombs intentionally on the city of Honolulu. They knew that Japanese comprised over half of the population. Stray or not, it scared the H… out of my father; he ran out into the street, hot-wired the nearest car, actually stole it off the street, and drove the fifteen miles home at breakneck speed. My mother stopped for groceries and sauntered in later, totally unaware her world was at war.

That is how I remember things started. Later that day, many of my mother's relatives (Mother was the youngest daughter of thirteen children, all living in Honolulu) came to our home for refuge, as they all thought invasion was imminent. We listened to the radio all day; we papered our windows for the blackout ordered for that night. My father had to go to Pearl Harbor later that day, he was a reserve Coast Guard Commander. He also had to return the stolen car! I don't remember being scared; my mother was calm all day. The radio news was not very complete and they kept playing popular songs. I remember the Ink Spots' hit "I Don't Want to Set the World on Fire" played over and over. There were only two stations, KGU and KGMB; neither told us much except to boil all drinking water. And that is how I remember December 7th, 1941.

Later, in June 1942, my family was evacuated to the Mainland. We traveled by convoy on a troop ship. Ron Brunk (whose recollection appears in this book) and his mother were on the same ship. But that is another story.

Few 1942 Fords were produced because of the shift to war-related production. The 1942 Ford "command car" on the left was seen in London in 1995, that on the right was used by the Bowles family until 1946 (photos by JBB).

Recollections of Malcolm Ing

I finished premed at Harvard and medical school at Yale, and pediatric ophthalmology in Washington, D.C. After the Vietnam War, I began my practice in Honolulu. We have three daughters and three grandchildren.

My family origin in Hawai`i began with my grandfather arriving in the 1880s to work as a field hand on the Ulupalakua Ranch on Maui at the age of fifteen. My grandfather, In Toon Akana, was among the many young males who were urged to leave their homeland during the great famine period of the 1880s in southern China. He was a master of the art of Kung fu, Chinese medicine and midwifery by the time he was twenty-five years old. My father was born on Kaua`i in 1902 in Hanalei and became a physician. When he was in his urology residency at the University of Pennsylvania in Philadelphia, he met my mother and after they married in 1932, he returned to Hawai`i to open his practice. He was the first resident-trained urologist in the Territory of Hawai`i.

On December 7, 1941, I remember getting ready for church with my brother and mother. At 8 a.m. we drove down to Central Union, where my mother taught Sunday School. A woman greeted us with the question, "Why are you here, don't you know we are under attack by the Japanese?" My mother said, "We thought the noise we heard this morning was U.S. Navy gun practice!" At this point she called home and spoke with my father briefly because the phone lines were being cleared for emergency use only. We found out that Dad, who was in the U.S. Army Reserve Medical Corps, had been called to active duty to serve at an emergency room station in one of the local hospitals.

Next, my mother offered to drive Maydene Liu to her home in the McCully Street area. Maydene was the only other person at Sunday school that day, having walked the six blocks to Central Union from her home. Ironically, the home next door was burning down, apparently after being hit by a stray U.S. Naval shell (not a bomb). What I remember most about that time was a visit by an American Legionnaire who came into the Liu's house for a glass of water. The American Legion headquarters was two doors away. His hand was shaking as he sipped his water, and he kept saying over and over, "This is the real thing!"

Our drive home that morning was uneventful, but I remember a lot of us sitting around the radio with all the lights out that night and listening to the reports of the devastation the bombing had caused. I'll never forget the smell of disinfectant that exuded from my father when he returned home that night. We were worried about an invasion, but that, of course, never occurred. Our fortunate circumstance was that my grandfather, who had a job at Pearl Harbor, had the day off on December 7th.

Little did we know then, that the Japanese Naval Forces and the invading troops would be turned back at Midway Island on June 4, 1942, just six months later in what can be considered the turning point of the Japanese-U.S. conflict. This aircraft carrier battle cost 362 American lives, but the Japanese forces lost ten times that many and lost all four of the aircraft carriers they planned to use in the Midway invasion.

Etched in my memory is the statement I heard at age seven, while standing with my mother in our "breakfast nook," which she used for ironing clothes because it was cooler there than anywhere else in the house: "We interrupt this broadcast to let our radio audience know, the Japanese invading fleet has been defeated at Midway Island by the U.S. Naval Forces." I thought, "Hooray for the U.S.!" What had begun as a sneak attack on Pearl Harbor had been avenged by the U.S. in the battle of Midway Island!

MIDWAY BATTLE TOLL: JAPANESE SHIPS SUNK!

2 Or 3 Carriers Down; Battleships, Cruisers Hard Hit; U. S. Losses 'Light'

American Casualties Are Small, As Enemy Forces Are Crushed, Scattered

Japanese losses heavy—indeed, disastrous; American losses relatively small—American personnel casualties "light."

That summed up a communique issued by Admiral Nimitz at 12:45 this afternoon at his fleet headquarters.

The Battle of Midway is not completely over—but the main score has been checked up—and it is heavily against Japan and the powerful fleet she sent into the Midway and mid-Pacific area.

Admiral Nimitz's communique follows:

"Through the skill and devotion to duty of our armed forces of all branches in the Midway area, our citizens can now rejoice that a momentous victory is in the making.

"It was on a Sunday just six months ago that the Japanese made their peacetime attack on our fleet and army activities on Oahu.

"At that time they created heavy dam-

"In addition one or two carriers badly damaged and most of their aircraft lost.

"Three battleships damaged, at least one badly.

"Four cruisers damaged, two heavily.

"Three transports damaged.

"It is possible that some of these wounded ships will not be able to reach their bases.

"One of our carriers was hit and some planes were lost. Our personnel casualties were light.

"This is the balance sheet that the army, navy and marine forces in this area offer their country this morning.

(Signed) "C. W. NIMITZ,

"Commander in Chief, U. S. Pacific Fleet and the Pacific Ocean area."

Text Of Coral Sea Communique

Gen. Tinker's Plane Falls Near Midway

Japan Loses Half of Her Carriers

Image above courtesy of E.M. Luhrs

Recollections of Roland Jackson

I received my BS and MA from the University of Hawai`i (Mānoa). I worked in Research and Design at Hewlett Packard for many years and recently retired.

I was born in Hilo, Hawai`i on December 5, 1933; the day prohibition was repealed. My maternal grandparents moved to Hawai`i at the turn of the 20th century when my grandfather was hired as a civil engineer to work on the narrow gauge railroad being built from Hilo along the Hamakua Coast to serve the sugar plantations. Grandmother Sisson became a teacher and later a principal in the Hawai`i school system after my grandfather died in a surveying accident. My mother became a teacher after graduating from University of Hawai`i. She met my father, newly arrived from Nebraska, when both were teaching at the same Kona School. After they married, both taught in several Island districts and were transferred to the Honolulu school district in 1937. I started school at Lincoln Elementary in 1939 and transferred to Punahou during fourth grade.

My family was eating a late breakfast on December 7, 1941, when guns began firing from Punchbowl Crater, a half mile away. We ran into the yard in time to see several Japanese planes fly through the black puffs made by exploding shells. A stray round exploded in an empty lot a block away and ended our outdoor "sightseeing." My dad ordered everybody back inside where we gathered around the radio to listen to the confused, contradictory and frightening reports of the attacks on Pearl Harbor and Guam Island. The radio reported rumors of the Nu`uanu reservoir being poisoned, of enemy parachutists landing, and planes bombing and strafing city streets. Authorities suggested that bathtubs be filled with water in case the water supply was damaged. Sometime during the morning we heard that my Uncle Jack, a civilian government official on Guam, was missing and believed killed during the Guam invasion. The war had become very personal to my family.

By late afternoon some schools were being opened to shelter refugees from Pearl Harbor. My grandmother, the principal of Royal School, was asked to open her school. That night my grandmother, dad and others helped organize shelter and food service for the evacuees. In the early morning of December 8th, one of the evacuated service wives gave birth to a boy who was given the nickname "Blackie" after the blackouts that existed for many months after the attack. Blackie and his mom lived with our family for several months afterwards.

Recollections of Edward W.L. "Eddie" Kam

I received my BA from Boston University and my JD-MBA from UCLA. I have been an Associate Professor of Law at University of Hawai`i-Mānoa. In 1998 I completed the U.S. Naval Justice School's Officer Basic program by correspondence. My wife, Beatrice is from Wahiawā, where she attended high school. She graduated from the University of Rochester in nursing and has worked as a nurse in New York City and at Queen's Medical Center. We have two sons, Steve and Charles. Both went to Punahou and were active in ROTC. Steven served seven years in the Marine Corps and works for the FBI. Charles runs his own computer repair business.

My grandfather, Charles Seu Kam, was born and raised in San Francisco in 1858. He came to the Islands in 1883 aboard the Falls of Clyde, *the three-masted Matson freighter now moored in Honolulu Harbor as a tourist attraction. He served as the ship's cook and took turns at the helm as well.*

My grandmother, Kam Goo Shee, was also born in San Francisco in 1867. She married my grandfather there in 1885 and returned with him to Hawai`i. Grand-dad bought a homestead in Kalihi Valley. A few years later they moved into a new home on the corner of Queen Emma and School streets in Honolulu and purchased the grocery store next door.

Grand-dad was a devout Christian and joined the original Chinese Christian community in Honolulu. He died in 1916, leaving five sons and a daughter.

My father, Edward Kam, was an accountant, a stockbroker and a reserve police officer before serving as an officer in the U.S. Army. He married my mother in 1933 after she had graduated from Boston University with Dad's sister. I was born in 1934 and went to Punahou from the seventh through eleventh grades. I graduated from Kemper Military School in Boonville, MO.

My recollections of Sunday, December 7, 1941, as a seven-year-old second grader in Mrs. Lutkin's class at Hanahau`oli School, started when I got up early to go out to play with friendly neighbors. My dad, Edward W. L. Kam, had also gotten up about 6:30 a.m. that morning to pick up a yard boy and take him out to our empty rental house along `Aiea Heights Road so that he could tend the yard. We lived on Rooke Avenue, in the Pu`unui section of Honolulu, at the end of Liliha Street, about two blocks below the O`ahu Country Club.

A little later, I was attracted by the sight of older neighbors looking through binoculars at Japanese airplanes with the Rising Sun insignia on their fuselage and wings. I ran into the house at my mother's calls to sit and listen to the radio while an excited announcer called out, "This is the real McCoy! Hawai`i is being attacked by Japanese planes!"

About mid-morning, Dad returned in his 1941 dark-green Buick Special coupe, wondering if he had seen the real thing or war maneuvers over Pearl Harbor. He had no radio in his car and had not talked to anyone except the yard boy. He said that he had parked beside a bridge on Kamehameha Highway, on the return from `Aiea, close to the entrance to the Pearl Harbor Sub Base (now the Arizona Memorial), and watched the attack on ships at Ford Island. Luckily, he was not attacked by the Japanese planes, and drove off, wondering if it was real. He said that smoke and flames filled the air and the sounds were loud and real. If it had been for training, it was very realistic. Mother rushed him into the house to listen to the radio, where he gasped at the thought of real combat reaching the Islands. Dad was the Office Manager for Dean Witter & Co. on Merchant Street in Honolulu, doing much of their accounting, as well as selling stocks and bonds.

Both Dad and I went out into the back yard, so that he could mow it while I played. A plane's engine roared low, and a machine gun sounded, followed by a whistling sound, then an explosion spraying mud down on us, after shaking the ground. We both ran into the house. We looked out of the front door and saw that there was a crater in the front yard of a house two or three doors up on the opposite side of the street. The crater was about five feet deep, ten feet in diameter, and had caved in the side of a single carport and the front of a house. Neighbors phoned for an ambulance, as did my mother, but the phone was busy at nearby hospitals. About thirty minutes later, an ambulance came up Rooke Avenue and the injured inhabitants were taken to the hospital. In later days, an older neighbor said he thought the explosion was probably due to an artillery shell fired at a plane in the excitement of combat from Pearl Harbor. He had searched, but found no tail fins, which guide bombs down much like mortar shells. He concluded that it could not have been a bomb.

In the early afternoon, after the two waves of attacking planes had become history, Dad drove out to `Aiea to pick up the yard boy. We stopped at an old grocery store, the Kalihi Store on North King Street, to buy canned goods for the emergency, as the radio had directed. After reaching `Aiea, we started up the old winding road and saw a group of people on the side of this roadway, close to an old water tank, strung out alongside it and looking *mauka* (toward the mountains) into the sugar cane fields. A U.S. Army two-and-a-half ton truck was parked off the road on the *makai* (ocean side) or right side, and a young Second Lieutenant, who said he had come from the Midwest about a year before, now led a group of eight riflemen who had accompanied him from Schofield Barracks to recover whatever they could of a downed Japanese Zero fighter. It was about sixty or seventy yards off the road, in the furrowed cane fields, with very little damage. Some people thought that the pilot was still alive. Most of them were Japanese-Americans who owned a home in the town of `Aiea and worked for `Aiea Plantation, with its sugar mill and workshop. They were called field *lunas*, or skilled plantation workers. They said they would not help the Zero pilot escape and told the American lieutenant that they were loyal to the United States. Some had emigrated from Japan about twenty-five years before, around the time of World War I. They said they were loyal to the U.S. as they were Americans now. My father, a third generation Chinese-American, witnessed this and relayed it to some Americans after some Japanese-Americans were put into internment camps on the Mainland for the duration of the war.

The lieutenant arrayed his men into a flank line and had them walk into the cane fields with rifles ready. He had his .45 caliber pistol out and walked with them. For a while there was silence, than a shot rang out and a man cried that he had been hit in the leg and that it was numb. He had fallen and couldn't get up. The Lieutenant thought that he saw someone ahead, next to a plane, and others yelled that someone was trying to crawl off from around the downed airplane. Three shots sounded. Shortly, two American soldiers reappeared from the sugar cane rows carrying the body of a dead Japanese pilot, slung between them. Others carried his equipment: a canteen, mess kit and personal sidearm, which, according to the Lieutenant, was a Japanese Nambu pistol with short training bullets in the magazine. The pilot had shot one American soldier in the thigh and he had to be helped back to the truck. I gasped as I looked at the dead Japanese pilot. When the soldiers carried him close to me, I saw that he had reddish brown hair, quite bright in the early afternoon sun, and that he was fair skinned. After inspecting his mess kit, the lieutenant said it contained rice, pickles and fish. His canteen was partly full.

As the soldiers loaded the pilot's body into the truck, people buzzed about what had occurred. After the plane had crash-landed into the cane fields, those who had seen it phoned the police who relayed the message to the Army. The pilot tried to find his way to the shoreline to catch a Japanese submarine. The Japanese-Americans refused to aid his escape!

Shortly after this, we picked up the yard boy. He told Dad that he had watched the attack on Pearl Harbor that morning from the front yard of the house, which had an excellent view of the harbor and Ford Island. The yard boy also saw a Japanese Zero with its canopy open, fly up the hill. This may have been the plane that had crashed in the cane fields. It could have been out of gas.

Dad drove the American-Japanese yard boy home and paid him. After we were back at our Rooke Avenue home, we realized that this was the start of a war which could last a long time. Mother insisted on keeping the radio on in order to keep abreast of the current news. A curfew and blackout were enforced for the first time that night. Hawai`i was under martial law.

Recollections of Ann Kirsch Latham

I left Hawai`i for the first time to go to the University of Colorado in Boulder where I majored in Medical Technology (an obsolete profession now). I married my college sweetheart, David Latham, and we have four children and two grandchildren.

My dad was born in Vienna, Austria, and my mother in Germany. They endured WWI in Europe and emigrated to the U.S. in the early 1920s. Mother was seventeen. She worked in New York for a while, and then took the first ever cross-country Greyhound bus to Indiana to see her older brother. She then took the second Greyhound all the way to California. Dad had grown orchids from the time he was fifteen. He studied horticulture in college and, after arriving in the U.S., he worked at Harvard at the Arnold Arboretum. Later, he traveled to California to work in a well-known orchid nursery. My parents met in California, in an evening photography class. They were married in Santa Monica and not long after, sailed to Hawai`i. Dad was offered a job caring for Frank Atherton's orchid collection. Since California was really suffering in the depression, it seemed like a good opportunity. The job expanded to include supervision of the grounds and gardens of other properties owned by the Atherton 'ohana (extended family). He remained there until after Mr. Atherton died. In 1945, Dad had his own orchid business, hybridizing hundreds of "crosses" and shipping plants and flowers all over the world. My mother was very involved with the business and worked long hours. Between them, they had the language ability to communicate with orchid collectors from all over. My mother still enjoys working in her garden in Kahalu`u.

On December 7, 1941, we lived in Mānoa in the last house on `Anuenue Street, a dead-end street. Along the back boundary of our property was the old Mānoa School, a non-English Standard school (see Wood recollection). On one side of the lot, the Japanese language school on East Mānoa Road abutted our place. The Inoguchi family ran the school and they lived in a house next to the school. *Otō-san* was the headmaster. They occasionally brought us eggs, and my parents gave them orchid flowers. We were always invited to the outdoor Japanese movies.

My sister Elizabeth and I were students at Lincoln School (now the Academy Art Center on Victoria Street) because it was the closest public English standard school. The Adell family lived next door to us on `Anuenue Street. Commander Adell was the executive officer on the *Chicago*, a cruiser in Pearl Harbor. Their son, Randy, was eight years old and our playmate.

On December 5, 1941, Liz and I were invited to have dinner on board in the wardroom. It was Mrs. Adell's birthday and the *Chicago* was to get underway later that night to accompany the *Lexington*, bound for Midway. It was quite an adventure for us to be aboard and to be served dinner by the steward. Mrs. Adell knew him and called him *Schatzi*, German for "sweetheart." He was very tall and dignified, and the first African-American Liz and I had ever seen! For several months prior to December 7th, we had regular Sunday visits from several young sailors, stationed on board the *Arizona*. One of them was the kid brother of a close friend of my mother on the Mainland. They were so young, eighteen or nineteen, and really enjoyed having a local family to visit. Sometimes Dad would take everyone for a ride in the car; sometimes we would stay home and visit. My sister and I found them fascinating.

On that Sunday morning, Liz and I were in the garden with Dad and Mother was making breakfast when Randy Adell came running from next-door shouting, "The Japanese are bombing Pearl Harbor! Turn on your radio!" We were in more danger from our own anti-aircraft shells than the bombers. One explosion caused a big flash of light to reflect off our glass orchid house and the Gibson family, farther up Mānoa Valley, saw it and said, "Well, there go the Kirsches!" Our radio was one of those huge monsters with the green tuning eye and short wave capability. That night all the neighbors sat in the dark in our living room, all the kids on the *lauhala* mat, and listened to the reports from around the world. The news was awful, and we knew all our friends on the *Arizona* were gone.

A good friend, Phil Beggs, headed the local FBI office. He stopped by one day soon after December 7th to tell my father to destroy all his darkroom equipment—which he did, with a heavy heart. My parents, German and Austrian born, were probably looked upon with suspicion. They endured silly comments at the beginning of the war. It was Mr. Beggs' sad duty to go to the language school next door and pick up our neighbor. He told us later that Mr. Inoguchi was waiting for him, dressed in his best clothes and sitting in a chair with his packed suitcase next to him. He was sent to an internment camp in California.

In the days that followed, fear and rumors gave way to new routines. School was cancelled for six weeks and when we returned to class, it was to Mānoa School because all children were instructed to go to the school closest to their home. We had Martial Law, blackout at night, gas masks to lug around, bomb shelters, rationing, mass inoculations, censored mail, fingerprints on ID's, barbed wire on the beach and shortages of everything. Somehow our parents and other adults around us saw to it that we had a good, happy childhood. The Adell family was sent to the Mainland, as were all Navy dependents, and later in 1942 the Smith family, including classmate Charles Phillip Smith (1934-1975), moved into that house. Liz and I transferred to Punahou in 1945, before the war ended. Classes were still being held at the University of Hawai`i campus.

Recollections of Adrienne Madden

My paternal great-great-grandfather, Dr. James Wight, and his wife came to the Island of Hawai`i in the 1800s. He settled in Kohala and built a home named "Greenback." He brought with him many unusual species of trees and flowers which are still on the property around the family cemetery. Dr. Wight had thirteen children. The boys did not survive, but the girls did. One of the girls, Eliza Yates Wight, married an Alexander and bore my grandmother, Mary Eliza, who attended Punahou from 1889-90. Mary Eliza bore two children, Grace Violet Madden, who attended Punahou from 1906-13 and my father, John Alexander Madden, who attended Punahou from 1917-1918. My mother, Camille Gillard, born in Leige, Belgium, came to Honolulu in 1920. John and Camille had two girls, Jeannine Madden Pummer, Punahou Class of 1948 and myself, Punahou Class of 1952. I am proud to be a fifth generation kama`aina *(literally, "child of the land).*

Following Punahou I received my degree and became a Radiological Technician in San Antonio, TX. I retired in 1985 and now travel as much as possible.

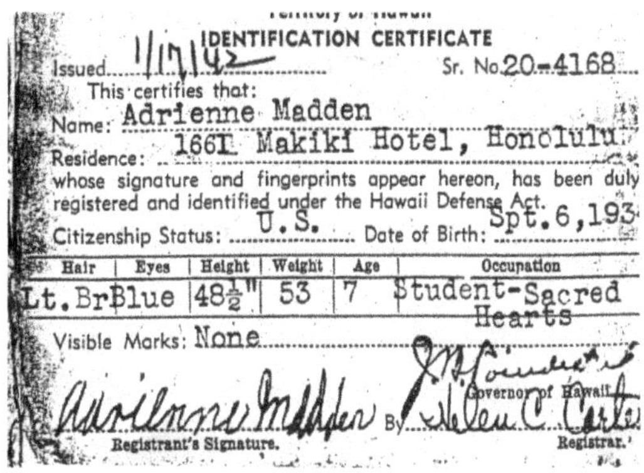

IDENTIFICATION CERTIFICATE

Issued 1/17/42 Sr. No. 20-4168

This certifies that:

Name: Adrienne Madden

Residence: 166I Makiki Hotel, Honolulu

whose signature and fingerprints appear hereon, has been duly registered and identified under the Hawaii Defense Act.

Citizenship Status: U.S. Date of Birth: Spt. 6, 193

Hair	Eyes	Height	Weight	Age	Occupation
Lt. Br	Blue	48½"	53	7	Student-Sacred Hearts

Visible Marks: None

Registrant's Signature. By Governor of Hawaii Registrar.

All of us were finger printed and issued identification cards that we always had to carry (Courtesy of A.Madden).

On December 7, 1941, I was at home with my mother because I was ill with pneumonia. My sister Jeannine ('48) and I were boarding students at Sacred Hearts Academy in Nu`uanu. When the bombs first fell, my mother, who had experienced World War I in Belgium, told people we were being bombed. She was told it was only target practice at Pearl Harbor. Not until it was broadcast over the radio did they believe her. My sister was at the Convent that day and told us the nuns took all of the children into the basement gym for prayers. A bomb fell quite close to old `Iolani School just up from Sacred Hearts Academy, and much praying took place in the gymnasium.

It was suggested during those first few months that all the women and children be evacuated to the Mainland. Mother took Jeannine and me aboard the *SS Permanante*, an old cement ship refurbished for passengers, on June 23, 1942. We sailed for San Francisco and ended up living in Los Angeles until 1944. We returned to Hawai`i while the war was still on. I can remember salt water baths on board the ship and being compelled to wear a life jacket at all times while outside our stateroom. On our return trip it took thirteen days to sail from Los Angeles to Honolulu. We were in a convoy and we kept a zigzag pattern to keep from being torpedoed.

When the war was over and the blackout lifted, I shall always remember the sight of lights at night. It was almost like seeing fireworks. I attended Punahou from seventh grade in 1947 through graduation in 1952.

Recollections of Diane McLean Stowell

I attended UCLA and Redlands. I have been a psychologist and therapist for many years and have done some teaching in Honolulu. I have two children and one grandchild. I am an active swimmer and have won many awards.

My father was born and raised in Hawai`i as were his dad and grandfather. They left Aberdeen, Scotland, and probably got here by whaling ship. Dad met Mom here when she was on a trip for a vacation. They both went to college in California—he at San Jose State and she at Cal-Berkeley. They did not finish and returned here to live and work. Dad was with the forest reserve and then worked for Del Monte after a swimming and surfing adolescence. He was removed from Punahou for some prank and ended up at Thatcher.

December 7, 1941, became a busy morning after we learned of the attack by listening to the radio. Petey (Peterson), my next door neighbor ('53) and I spent our morning on his porch watching the Zeros fly over. All of the smoke from Pearl Harbor was very visible to us (no high rise buildings then). We also lay on the ground and watched the flames. We had heard my dad talking earlier in the week and he seemed to know something was up—he overheard stuff at the Del Monte Pineapple cannery. The first half of the day everything seemed like a game, but as night came on fear presented itself boldly. I tried to sleep with both parents in a single bed. My dad's gun was on the floor under the bed. A bomb or something went off that night in the McCully area and our house shook all over. I thought it was the end. Of course our little house was not stable anyway—the termites were the real owners. After that first night, my heart would pound every time I heard a siren. However, the worst part of the following night was when we had to get into the bomb shelter with the spiders and dampness—it was awful—as was carrying gas masks to school.

View of Waikīkī Beach and hotels (Royal Hawaiian left and Moana right) similar to what many of us saw on December 7th. Pearl Harbor smoke, ack-ack, splashes and Japanese planes dubbed by J.B. Bowles (photo taken 1953).

Recollections of Peggy Moir Vollmann

My mother's father, Charles Arstad, was born in Norway. As a young man he moved to Glasgow, Scotland, with his mother. She was a seamstress for a furrier. While in Glasgow, he earned his papers to become a ship's engineer. He met my grandmother, Margaret Wilson, while in Glasgow. Charlie set off to sea to discover the world. After sailing around for a bit, he wrote to Margaret and asked her to marry him. She said yes, but would not join him until he found a place where he would like to live. Charlie found himself in Hilo, got off the ship, and went to work for one of the plantations on the Hamakua Coast. He wrote to Margaret and she set sail from Glasgow for Hawai`i with her worldly goods. She arrived in Nova Scotia at the time of the San Francisco (SF) earthquake. Her plans had been to take a train to SF and then a ship for the Islands. She was not allowed to travel to SF and instead had to travel across Canada to Vancouver where she waited for transportation. In the meantime, Charlie moved from Hilo to Honolulu and went to work for Dole, where he stayed until after the war. My mother May was born in 1907, went to Punahou and graduated with the class of '26. She was an only child.

I know very little about my father's side of the family. His name was Charles Neal and his family was from Rotterdam, Holland. I believe his father worked for the post office. His mother was widowed at a young age and went to work for Coyne Mattress Company in Honolulu. Charlie (Neal) worked for Thomas Cook, a travel company, and then for Inter Island Steamship Company, as a representative greeting the ships as they arrived in Honolulu from the mainland. He died at a young age.

I was at home on the Sunday morning of December 7th, getting ready to go to Sunday school. The Devereaux kids (all Punahou students) were with me waiting for our ride to St. Clemens, when we all looked up and saw black puffs of smoke in the sky. We were living in Mānoa, near where the Safeway store is now, so we were quite removed from things. My father, who was a reserve police officer, along with Bobby Vieira's ('52) father, took off for the police station downtown on Merchant Street. Dr. Devereaux left immediately for Queen's Hospital and long hours of work. The two wives walked to Mānoa School, which was out our backdoor, and began to roll bandages as they had been doing for months already. I was left with my grandmother, and I think that I spent the better part of the day under the table trying to figure out what was going on.

My mother had a huge Victory Garden planted on the bomb shelter, and Peter Canlis (of the famous Canlis Broiler), who was the general manager of the army "Y," would take the produce to the "Y" and would always come back with hard-to-get goodies for the household. I think we had coffee and lots of sugar when others didn't. My grandfather worked at Dole at the time and the cannery made candies with names like Midway and Tarawa. We always had those treats to enjoy.

I also remember playing Army with Jan Phaender, ('52) Bob Fase ('49), the Devereaux kids and others in our front yard on a huge load of dirt my mother was going to use in her garden. We sang all the patriotic songs.

Of course, we all remember going to private homes for school for the first months of the war. I was at the Halfords' home behind Rocky Hill until we moved to the University site.

The war years were pretty uneventful as I remember, but we always had many "single men" around whose families had been sent to the Mainland. I recall my mother saying that she was so happy that I was just a youngster during the war because of all the single young men on the loose. I'm sure mothers with older girls were not quite so happy!

Fort Street in downtown Honolulu was crowded with service men through out the war. Sailors seemed to be everywhere when the fleet was in; chop suey was a favored food. (left photo, Hawai`i State Archives, 1944; right photo, JBB, 1952).

Recollections of Barbara Moody Hudman

I have three children and five grandchildren. My occupation is whatever I am involved with at the moment…I'm still back-packing around the world by myself.

My father, Preston L. Moody, a civil engineer graduate of Rennselaer Polytechnic (Troy, New York), was employed by the Turner Construction Co. He was offered a 5-year contract to go to Russia with all expenses paid or to Hawai`i to work for Hawaiian Dredging, but paying his own way. He chose the latter.

We arrived on the Matsonia *on January 2, 1940. In 1947, he helped start several companies, including Hawaiian Dredging and Walker-Moody. Among the most visible of his projects are the Italian marble statue in Punchbowl Memorial Cemetery and the application of Gunite to the Arizona Memorial.*

We lived on the right side of the St. Francis Hospital next to the entrance (2244 Liliha), a complex of four houses. Bob Vieira lived on the left side (see his story in this book). Dad was bringing the car from the garage to take my brother and me to St. Christopher's Church near Punahou. We were ready to hop in the car when all of a sudden there was a knock on the door; our landlady was screaming, "The Japanese are bombing the Island!" Well, no Sunday School that day. Unbelievably, Dad drove up `Alewa Heights to take movies; the rest of us sat out in the yard and watched planes go overhead. A bomb dropped down by Judd Street but it never went off. That night fear took over and all windows were blackened.

Two weeks later, Dad had my mother, brother and me on the troop ship, *President Garfield*, in the middle of a convoy of six other ships. Upon arrival in San Francisco, we learned that we had been lost from the convoy for several hours at one time. We were given the all clear to be homeward bound in the summer of '43. Dad stayed and left his own legacy. His company built the Punchbowl Cemetery Memorial. Ironically, Ernie Pyle, for whom the cemetery is dedicated, was born on my brother's birthday and killed on mine; 8/3 and 4/18 [respectively].

The extinct crater, Punchbowl, became the National Cemetery (1952).

Recollections of Rita Paris

I received my BA from Whittier College. I did some real-estate work and now operate a coffee farm in Kona with my husband, Skip. We have three children and four grandchildren.

My family history is all in Hawai`i, yet I cannot call myself Hawaiian. On my mother's side are Cookes, Rices, and Loves. The Cookes and the Rices came from New England as missionaries. Amos and Julliette Cooke were teachers to the children of the Hawaiian Royalty. The story I heard was that the Rices were on a ship bound for Oregon that stopped in Hawai`i. They were on their way to Oregon to join the Whitman party. When they landed at Honu`ainu near Na`alehu on Hawai`i, they were told of the massacre of the Whitman mission and implored to stay in Hawai`i and join the mission here. Also with them was the Reverend J.D. Paris. He is not a lineal ancestor, but his younger brother, Thomas, my great-grandfather on my father's side, came later and stayed in Hawai`i as a surveyor and businessman. Robert Love was on his way from Australia to the California gold rush and stopped in Hawai`i. Robert married Fanny Johnston, whose father was an early furniture maker at the Palace. They founded a small bakery on Nu`uanu Avenue. That bakery, although no longer family-owned, is still known as Love's Bakery.

On my father's side were Paris, Lewers, Schmidts and Weights families. The Weight family came from England to work in the sugar industry. William Weight is credited with designing the irrigation ditch around Haleakala. Heinrich Schmidt came from Germany to work with Hackfield & Co., which later became American Factors. The Lewers family came to Hawai`i early and went into business in Honolulu.

My memories of the actual attack are vague. We were so young and unaware of danger. It was a quiet Sunday morning and we were at breakfast in our home in Nu`uanu Valley. Daddy was called to his office at Lewers and Cooke downtown, as the sprinkler system had gone off. When he got there he found that the cause was that the building had been hit by anti-aircraft fire. He called to tell us of the attack and told us not to stay in our house with its large metal roof as it might be mistaken for a water tank. So my mother, my sisters and I all went down to the stream below our house and spent the morning there. Planes came through the Pali (the pass over Nu`uanu Valley) and flew over the house, but we were in no danger. Later that day we went up to my grandfather's house to meet the family he had staying with him who had evacuated from Pearl Harbor.

I remember more from the ongoing war. Of course, we built a bomb shelter, which was horribly moldy, yet an adventurous place to play. I remember the air raid sirens in the night. I must have learned fear then; I still get "chicken-skin" when the sirens are tested each month. We all got our own ID cards, and identification bracelets and carried gas masks. When the war started, I was attending Hanaha`oli school. When it was closed, we held classes in neighborhood homes. I went to school at a house on Nu`uanu Avenue.

My father became a reserve policeman, and went out for patrol at night with his headlights painted out except for a small dot. We were under blackout at night. Since our living room was large and had too many windows, our playroom was converted to the blackout room with blue denim curtains. When we went back to school, the playground had bomb shelters under it and we had air raid drills rather than fire drills. Our house at Lanikai was converted to a military rest camp. When we were able to go to the beach, we had to crawl through the barbed wire. The islands off Malaekahana Beach became bomb targets, and we watched the practice bombings there. Many of our friends and family left to live on the Mainland for a while, and we missed them. Our family entertained many servicemen who were passing through; regretfully, some that never came back. We had a Victory Garden. In keeping with the current scare, there was a "Dengue man" who came around to check our water-filled flower pots and an old tire casing as it was feared that the dreaded mosquito would come in from the South Pacific. Best of all, I remember V-J day and going down to Lewers and Cooke to watch the parade and throw confetti.

Skip (my husband) was living in Waipahu at the time of the attack, and has much more vivid memories of the planes flying over. Between the first and second wave he was on his way to his neighbors, and when the second wave came in, his father had to "rescue" him from the garage.

We often encountered military convoys and occasionally got a ride in a tank or half-track (Hawai`i State Archives).

Recollections of Beryl M. Peters

My parents moved to Hawai`i in the 1920s from California. My father was an attorney, my mother a teacher. In the late 1930s, they were divorced. On December 7th, my mother and I were living on Lewers Road, probably a couple of blocks from the Ala Wai, though it could have been farther makai *(towards the ocean). As was typical at that time, kids could roam the neighborhood, if they understood how to cross streets safely.*

After graduation from Punahou, I went to nursing school at Stanford and received a Baccalaureate degree in Nursing. Eventually I received a Master's degree in Nursing from the University of California, San Francisco and a Ph.D. in Nursing from the University of Pittsburgh. I retired after close to twenty years from the faculty of the University of Utah, College of Nursing in 1994. I am still living in Salt Lake City, Utah.

My memories of December 7, 1941, are sketchy, but those I do have are vivid. That morning I was up at an early hour. Mother was still asleep. I met a neighborhood friend of my age, seven, and we roamed Kalākaua Avenue. I have no idea now what our plans were, how long we were there or how we learned that we were under attack.

We must have been told to go home because we did. We had seen a British war movie the day before at the Waikīkī Theater and for some reason I have very clear memories of air battles in the film. On the way home, we fantasized about the heroics we would be involved in should a bomb drop in our vicinity. We obviously understood that something was happening, but it did not seriously involve us. We happily went towards home.

When I got home, Mother was on the phone. A friend living in Mānoa Valley had called and told her that we were under attack by Japanese planes and that her husband was coming to get us, because Mother did not have a car. She considered them alarmists and refused to believe them. I arrived saying, "We're being attacked." I had no idea what that meant; I was repeating what I had heard. She still was not convinced, but did pack a suitcase. At the same time, she insisted on showering and having breakfast. When the friend arrived, he tried to convince her to hurry as the situation was serious. Mom serenely held to her schedule, thinking this was all nonsense.

When Mother was ready, I was loaded into the car with my canary in a cage. The friend was panicked and tried to get Mother into the car without the suitcase. Mother insisted on the suitcase. They stood at the trunk, trying to load the suitcase, which was stuck halfway in, still arguing about the situation. Just as the suitcase decided to cooperate, there was an explosion and the road erupted about a half a block in front of us. No one was injured, but it made a believer of Mother. (Later it was confirmed to be an anti-aircraft shell.) That "seven-year-old" bomb heroics fantasy on my part dissolved into sheer panic. At that point, Mom was yelling, "Leave the suitcase." The friend then tried, unsuccessfully, to remove it from the trunk. It was stuck again, inside this time. Reason soon prevailed and we drove off with the suitcase.

I have no recollection of what route we took to Mānoa Valley, but I do remember passing at least one home on fire, maybe two. I also remember standing by the front door of the Mānoa home watching a distant aerial dogfight, until both planes drifted out of sight.

I recall sitting in the dark that evening and night, listening to the radio (commercial or short wave, I have no idea) reporting parachute and submarine sightings, as well as other threats of invasion. All turned out to be rumors, but we could only believe them and feel helpless at the time. We felt helpless then and a long time after.

Before December 7th, we often heard the 155 mm coast defense guns during target practice (Hawai`i State Archives).

Recollections of Donald Smith

My Grandfather, William Elliot Smith, was the son of an American father and a French mother. He grew up in Peru in a shipbuilding family. His sister was a milliner in Peru. I do not know how he came to the U.S. or when. I show him coming to Hawai`i on a ship. He married a pure Hawaiian woman who bore him five children. She died. He married a Portuguese woman who died... no children. Then he married my grandmother, Marion Kaina Lovell. She had five sons, including my father, and died. She was 16 when she married him. He was 46. (Subsequently he moved to Honolulu... met a Japanese woman... had one child from her. Later he moved back to Kaua`i and married a Puerto Rican woman. She bore him five children, contracted Hansen's disease and was sent to Kalaupapa where she died). My maternal grandfather was William Francis Thompson from New York City. He took his inheritance, traveled the world, liked Hawai`i, and settled there. Then as first-mate and Captain of the "Piltz," he traveled from Hawai`i to Guam and all islands in between. He married my grandmother, Emily Kalah`olewa Manu and fathered nine children, including my mother. Emily's father was the illegitimate son of Prince Leileohoku (Kalākaua's brother) and his mother was a [illegible] to the Prince.

It was a regular Sunday morning. Mom was making waffles with real whipped cream and some strawberry preserves; also scrambled eggs and some homemade honey for the waffles. My older brother and I were across the street at a park in Kalihi, where we lived. We saw the planes flying overhead and heard sounds of gunfire. We pretended to be anti-aircraft fighters and were trying to shoot down the planes with our fingers. In the distance we could see the black smoke coming from Pearl Harbor. A white-haired woman came to her front porch and yelled at us, "get the hell off the streets, we're at war." We stopped playing. The woman was the mother of E.K. Fernandez (a local promoter and carnival operator). We were called home. My uncle, who was on his way to work at Pearl Harbor, stopped by our home. We all sat on the lava rock wall fronting our property. My uncle and parents spoke quietly and we knew better than to say anything. Later we found out that Japan had dropped bombs on Pearl Harbor. There was a mad scramble to get canned goods, first aid supplies and water. Everything was put into a small hallway. That night we all slept in that small hallway. That was the only room from which no light would show outside. There were lots of rumors of Japanese landing at different parts of the island. None were true.

I attended Washington State College, now known as Washington State University, majored in Architecture & minored in Speech. After graduation, ('57), I attended Officer's Basic Training in Ft. Benning, Ga. Our company was designated to be the honor company in the dedication of the minuteman statue. My first duty station at Ft. Chaffee, AK was a culture shock. I taught basic training, a good job, and got in with the "Country Club gang"—nice people; they kept me sane. When Ft. Chafee was closed, I was the last officer out. I was transferred to Ft. Shafter. Ahhh! Home again. I was put with a battle group & then to basic training until I retired.

After several engineering jobs I injured my back and took a substitute teachng job at Wai`anae High. I loved teaching; went to UH got my teaching certificate and taught at Wai`anae until I got sick and had to retire in 1990.

Recollections of Robert (Bobby) Vieira

Our family migrated to Hawai`i over four generations ago from the Island of Madeira (famous for Madeira Port), 280 miles out into the Atlantic from Lisbon, Portugal. My father's father had a barbershop in downtown Honolulu near the old Alexander Young Hotel. It was later named the Silent Barbershop. My mother's father, Thomas Gouveia, was a cattle rancher and owned a large ranch in Hōlualoa, Kona, directly across from the Hōlualoa School. He also owned a butcher shop which still stands today in front of Mom's birthplace home, now owned by the Catholic Church. Mom used to sail to school at Sacred Hearts Academy in Honolulu on the old steamers the Humu`ula *and the* Hualālai. *Grandfather's cattle would also be on board going to the slaughterhouse in Honolulu. Mom boarded at the Academy. We have been to Portugal twice, and it is a wonderful place to visit. Sight-seeing in Madeira is like being on Kaua`i. The islands look like they are twins. I believe our ancestors must have arrived around 1840 or thereabouts.*

On December 7, 1941, Dad, Mom and I lived on Wylie Street, two doors from old Nu`uanu avenue. Dad was manager of Honolulu Finance and Thrift Company located on the corner of King and Alakea streets, kitty corner from what is now the new First Hawaiian Tower. Dad was also into real estate development and became a partner with Thomas McCormack in what was to be one of O`ahu's first subdivisions, Ka Hanahou Circle on Kāne`ohe Bay across from Coconut Island. This property was owned by the father of one of our deceased classmates, Louie Gaspar. (Dr. Louis Antonio Rodrigues Gaspar, M.D., then Chief of Surgery at the Queens Medical Center.) Some of you might remember swimming at Louie's house at the end of Dewey Way in Waikīkī. We had some great times in those days swimming to the raft in front of the house. As most of you know, our classmate Mike McCormack (see his recollection) was Tom McCormack's son. Anyway, back to that Sunday morning, Mom had gone to Church at the Cathedral of the Lady of Peace on Fort Street. Dad was home reading the paper. It was early, around seven o'clock. I was riding my Irish Male, which is a type of four-wheeled vehicle, like a wagon that you sat on and pumped back and forth to achieve forward motion. I was directly across from Ma`ema`e Elementary School heading down the sidewalk towards the Borthwick home on

I attended the University of Washington and earned BA degree in General Business/AS and then joined the Army as a second lieutenant. Upon return to Hawai`i, I worked in various management positions at HC&D (a construction company), two years at Hawaiian Electric and thirty-two years as Director of Purchasing and Director of Economic Development. I married Virginia Winfree from Daytona Beach, FL. I have two children from previous marriages and two children with Virginia. I am actively involved in selling real estate as a licensed real estate broker with Stott Realty in Kailua, O`ahu, Hawai`i. I am an active Rotarian, a member of the Kailua Neighborhood Board. We belong to the Outrigger Canoe Club and the Kāne`ohe Yacht Club where we enjoy boating on Kāne`ohe Bay with our young family.

Wylie. (This is now the Girl Scout headquarters.) All of a sudden I heard the drone of low flying airplanes coming down Nu`uanu Valley. I looked up to see two airplanes (Zeros) flying wing tip to wing tip, very low. There were big red circles on their wings. I am sure the pilot of one of the planes saw me looking up at him as he dipped his wings from side to side. Then I saw something fall from one of the planes. It landed with a big thud in the back yard of the house three doors from ours. It was a 300-pound bomb that, for some reason, failed to explode. Dad came running out of the house saying that he had heard on the KGU radio that Pearl Harbor was under attack.

In the 1930s & 1940s small ships like the *Hualālai* (top) and the *Humu`ula* (middle & bottom) carried passengers and cargo among the islands-including cattle (JBB, 1947).

We could both hear dull muffled explosions from Pearl, which was approximately twelve miles from Nu`uanu. At the Cathedral, the priest halted mass and told the congregation to return to their homes. Mom's car was commandeered by some navy sailors stationed at Kāne`ohe Naval Air Station. She drove them to the Pali lookout where they were picked up by a truck. After that day, we went to school at the old Cooke house on Nu`uanu Avenue. We wore gas masks to school.

Our windows were blacked out. We built a bomb shelter in our back yard. Dad joined the reserve police officers. Sometime after the seventh, we, along with other families of women and children, took the *Lurline* in a camouflaged convoy with war ships to San Francisco where we lived for a year fearing an invasion by the Japanese.

Recollections of Joan Wood Fleming

My family came to Hawai`i at the turn of the century when my maternal grandfather, an accountant, came from England to work at Waialua Sugar Plantation, where my mother and her siblings were all born. My paternal grandfather, architect Hart Wood, brought his family from San Francisco in 1919 when he accepted a job as partner with C.W. Dickey, then formed his own firm, designing a number of well-known buildings throughout Hawai`i. Both my parents and their siblings were Punahou graduates. My sister ('57) and I were born and raised here in Hawai`i, and like many of us, didn't leave Hawai`i until college. My family lived in Mānoa at the time of the attack, having moved into what is best described as a "fixer-upper" the previous summer. We moved to Maui in 1949.

The winds of war were already circulating, for I remember saying to my parents at the time we moved into our Mānoa home, "I sure hope there isn't going to be a war" and their concurring. (Funny how you remember these things!) I was a student—and so was Ann Kirsch Latham (see her account)—at Lincoln School on Beretania street across from the Academy of Arts and Thomas Square, the only English Standard elementary school in the Honolulu district. This school is now Linekona, the facility where the Academy of Arts conducts classes for the community.

On the morning of the attack we were, like countless other Honolulu residents, sitting down to Sunday breakfast (always waffles, which stuck to the waffle maker) when our gothic-arched wooden table radio announced the famous news: "Pearl Harbor is being bombed! This is WAR! This is the REAL McCOY!" We could hear the noises of the attack, sounding like thunder in the distance, and they seemed to go on forever. I went outside to feed my pet rabbits and a shell screamed overhead and landed in the property across the street. We found out later it was from "friendly fire." My parents must have been scared to death, for everyone thought the Japanese could and would take over the Territory immediately. But do you know, they never communicated their panic to us children at all. It must have taken tremendous will power to remain so calm and to go about our lives in a close to ordinary manner.

I am currently living "happily ever after" in Kailua. Both my husband and I are retired. He ran the Navy's nuclear submarine overhaul and refueling program at Pearl Harbor. I was a graphic design specialist at Punahou. We keep busy with various hobbies and community organizations. Our four kids are all grown and we have five of "the world's cutest grand-children" who, unfortunately, live in California.

English Standard Schools had been set up for students who could pass a test of fluency in English, the language of instruction, as opposed to students whose immigrant families spoke other languages at home and who still needed to learn enough English to survive in the regular classroom. While our 21st Century hindsight views this system

Later on that morning, a truck with a loudspeaker roamed the streets proclaiming that the water had been poisoned, but that proved to be a false alarm.

That night, friends who lived on Tantalus, fearful of another attack, came to stay with us. Like many nights to come, a complete blackout was ordered. This meant no lights whatsoever after dark, and I remember my mother trying to fry hamburgers in the dark kitchen. As it was winter, it got dark early, about 6 PM.

Of course, life as we knew it was utterly changed. At first we had many air raid scares. Many times we awoke at night to sirens and searchlights anxiously scanning the skies, occasionally to accompanying gunfire. The blackout remained in effect for many years, and we had to curtain the windows with dark fabric to keep the indoor light from showing. This could be a hardship during hot weather when we needed every cool breeze. Even the headlights of the cars were blackened on the top half and looked like sleepy eyes. Martial law prevailed and we also had a curfew; no one was allowed on the streets after 10 PM.

In the early days of the war, everyone was convinced the Japanese were coming back and it wasn't until after the Battle of Midway in April of 1942 that we considered Hawai`i safe from another attack or occupation. We were all required to have a bomb shelter where we could hide if we were attacked. Ours was a neighbor's garage, which had previously been dug into the hillside, with sandbags along the only open end. Thank heaven we never had to use it. Its permanent residents included a few centipedes and scorpions! Bomb shelters, planted with sweet potatoes on top, were a feature of our school playground too—dark, damp, dirty, spooky caves. Even the memory makes me shudder!

All schools were closed for a couple of months while Hawai`i mobilized, and served an important purpose. That was when we were immunized and issued ID cards and gas masks ("bunny masks" for the littlest citizens), which at first we were required to carry with us at all times. Like Punahou, many school fa-

as "racist" and "segregationist," I recall children of all races who were my classmates in the English standard school, for many families, realizing that this was the key to advancement in our society, tried hard to have their children learn to use English well. The importance of this system is illustrated by my husband's experience when he and his twin brother entered first grade at Honolua School, 15 miles beyond Lahaina, where his father was the plantation doctor. They found that they couldn't understand what the teacher or the other students were talking about, so they were placed in second grade where English language skills were only marginally better. The following year the family moved to a more urban area and they went to the English standard school. Many of the boarding students at Punahou also came from plantations in remote areas where the local schools served large immigrant populations with different needs. In the early days, it was necessary for those living in rural O`ahu to ride the

cilities were commandeered for war-related purposes for the duration of the war.

When the public schools re-opened following the attack, Ann Kirsch Latham (see her recollection) and I found ourselves at our neighborhood school, Mānoa School, within walking distance. We English standard students were "segregated" from the others and put into crumbling classrooms that fronted East Mānoa Road. Two grades were put in one room with one teacher and our class size was small. I recall that for the combined fifth and sixth grades, we had a total of fourteen students. Math and reading were ability grouped, while social studies and science included the whole class. I think we benefited from this setup.

After the war, in response to burgeoning population growth in Mānoa, a new elementary school was built further up the valley and the classrooms we used reverted back to their original use as the Japanese language and culture school. By the 1950's the English Standard school system was no longer needed and was abolished. When Punahou's campus was returned to the school at the end of the war, my parents enrolled me there for sixth grade.

My mother worked as secretary to the head of the Office of Civil Defense. Their office was in `Iolani Palace and I often took the bus downtown to hang out in the Children's Room of the library next door until her day was finished. My younger sister attended a number of day care centers set up around town, but I was a "latchkey child" in a much safer era. My father worked for the Army Corps of Engineers. under J. W. Mahoney on the Punahou Campus at the J. B. Castle shop, creating ancillary war material for the Pacific Theater. Later, he used to tell us interesting stories about what they made and where it ended up. Both my parents worked ten hours a day, six days a week, probably not an unusual schedule when the whole country was focused in a massive effort to win the war.

Rationing became a reality: I remember my mother standing in line for what seemed like hours to buy a round one-pound tin of New Zealand butter, a highly prized item in a world that did not include colored margarine sticks. Similar queues arose

O`ahu Railway and Land Company trains around Ka`ena Point to Honolulu. The train service was terminated in 1947; by that time most people went by car anyway.

for meat. "Swiss steak" was a real treat. I think the reason Spam is a popular item on local plates today is because a whole generation grew up eating it for dinner during the war! Unlike the mainland, shoes were never rationed (we kids never wore them anyway), but gasoline was, and cars were in short supply as they weren't being made for the duration of the war. So we took the bus or streetcar and carefully planned our trips to visit the grandparents on the North Shore.

My parents hung a large map of the world in our living room and we used it to track the course of the war. Several of my uncles and family friends came through Honolulu occasionally on leave, and the adults spent a lot of time speculating about where the next battles would be fought, especially in the Pacific when the U. S. was island-hopping toward the Japanese mainland.

Sometime during this period my father was seriously injured while at work, breaking every bone in his right foot. He spent nearly two months hospitalized at St. Louis School, which had been turned into a hospital facility. He was in a huge ward with 20 or 30 war casualties. Fortunately he made a complete recovery. I certainly hope the other men in that ward did too.

Fuel and food rationing brought a ceiling on prices (above). Island fish prices during the war were controlled by the Office of Price Administration (courtesy of E.M. Luhrs).

Recollections of Jackie Young

I received my BS from the University of Hawai`i (Mānoa), MS from Old Dominion, and Ph.D. from Union Institute. I am currently the Director of Communications for the American Cancer Society Hawai`i Pacific. I was a former legislator and ran for the State Senate in the 2002 elections.

My grandfather, Pyung Yo Cho and his wife, Kum Soon, came to Hawai`i from Korea in August 1904 to escape political oppression as Japan was in the process of colonizing Korea. My grandfather was a university-educated soldier and married my grandmother just before leaving for Hawai`i. Boatloads of Koreans arrived from January 1903 through 1905, but when the king learned that they were working on plantations, he wouldn't allow any more Koreans to leave. Because my grandfather was a political activist, he left the plantation within a year and came to Honolulu where he worked at Punahou School as a cook and then attended `Iolani School, becoming an immigration translator, then a businessman. From 1938 to 1950 he served as President of the Korean National Association, a political group advocating the independence of Korea from Japan. In 1996 the President of Korea awarded the Patriot's Medal posthumously to my grandfather for his political activism. January 2003 was the 100th-year anniversary of the first Koreans to arrive in the United States.

In my jewelry box is a faded red, white and blue pin embedded with a small pearl that says, "Remember Pearl Harbor." I was seven years old on that day, an impressionable age. So I remember. I remember Pearl Harbor. I remember the attack.

Today, the recollections play back like an old silent movie. Vivid visual images remain frozen in my mind's eye—frozen and framed to play back upon demand.

The moment before I was aware of the attack, I was happily eating my favorite breakfast of fluffy pancakes, crispy bacon and cold milk. My older brother Bob was at the table with me. My grandparents were getting ready for church and my aunt was in the kitchen. They had already eaten their breakfast of tea, hot rice, *kimchee* (a Korean condiment consisting of Asian cabbage pickled in salt, hot peppers and garlic) and vegetables.

I looked out the dining room window, past the low stone wall in front of our house and saw our neighbors standing in the middle of the street, arms flailing about, pointing at the sky.

I shook Bob, "Look outside."

His head turned and he jumped up and bolted for the front door. I was right behind him. By the time the screen door slammed behind me, we had sprinted across the yard.

Our home was on `Ālewa Heights, high above the city. It was a clear day and out towards the ocean, past Honolulu Harbor and beyond the next mountain ridge, was Pearl Harbor. Columns of billowing, dark gray smoke rose high into the sky.

I remember being confused by what I was seeing. The only sound I can recall hearing is the high-pitched buzzing of planes. Far off in the distance, they looked and sounded like frenzied mosquitoes—diving, climbing and diving again.

I looked around and saw people's mouths moving with their faces contorted, tears streaming down their cheeks. Their lips were forming the words, "Oh my God, oh my God, we're being attacked." Still, I recall hearing no sound except for the strange buzzing.

Chills were running up and down my body. I felt bewildered, looking to the adults around me for clues as to what was happening.

No one paid attention to me. I stared at people's faces and the quick movements of darting eyes, the tautness of neck muscles, the hunched over shoulders all told me what was not being said.

My grandfather had come outside and was standing in the crowd with us. Suddenly he grabbed my hand and motioned to Bob while pulling me towards our driveway. My grandmother and my aunt came running out of the house. We all got into the large green Packard sedan that was his birthday present from my mother just a few months before.

My grandparents were talking excitedly to each other in rapid Korean, "We have to go, we have to go," He was saying.

My grandmother scowled, arguing, "It looks dangerous; we need to wait."

As we wound our way down `Ālewa Heights Drive I saw some people running into and out of homes, like they didn't know where to go. My skin felt prickly, I wondered what was happening, why were we being attacked? Isn't that what people were screaming? "Attack!" What does that mean, "attack?" What does it mean when it comes from the sky?

We drove down Middle Street, passing Fort Shafter, and then joined a throng of cars. But now we were at ground level, only a few miles from Pearl Harbor and the view was even more frightening. The planes, which looked like mosquitoes from our hilltop home, loomed bigger and fiercer, and the buzzing was now a shrill and grinding sound. I know there were more sounds—high, loud, screaming sounds, low, persistent booming sounds. But, perhaps, as a survival mechanism, my mind refused to record the frightening, deafening sounds.

A big man wearing a hard-hat and an armband that read "MP" came up to our car. He told us to turn back. My grandfather was firm and spoke in precise, though halting, English, arguing that we had to get to Wahiawā, which was ten miles past Pearl Harbor in the central highlands of the Island of O`ahu, next to Schofield Barracks. He told the military policeman that we owned a laundry business in Wahiawā. He pointed to Bob and me sitting in the back seat and said that our parents lived there. The soldier kept saying the words "attack" and "Japs" and yelled something about "war" and waved his arms, motioning for us to turn back.

My grandfather turned the car around. No one spoke. The silence was scary. As soon as we got back in the house my grandfather turned on the radio. The announcer said not to drink the water from the faucet—it might be poisoned. I knew that word. Poison. Poison in our water? My grandmother rushed to the kitchen yelling at my aunt to help her fill pots with water. She put a big kettle on the stove. My grandfather was on the phone, calling my parents in Wahiawā. He kept dialing and dialing.

Bob shouted from the back porch. He was shooting BB pellets from his Daisy rifle at a plane that was buzzing low overhead. He kept shouting that it was a Japanese plane. I knew he could hit it if he wanted to as he always practiced shooting tin cans hanging from a tree branch in our yard, excited whenever it pinged and then afterwards counting all the holes in the can. He insists to this day, that the plane was so close to the house he could see the pilot looking at him, so he stopped shooting. He didn't want to kill anyone; he just wanted to shoot the plane down.

We spent that day bathed in fear and worry. We had no news from my parents in Wahiawā. The telephones weren't working. The radio was silent for long periods and when we did hear news it was to tell us to lock ourselves in the house, that there might be spies all around us.

Late Sunday evening my parents finally arrived looking exhausted and worried. Bob and I were immediately sent to our rooms but a few minutes later we snuck out the kitchen door and sat on the narrow wooden stairs, close to the open living room windows where we could hear the strained conversation.

My mother, who ran the family business managing forty employees, was sobbing that one of our workers at the laundry was dead; "Mr. Lee wouldn't take cover. He ran outside and was shaking his fist at the Japanese planes, when suddenly we saw bullets ripping through his body."

My father's voice, normally soft and low, was unusually high pitched and he was speaking rapidly. Our house in Wahiawā was riddled with bullets. He said,

"There are bullet holes in the bedroom ceiling. We heard a crash and a Japanese plane landed in the reservoir in back of the laundry." He said that many soldiers at Schofield Barracks had been killed.

Years later my parents related the story of their experiences on December 7th to a writer who titled his book, *The Day of Infamy*. It was a day of infamy. Something terrible had happened to all of us. Everyone.

It was hard to believe that the night before the surprise attack on Pearl Harbor my life had been so calm and predictable. On December 6th, as we did on many evenings, my brother Bob and I had sat on a wall which divided our property on `Ālewa Heights from the popular Natsunoya Tea House. We had watched limousines drive up with military men in uniforms, their breasts covered with medals. We made a game of guessing their rank and branch of service.

Later there were rumors that the only spy discovered in Hawai`i was a Japanese naval officer, posing as a student, who had lived in an attic of a hilltop teahouse.

Okinawa-born Gima-san hangs up laundry on the Bowles' property at Sunset Beach (North Shore) against the backdrop of a dummy airfield with plywood and canvas B-25s (JBB, early 1940s).

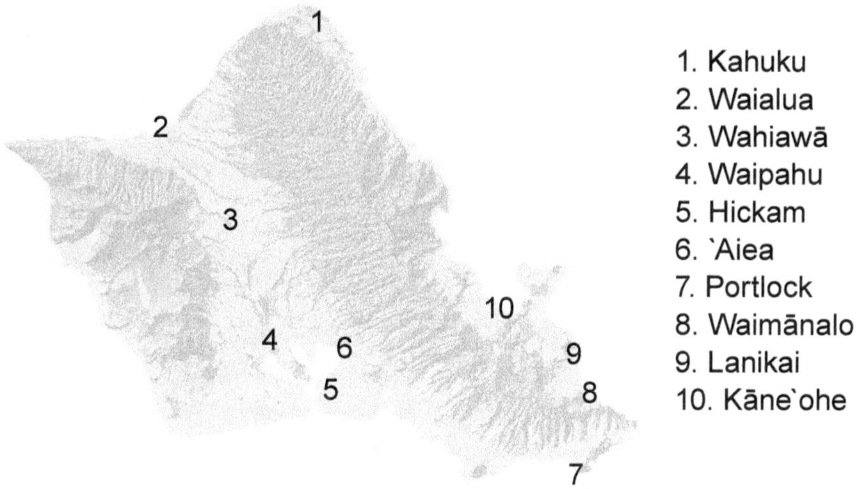

Rural O`ahu

Betsy (Beets) Alfiche Castillo—Kahuku
Dale Barrett—Kāne`ohe
Roger Dow—Waipahu
Homer F. Eaton—Lanikai
Valmer Hollinger Takahashi—`Aiea
& Harry Takaashi—Wahiawā
Bea Horner Toomer—Hickam
Cynthia King Sorenson—Portlock
Vernon Knight—Kāne`ohe
Muriel Matson—Waialua
Willie Morioka—Wahiawā
John O'Donnell—Waialua
Delia Wilson Schmedding—Waimānalo

Recollections of Betsy (Beets) Alfiche Castillo (1934-2004)

Both my parents came from Cebu, Philippine Islands in 1919. My father was a sugar plantation luna, *(foreman).*

I attended University of Hawai`i (Bachelor's degree in Business Personnel and Industrial Relations). I have a wonderful marriage to Hilo native Ed Castillo (forty-three years in 2002.) We produced two children: Ruth, (Punahou '80, now living in San Diego, CA) and Mark, (Punahou '82, now living in Benicia, CA). I retired from Sheraton Hotels at the end of 1991 after twenty-five years as Royal Hawaiian Hotel Personnel Director. We moved to San Francisco in 1999 to be closer to our children and three grandsons.

It was a typical sunny Sunday morning in Kahuku. After breakfast my parents, as usual, sent my five sisters—Connie (16) Pumkin (14) Edna (12) Lee (10) Madge (9) and me (7) off to attend Sunday services at Kahuku Methodist Church. We lived on Kamehameha Highway, a ten-minute walk from church. After church, we looked forward to stopping at the nearby Owan Store to buy red coconut candy, which we would devour on the way home.

But this Sunday was different. As Lee, Madge and I skipped on the dirt roads and balanced ourselves on the railroad tracks, I noticed the cars uncharacteristically whizzing by. I asked Lee and Madge, "Why are the cars going so fast?" Our beautiful mother, who had been in ailing health for years, met us at the front door with a worried look on her face. "Something bad has happened. Pearl Harbor has been attacked!" Stunned, we turned on the radio to station KGMB and heard President Roosevelt announce that the Japanese had attacked Pearl Harbor without warning. Mama said she had heard airplanes earlier that morning "that did not sound like American planes" flying over our house. She mentioned to Papa that she was concerned and sensed that something was wrong, but Papa insisted it was only her imagination and that their daughters would attend church as usual.

We spent the rest of the day filling bottles, containers and our bathtub with water. Blackout started that night. Our family huddled in the darkened living room, frightened and not really understanding what was happening. As a seven-year-old, I wondered how the Japanese were able to travel in their airplanes all the way from Japan! Mama, on her trusty old rocking chair with Lee and me on her lap, sang Philippine lullabies and told us of growing up in her native Cebu.

Papa thought the Japanese would return and attack us again. With keen foresight, Papa admonished us not to hate our neighbors, the Shigimitsus and Haidas, who were not responsible for the attack. The war took a heavy toll on Mama's fragile health. Two months later, on Valentine's Day and only nine days after my eighth birthday, Mama was gone. She was only thirty-eight.

Recollections of Dale Barrett

Dale was born in Los Angeles, but his folks decided LA was getting too crowded, so they took the Lurline *to Hawai`i in 1934 or 1935. After December 7th, the family left Hawai`i on the Pan American Clipper and eventually ended up in southern Florida, a town near Miami called Coral Gables, and opened up a curio shop in Coconut Grove. After a few years, they came back to Waikīkī and built their Diamond Head home near the beach at the end of Kalākaua Avenue. Dale returned to Thomas Jefferson School. He said he was the resident* haole *(Hawaiian slang for Caucasian) and that it seemed that every day was "kill* haole *day."*

The family opened up the Waikīkī Curio Store on Kalākaua Avenue across from the Waikīkī Tavern. Dale was at Thomas Jefferson School on the day Roosevelt died—that was 1945. Dale entered Punahou in the seventh grade in 1946 and stayed until 1951—his junior year.

Dale graduated from Roosevelt High School in 1952 and married Dido Kekoolani in 1953. He attended Riddle Aviation School and started flying commercially for Delta Airlines in 1956 at age 21, the youngest pilot in the system. He retired in 1994. He and Dido have traveled all over the U.S.A. for about 25 years in their motor home. They bought a home in Haiku Plantations in 1987 and their son John and his family took it over in 2000. Dale and Dido now live in Santa Paula, CA and their daughter Dana is with them.

On December 7, 1941, Dale and his parents were in their weekend house on Lilipuna Drive overlooking Kāne`ohe bay and so observed Japanese planes dropping bombs on Kāne`ohe Naval Air Station. Their town home was in Waikīkī on Kapili Street. He went to Thomas Jefferson Elementary School on Kapahulu Avenue.

The Pan American Clipper was our primary means of air travel in the 1930s, making regular runs between Honolulu and to the Mainland (Tai Tsing Loo, Bishop Museum, 1953).

Recollections of Roger Dow

Having taught in the DOE primarily at Aiea High School since 1959, I retired in 1994. In 1999 we relocated to Bellingham, WA. Our three children all live in the state and frankly, we wanted a change of environment. Yes, we like the weather and yes, we do miss our friends. (d. 2000)

Having survived WWI and having been shot once by the Germans and twice by the Irish, Dad hoped to rejoin the ranks of civilians by seeking to return to a normal civilian occupation in Scotland. However, normal was not to be; with worker unrest and rebellion just below the surface, Scotland was particularly hard hit. Jobs were few and job seekers many. He was able to find work as a bookkeeper with a fishing wholesaler in Ayr. The work was stultifying and Dad had given himself five years to improve his situation before accepting a job offer which he had received from his cousin, who was working for O`ahu Sugar Company in Waipahu. Things did not improve, so in 1923 he found himself working in the office at O`ahu Sugar Company. He was surrounded by many other Scottish " reprobates" and so the "old country" was never far away.

The morning of December 7th followed an afternoon at the Shriner's football game and a morning at my first (and last) piano lesson. We were up by 6:30 a.m. and had just begun weeding the front flower bed when we realized that all hell was breaking loose just under two miles from the house. The sugar cane hid Pearl Harbor from view, but not the noise. That, and the fact that the planes circling over the house had red markings on the wings and fuselages, gave us some clue that all was not well. At the same time, our Japanese maid came rushing out from the house to inform us of the attack, and was distraught that the *haoles* (Caucasians) might think that the local Japanese had something to do with this disaster. Dad and Mother had to assure her that no such thoughts could possibly ever exist. Dad then rushed into the field and started taking pot shots at the planes as they swooped overhead. This was fine until one of the planes did a quick turn and returned his fire. Dad took one look at the road, which was torn to shreds, and decided that it was an uneven match, and time to quit being a hero. He grabbed me and pushed Mitsui back into the house. The men in the neighborhood were all WWI veterans, most from Scottish regiments, so that afternoon was spent getting ready to head up into the Wai`anae Range if and when the invasion came. Everybody thought that the huge plume of smoke that erupted from the harbor was one of the large fuel tanks getting hit. No one considered that a ship could go up like that. We spent the rest of the day glued to the radio and prepared for flight.

Recollections of Homer F. Eaton

After Punahou, I went to Princeton, receiving a BSE degree in 1956 in Civil Engineering. After serving in the Navy in the Marshall Islands, Alaska and Southern California, I married Evie. I got an MBA at Harvard in 1962 and we returned to Hawai`i for ten years and had two daughters. I worked for Castle & Cooke until 1984, then purchased J. DiCristina & Son, a manufacturer and installer of custom wood in California. I retired in 2002.

My father was born and raised in San Francisco. He moved to Hawai`i in the 1920s—as a divorced Irish Catholic. I think we know why he had to go west! He was a CPA and, at the time of his death in 1936, was auditor of the Public Utilities Commission. My mother was born and raised in Upper Michigan. She came from a large family and ran away from home to go to nursing school in Milwaukee, Wisconsin. She then decided, for reasons unknown to my sister or me, to go to Hawai`i where she met and married our father.

My sister (Dobie, Punahou '49), mother, stepfather and I lived at 919 Mokulua Drive, Lanikai, across the street from the beach. My mother came from Channing, a very small town in Michigan's Upper Peninsula. We had a childhood friend of hers from Channing as a house guest that weekend. He was an enlisted man in the Army Air Corps, stationed at Hickam. His being our guest that weekend apparently saved his life, as his barracks reportedly sustained a direct bomb hit in the initial attack.

My memory of the day begins with our becoming aware, around breakfast time, that there were a lot of airplanes in the air and a lot of noise coming from the Kāne`ohe Naval Air Station, across Kailua Bay from Lanikai Beach. To get a better view of what the adults considered "the maneuvers," we walked a couple of blocks up to a vacant lot my family owned on the hillside behind our house. I recall hearing explosions, and seeing smoke coming from Kāne`ohe and airplanes flying in apparent confusion over Kailua Bay. At one point several planes flew low over our hillside location. Our Army Air Corps friend didn't recognize the insignia ("The maneuvers sure are realistic this time!") and, of course, we waved at them. (Did they wave back?) Only later when we sat down to breakfast and turned the radio on did we hear the announcement, repeated over and over again, to the effect that "all armed forces personnel are to return to their bases—the Hawaiian Islands have been attacked. This is no drill." Years later, watching the movie *From Here to Eternity* for the first time, I remember the hair on the back of my neck standing up when they repeated that same radio announcement.

That day and subsequent events remain very exciting times in my memory. Subsequent events included barbed wire and machine guns placed on Lanikai Beach and us taking homemade cookies to the soldiers on the beach in return for getting to sit behind the machine gun. Also, being issued World War I helmets and gas masks and going to school (Kailua Elementary) with them—boy, were they heavy. Dobie and I traveled to California with a friend of my mother's on the *Aquitania*, in convoy (English teas and abandon ship drills!), followed by a long train ride with an uncle from Los Angeles to Channing. We experienced true culture shock for the first time when Dobie and I arrived in Channing, in the snow, in February 1942.

Sidebar: Years later, in the Princeton Library, I came across a book on civilian experiences on December 7th, and in it was an episode related by Erling Hedeman, who lived directly across the street from us in Lanikai. He and several of his buddies were out surfing, I think on the North Shore, that morning and their car got chased and shot at by a Japanese plane. They ran off the road but no one was seriously hurt. I knew Erling when we moved back to Hawai`i in 1947, but never heard the story directly from him.

Even before December 7, 1941 we saw search lights that the U.S. Army used during anti-aircraft maneuvers (Pan Pacific Press Bureau, Hawai`i State Archives).

Schools Closed

All schools on Oahu, both public and private, will remain closed until further notice, Edouard L. Doty, territorial director of civilian defense, announced at 11 a. m. today. This does not apply elsewhere in the territory.

Honolulu Star Bulletin, December 7, 1941

Recollections of Valmer Hollinger Takahasi & Harry Takahasi

Harry Takahashi (1934-1992): Harry's grandparents, both maternal and paternal, came from Japan.

Valmer Hollinger: My maternal grandparents were born and raised on the Island of Hawai`i. My paternal grandparents came from Europe—my grandfather from Ireland via Germany, my grandmother from the Azores. They met and married on O`ahu and raised a family of thirteen.

I retired from Pan American World Airways in 1989 after twenty-two years.

Harry retired from his freight forwarding and yogurt businesses in December 1991 due to his illness.

As told by Valmer Hollinger Takahashi:

Harry's family was living in Wahiawā on December 7, 1941 and, although they did not have the unbelievable view of the whole bombing of Pearl Harbor that my family had, they could hear the bombing and shooting that went on at Schofield, an Army base just outside of Wahiawā. Being of Japanese descent, my father-in-law thought it best to bury all of their Japanese memorabilia (samurai swords, especially). Unfortunately, he couldn't remember exactly where he had buried them so he was unable to dig them up after the war was over. My mother-in-law's brother was in Honolulu and drove home to Waialua to check on his parents. He used the "haul cane" roads through the cane fields and was strafed with bullets but luckily was not injured. He was the only member of the family to join the "442." (The much-decorated infantry division, primarily made up of Japanese-Americans, the "442" saw extensive action in the European theaters of World War II.)

I wish I could add more, but most families did not talk about their war experiences. I am sure the adults talked among themselves but we were all pretty young at the time.

I really didn't know much about internment camps until I moved to California. Many of Harry's *katonk* (Mainland Japanese) friends had been in camp but didn't share much about their experiences. I think most of them did not want to dwell on those years but preferred to get on with their lives.

My family and I were living in `Aiea Heights on December 7, 1941. We saw the entire attack on Pearl Harbor from beginning to end. It is something I will never forget. We had an unobstructed view.

Recollections of Bea Horner Toomer

My father's family were immigrants from Germany in the 1800s. They bought passage to New Jersey. They were farmers, so they worked their way to the heartland and set up their families. As the dust bowl hit, they worked their way west. My grandfather bought passage to O`ahu and then to Kaua`i where he set up business in sugar and pineapple. He left his oldest son in charge on Kaua`i and he went to Honolulu and ran the business. My father was one of five children.

My mother's family came from England in the 1800s by boat and landed in Massachusetts. They also were merchants and came across the country to California and set up vegetable farms to feed the miners. Eventually they bought a fleet of ships and sailed for the Islands. One went to Maui and bought land from the Queen. My mother's father set up a mercantile business and trade goods store. My father was a chemist and worked on the plantations. My mother was a schoolteacher and then was a machine inventory clerk for Hickam Field and Pearl Harbor. I have two sisters, one in Kansas, the other on O`ahu. My parents are deceased.

I now live in McMinnville, Oregon. I went to Oregon State University for two years after high school, and then got a teaching position at the local high school where I taught agriculture, small engine repair and auto technology for twenty years. It was a blast. I am now retired due to progressive eye loss. I am widowed with three children: a son, John, who is a Lieutenant Colonel in the Air Force and teaching at the War College in Kansas City, Kansas; two daughters, Janean O'Connor and Carol Bryan; and two granddaughters, ages four and seven.

December 7th was a real awakening for my family. My father was on the isle of Kaua`i working for my uncle. My mother was getting ready for work at Hickam Field. We heard a lot of booms (shooting outside). Mom turned on the radio and heard we were under attack by the Japanese and we were to go to our bomb shelter.

I went outside and the sky was full of flak and Japanese and American planes were shooting at each other. Some planes were on fire and coming down. A Japanese plane flew over the house and dropped a bomb that skimmed the roof of our house and went into the house behind ours. It blew up and a big piece of shrapnel came into our yard and cut off a branch about twelve inches thick, just missing me. The neighbor had just stepped into the house that was hit and, unfortunately, was killed.

My dog got out, so I went to get her. I fell to the ground with the dog and then ran for the house. I almost got hit by bullets strafing our yard. My mother had a fit. We then had to go with our gas masks to the neighborhood school. We were issued coupons and coins so we could buy things if they were available. We put up tarpaper in our house windows so no light could be seen.

During that morning we could see the fires and hear the explosions of batteries on the boats. We lived on the other side of a ridge that separated us from Pearl Harbor. I wanted to tell my story, as I could have been a victim. I have the bullets and bomb fragments at the family home on O`ahu.

It is surprising to me how vivid my memories are about going to Punchbowl Cemetery and hearing my mom speak of the many dead buried there that she knew. What I remember most about Punahou was the military taking over the school, parking military vehicles on the lower campus and stripping Dillingham Hall of seats to allow storage of weapons and ammo.

Only a few classmates lived close enough to Pearl Harbor to see the fires that produced the black smoke from the burning ships (photo modified to simulate the actual fires, photo source unknown).

Recollections of Cynthia King Sorenson

Eddie Sorenson and I have been in Hilo since 1972 and have a daughter who lives and works in Walnut Creek, CA. Eddie retired from Theo H. Davies about ten years ago and I have volunteered in various capacities. Now I concentrate more on my eighty-eight-year-old mother's personal care. I can always find time to pick up my tennis racquet.

My father's ancestors began their odysseys in Germany (Hanover), England, Ireland and Nova Scotia...some wending their way across our Country in or riding next to the Conestoga wagons to California (1842). Others settled in Australia (near Sydney)...and a female ancestor, Anne Mo`orea Henry, the daughter of a missionary to Tahiti and the first white child born on Mo'orea, eventually settled at Hanalei, on Kaua`i. The German connection was through an ancestor (G.F. Wündenberg) who was brought over to manage Princeville Plantation on Kaua`i after serving in the Napoleonic wars. In 1845, Mr. Wündenberg married the aforementioned Anne Henry who had come from Tahiti to visit her sister. The Wündenbergs raised their family at Hanalei.

The King Family arrived in California via those Conestoga wagons in 1842-43. Richard King was a contractor and started a planing mill in the San Francisco area. Richard's son, Thomas J., came to Honolulu in 1883 to work for a feed company and eventually started his own "California Feed Co." in 1895 with his brother-in-law, J.N. Wright. In 1870, Thomas J. King married Josephine Wündenberg of Hanalei (G.F. Wündenberg and Anne Henry's daughter). Their five children included my grandfather, Thomas V. King, and Mrs. Clifford Kimball, who, with her husband, owned and operated the Hale`iwa Hotel and later the Halekulani. Grandmother King was Ada Newbegin from San Francisco and Mill Valley, California, whose ancestors were from England and Nova Scotia. Her father started Newbegin's Bookstore in San Francisco. My father, Thomas D. King, was born in Honolulu at the family's home on Pi`ikoi Street.

My maternal great-grandfather was born in 1826 in Londonderry, Ireland. I have recently learned from a cousin in England that his family was one of a group called "Ulster Scots," these being Scots who traveled back and forth between Northern Ireland and Scotland over many generations. One of twelve children, James Campbell left Ireland at thirteen, a stowaway on a ship headed for America. Some of his male siblings had preceded him to America. In 1841 he hired on as a ship's carpenter on a whaler bound for the whaling grounds in the Pacific. After some hair-raising experiences at various locales in the Pacific, including a shipwreck in the Tuamotus, he settled in Lahaina. He and two partners established Pioneer Mill Co., raising and processing sugar cane. In 1877 he sold his interest in Pioneer Mill and moved to Honolulu where he lived with his wife, Abigail Kuaihelani Maipinepine, a nineteen-year-old Lahaina woman for whom Campbell had built a cradle nineteen years earlier at the request of her father. Mr. Campbell purchased land in various parts of O`ahu and on some outer islands, as well as in California. The Campbells had four daughters who survived the various childhood diseases that seemed to have ravaged the infant population at that time. One daughter was Muriel Shingle (later Amalu), my grandmother and also that of Auwe Sutherland Morris (my first cousin); another daughter was Alice Kamokila Campbell Macfarlane (Alice Flanders Guild's grandmother). Both Auwe and Alice were my classmates. Thus, my parents' families have been rooted in Hawai`i for a number of years.

Our family was living at Portlock Road (in those days, way past the end of the "car line")... we did see a few "dog fights" in the air after the bombing began, but I don't remember being aware of the mess at Pearl Harbor, because we weren't near it. My mother was in the Red

Cross Motor Corps and was called to go out to drive/help where needed. My father was yanked into the Navy and stationed at Kāne`ohe as an ensign, since the Navy needed officers who knew Hawaiian waters. I recall that someone (a kid…Rocky Sack ('49) or Johnny McComas ('48) or maybe one of the Durant boys…any one or more of them could whip up a good story on a moment's notice) told us kids that there was an unexploded bomb in one of the empty lots down the street from our house. I don't even recall if I went to see it…probably not, as it would have been off-limits to us six, seven, or eight-year-olds, I'm sure. I remember that a night or two before the 7th, I saw search lights in the sky…my father explained that "they" were looking for lost planes.

One amusing story (I think) about my grandmother (who lived at the end of Mānoa Valley…again, beyond the end of the "car line"): Sometime before the war began, she had hired a Japanese alien ("Taki") as a yardman and then later pressed him into service as a cook. She had three unmarried sons living with her…all having enlisted in various sections of the Navy when the war began. Because Taki was an alien, he was hauled off to "headquarters" to be interrogated and was probably headed for Sand Island (he did have a picture of Tojo on the wall of his bedroom...plus a Japanese flag…and he supposedly had a short-wave radio set somewhere in that hovel). Well, my grandmother must have hit the panic button at the thought of losing her cook, even if he did overcook the string beans. She hiked up her *mu`umu`u* (loose-fitting dress), stuck some fresh ginger buds in the "bun" of hair at the back of her head, jumped into Taki's 1932 Packard sedan (that Taki couldn't drive as he had no license) with new yardman, "Keawe," at the wheel, and headed for the "commandant" (whoever that was…she may have gone to Admiral Nimitz, she was so upset). As the family story goes, she stormed into the commandant's office, demanded an audience, got one and proceeded to inform the power-that-was that she had three men in her household who were doing their part to fight the war. They needed to be properly fed and she damned well needed Taki back, and they'd better give him back if they knew what was good for them. And who did they think they were anyway? Taki came back in short order. For the rest of the war, Taki told anyone who would listen that Japan was destined to win the war. And for the rest of the war he overcooked the string beans, but no one complained.

Ginger grew wild along the roads and was a favorite flower for leis (JBB, 1962).

Recollections of Vernon Knight

Vernon graduated from the University of Hawai`i, worked for Boeing, (Seattle) and the Navy (Honolulu), as a computer software engineer/analyst.

In 1848, my great-great grandfather, John Thomas Waterhouse Jr. was due to leave Tasmania for Fiji. John Thomas Waterhouse was minister to Australia, New Zealand and Fiji. Following in his father's footsteps, J. T. Waterhouse Jr. trained as an English missionary and was sent to Fiji with a clergyman who, according to Aunt Eleanor Waterhouse Isenberg, was promptly eaten by the natives. John Jr. therefore prudently decided to take his family to Hawai`i.

Arriving in Honolulu with his nine-year old son J. T. Waterhouse III (my great grandfather), John Jr. opened a general store. The Waterhouse Company continued as a department store until 1895 when it became an investment company. John Waterhouse III had a son, Ernest B. Waterhouse, who was my grandfather. He married Helen Harding from Canada. They had three children—Amy, Leigh and Gwendolyn, my mother. The three children grew up in Nu`uanu on Judd Street very close to the Pratt family, who lived on the corner of Judd and Nu`uanu. Laura Pratt and my aunt Amy became close childhood friends.

In the late '20s, grandmother was killed in a car accident on Tantalus; my grandfather moved to Carmel, California. Meanwhile Aunt Gertrude Harding, sister of Helen Harding Waterhouse, had settled down in Bound Brook, New Jersey. After the accident, Gwendolyn went to New Jersey to be with her where she met and married Walter Kaufmann. In October of 1934, I was born. In November of 1936, Gwendolyn gave birth to my sister Helen.

The marriage did not go well and shortly after Helen was born, Gwen, aided by Auntie Gert, changed our name to Knight, left New Jersey and traveled cross-country to Carmel where we lived for several months. The basis of our new family name, Knight and the change of my first name is quite interesting—the Hardings' great grandfather was Joshua Knight who married Jane Vernon—so Helen and I really are Knight descendents.

We eventually arrived back in Hawai`i around 1938. We lived in Kāhala close to the Waterhouse family summer cottage. In the summer of 1939, because of my mother's poor health, I went to Kāne`ohe to live with Auntie Laura and Uncle Frank Bowers—they took care of me that summer along with many other children including children of friends, cousins and their own son and daughter Miki and Betty. The joy of growing up in the country with the Bowers is priceless and I am so fortunate, but that's another story.

My sister Helen ('54) and I had one more year living together as a family in Kāhala; I attended kindergarten somewhere in Kaimukī. The strain of the situation was too much for our mother; she had to leave Hawai`i for her health and she never returned. Helen went to live with Aunt Amy Waterhouse Gotshalk. Amy couldn't handle the two of us (actually it was me she couldn't handle) so she asked Laura, her childhood friend, if she would take me in. Anyone who knows Laura Bowers knows that her reaction was something like, "Of course, Amy, I would love to have him come to live with us as long as you want him to. I wouldn't have it any other way." I didn't know it at the time, but fortunately, from that time on my home and my family was to be in Kāne`ohe, forever with the Bowers. In 1942 my mother passed away—the Bowers took me on permanently; I became their hanai *(informally adopted) son. In September 1940, I entered the first grade at Punahou.*

The Kāne`ohe property then was about seven-and-a-half acres in the middle of Castle Estate land. Grandpa Pratt called it "Maka`alamihi" or "eye of the farseeing crab" for it was on a hill where in those days one could see for many miles, including most of Kāne`ohe Bay. There was a ridge coming down from one peak of the Ko'olau mountain range. Running on that ridge was a kahawai *(irrigation ditch), which supplied fresh water for the taro patch, an extensive vegetable garden, a banana patch and a large stand of papayas. It was post-depression time, and Dad moved the plant* *nursery business to Kāne`ohe, so the fruits and vegetables we grew and the rabbits and chickens we raised kept the family going.* [Editors note: Commercial feed for rabbits and chickens was limited. Those who raised animals for food received more than those who began after December 7th]

Early on the morning of December 7, 1941, I was helping my mom, Auntie Laura, in the back fields picking strawberries or string beans. I remember hearing the drone from the engines of the Japanese planes before I actually saw them coming from the north over our property; I guess they were in the middle of a large circle at about 500 to 1000 feet altitude. A few minutes later I could hear the bombs dropping on the Naval Air Station at Mōkapu. I definitely remember seeing the large red circle on the underside of each wing. Mom often said after the attack that she could see the faces of the pilots, I imagine I did also, but, having turned seven only one month prior to the attack, don't actually remember for sure. We thought the bombers were our planes practicing as they often did for a couple of years before the war (several of the Islands from Lanikai to the open water of Makapu'u were targets) although Mom said she couldn't understand why they did so on Sunday and so early in the day. The bombs were also falling near the mental institution that we kids called the *Pupule* House, about a mile to the east of us. That building, (currently The University of Hawai`i Windward Community College) had a red tile roof and must have looked like a military establishment. I saw the smoke from those bombs but only heard the bombs dropping in Kāne`ohe Bay, less than three miles away.

After the attack had started, my sister Betty came out to bring us back in to the house, she knew that the Japanese were attacking but neither she nor anyone else had any exact information or knew what to do. Unfortunately, both my mom and dad have passed away so I cannot "pick their brains" to piece together the events of that day, but Betty was eleven years old at the time and more aware than I of what had happened. After we all regrouped, my dad decided to take the old Chevy to try to see what was going on and to deliver the strawberries and string beans Mom and I had picked to give my Auntie Margie (Mrs. Wriston, our fifth and sixth grade teacher) who lived on Kailua Beach. Betty was allowed to tag along; I wanted to go but couldn't because I was "too young." My brother Miki, fifteen-years old, was installing a radio antenna on his cottage in back of the house. He did not go and instead continued the installation.

According to Betty, she and Dad first went to the telephone communications center in Kāne`ohe town. Men were outside of the building with rifles.

Dad talked to them for a few minutes and then left for Kailua. On the way they stopped on a hill above Mōkapu Drive, where Dad had just completed a landscaping job. He checked that out and must have considered that the property had a good view of Kāne`ohe Bay. When they got there, Betty remembers that she could see oil or fuel burning on the water in the bay in front of the Naval Air Station and remembers seeing men swimming through the flames to the shore. Dad and Betty drove back to the highway and proceeded to the Wristons' house in Kailua. We later learned that the Japanese fighter pilots had strafed that same road. Somehow, they made it back home later that morning.

Shortly after the attack the Army set up a training base camp mostly on our property. The Officers' Quarters, huts and mess hall were located right across from our porch in the front yard. There was also an enlisted men's mess hall (I remember a lot of "C" rations and "K" rations) and at least three barracks for the troops. It was exciting for me—I collected mess gear, cans of Spam, shell casings and, whenever I could, I just hung out. The engineers installed a pumping system and pipes for water. We were able to tap off of it and have drinking water. Previously, water had been brought from grandma's house in Honolulu over the Pali in two five-gallon glass jars. We used the *kahawai* (stream) water for showers, the toilet and dish washing.

My dad had ukuleles and a guitar, as well as an old violin; my sister Betty had her accordion. I remember that at least two of the doctors (medics) were good musicians. One of them had a mandolin—he impressed me. The other played my dad's violin. There was lots of good music after "curfew"—lights out. On occasion, my uncle, Carl Farden, who lived close by, would come over for *kaukau* (food) and music. Carl's sister, Auntie Irmgard, lived with us for a while; she worked for the war department as a home economist.

I mentioned how exciting it was for me to have the military all around us, but now that I reflect back to those times sixty years ago, I feel lots of empathy for all of those young soldiers who cycled through the hastily assembled training camp. Especially those men who were there in the first couple of years, because many of them must have died fighting on our behalf at Midway, Guadalcanal, Wake and Marianas.

Recollections of Muriel Matson

I attended Eastern Washington College and University of Colorado (Boulder), and then worked for Liberty House and the Hawaiian Telephone Company. At age twenty-one, I was an airlines stewardess in the Pacific arena for several years, and then worked for Trade Wind Tours in Seattle and Los Angeles. Next I was a secretary for an insurance brokerage in Europe and joined a Switzerland-connected ski club for outdoor fun! I worked in the Swiss Alps by night and skied by day! The last thirty years I have lived and worked in Los Angeles and enjoyed the ski slopes each winter!

Rudolph Muller arrived in Honolulu in 1895 on a clipper ship that came around Cape Horn in a record six-months time from Germany. He was eighteen years old, an apprentice chemist hired to work with the new sugar industry. His first assignment was Kaua`i. In a couple of years he returned to O`ahu and some time later met an Island-born caucasian girl named Agnes Carroll. Agnes was the daughter of settlers from Boston (a la the description in Michener's Book—no kidding!). Agnes had a sister named Maimie who also married a German man. He was in the horse and buggy business, which later became Schumann Carriage Company of Honolulu (a luxury car dealership)! Rudy and Agnes spent some time on Maui and returned to Honolulu. Their one child was born there…Sascha Muller. She later graduated from Punahou in 1926. Rudolph worked at Ewa Plantation upon his return from Maui and later became the Chief Auditor for Castle & Cooke in Honolulu.

Sascha went to the Mainland to college, became a kindergarten teacher and returned to Honolulu. There she met Joe Matson, a civil engineer who was building roads for the Territory of Hawai`i. It turned out that Joe was an "Army brat" born in Maine, but also a Punahou graduate, class of 1922. His father had command of Fort Kamehameha just before he retired to California. Joe then went to Cal Tech and returned to Hawai`i after working his way around the world on an oil tanker. Joe and Sascha married and moved to Kamuela on the Big Island. Joe was making their first paved roads. Sascha got hapai *(pregnant) and had to go all the way to Honolulu on a boat to have her baby, but they soon returned to Joe on the Big Island. Mom and Dad made eleven moves during MY first year of life as the road progressed! Then my dad got moved to Maui to build artesian wells for Moloka'i, Lanai and Maui. My two sisters were born on Maui: Kathy Matson Hewitt (married to Fritz Hewitt of '52) was a Roosevelt grad in '55 and Lorna Matson (now Muren) graduated from Punahou in 1957. Now both my parents are dead and my sisters live in California. Kathy in Laguna Leisure World and Lorna in Foster City, near San Mateo.*

Sixty years ago, I was seven years old and in the second grade. My parents had just moved to Waialua Sugar Plantation on O`ahu, North Shore, from Wailuku, Maui. My dad was the new Civil Engineer. There were no kids my age, except for classmate Temme Cheeley, at Mokulē`ia. His mom drove us to Leilehua School near Schofield every day. In the whole neighborhood there were about eleven kids, all of different ages. The only church on the plantation was Catholic, but none of us were Catholic and all the parents decided that all the kids, whatever age, needed to have a Sunday school nearby.

They finally got an OK from the plantation office to use the clubhouse every Sunday morning. The clubhouse had a big assembly room/dance-floor area with a big stage. There was even a piano in the corner. Also, there were several dressing/meeting rooms behind the stage area, and a bathroom. The parents decided these little rooms could be used for pre-school, first-third graders and fourth-sixth graders. They managed to collect some tables, chairs and Sunday school pamphlets, stories and songs for various ages from their own churches. In a few months they were ready to "open" the Sunday school. A lot of enthusiastic prompting went on in each household to prepare the kids for this very special Sunday class.

We all got new clothes to wear, and it wasn't yet Christmas. The only problem was that we had to wear black, shiny shoes, with socks. I remember my mother saying it would only be for a couple of hours and that if we were good, we could come home, have lunch and then go to the beach after our naps.

Finally the day arrived…the first Sunday in December 1941. The clubhouse was about a quarter mile from our house. My mom got us all dressed up and, since I was the oldest, I had many instructions to watch out for my little sister and be sure she didn't stray off and to always hold her hand on the street. (Since Mom had to stay home and take care of the baby, she would never know that I hid the shiny shoes in a neighbor's hedge on the way because they were so stiff to walk in.)

The more elderly ladies on the plantation were waiting for the kids. There were more of them than us! They sat us all down and said we would have community prayer and song before going to our separate classrooms. They promised that with their help we would soon know the Lord's Prayer and "Onward Christian Soldiers" by heart! So one lady played the song on the piano another lady used a mike and mouthed all the words for us to repeat. It was a song about soldiers marching into battle.

The phone rang…and rang. More rings—blaring!! Finally one lady went to answer it. We were all singing. When we finished, the lady that had answered the phone rushed forward yelling, "Quiet! Listen to me. We have an emergency. The Japanese are bombing Pearl Harbor and you must all go directly home and stay indoors. Do not sit down, go right home, right now!! Do not play on the way. Hurry, hurry home!"

We all fled. Luckily I had shed the shoes so I could really run fast! Everyone was running down the street with unknown fear pushing them forward. Of course, I forgot my little sister. Of course, my mother was angry with that. (She was really very scared, too, but didn't want to show it to the kids.) Of course, another lady drove her daughter and my little sister home.

My father had the radio blaring and he stood on the back porch watching greenish planes with orange circles on the wings go overhead. You could even see the pilots' heads inside because they were so low. If we tried to go on the porch, Dad was very stern and ordered us into the house. We felt we had been very naughty and didn't know why…my mother hadn't noticed the missing shoes and I had forgotten them.

I remember crawling under Dad's desk in the den. I felt very scared and refused to come out. It was or is my first recollection of real fear. All day long we could hear distant boom-booming. The radio had the same man talking all day…in a scared voice. The radio said: "Do not turn on lights at night. Do not go outside. Do not drive any cars." My mother dragged me out from under the desk and made us eat supper and go to bed early. Mom always read us a story, but not that night. I really WAS being punished, but why my sisters too? and why no lights? I didn't know why!! Was it something about the soldiers marching into battle? Was it because I was singing barefooted? Did we all sing it wrong? Even the grown-ups? Boy! We better try to learn it good for next time! But who could help us?

The next morning my mother lectured me on not caring for my little sister and then she discovered wet, soggy, new, UN-shiny shoes that floated down to our driveway from the neighbor's hedge. (How did I know they were going to water that morning?) Now SHE really had two reasons to be angry and forget her fears and I had a triple dose of being afraid!!

December 7th aftermath. The next two months after the bombing of Pearl Harbor were probably the most fear-inducing months for all of us living in Hawai`i, adults and children alike. Schools were closed until after New Year's, January 1942. Trenches were dug across the playgrounds. Bomb shelters were built in every yard, each equipped with emergency food, toilet paper and a change of clothes for family members. Blankets were removed from windows and replaced with blackout paper thumb-tacked to all the windows. Every community had an air raid warden who would check all the residential areas each night to be sure there were no cracks of light showing. Mainland food was in short supply and rationed. So was gasoline. People were cautioned not to venture out of their communities. All us kids had to go to the plantation elementary school, not the English Standard Leilehua of Wahiawā, ten miles away (see Joan Wood's note).

Everyone was issued a gas mask in a bag with a shoulder strap. We had to wear them everywhere, all the time. We had gas mask drills at school, and had to have individual evacuation bags. Whenever there was an air raid drill, we had to carry them to the trenches and sit there in the red dirt...waiting for the "all clear" signal. The sugar mill smoke stacks all were equipped with warning sirens. We all had to get a series of immunization shots. We had to wear ID tags with our blood type on them. I was classified as a "B" type; years later I discovered I am really "O-Negative," which says a lot about the mass blood-typing of everyone that went on those first few months after December 7th!

Military convoys were everywhere. All the beaches were barb-wired. (We soon learned to dig big holes under the fences and get to the water!) Suddenly there were tall search light towers all along the coastlines, and the soldier camps guarding them were everywhere. Out on the North Shore of O`ahu, people saved their gas rations and carpooled into Honolulu on rare occasions, to go to the dentist, or to see the grandparents. When we passed Pearl Harbor, all we could see were heaps of salvaged metal from the bombed ships being dredged from the waters.

For all of us of that era our elementary years were very restricted, to say the least. Perhaps that is why we are such a great, caring, sensitive group with a long-lasting camaraderie?

Most of the houses on sugar plantations were of the wood frame type (JBB, 1962).

Recollections of Willie Morioka

My father's parents arrived in Hawai`i from Iwakuni, Japan around 1899 to work on the sugar plantation at Laupāhoehoe, Hawai`i (The Big Island). My mother's parents arrived in Hawai`i around 1903 to work on the sugar plantation at Wailua, Hawai`i.

Willie went to Princeton for AB and MD. He is currently working as an otolaryngologist (ear, nose and throat) doctor. He is married, has four children and one grandchild.

On December 7th, I was at Sunday school (in Wahiawā) when our teachers informed us that the planes flying overhead were not on maneuvers but were part of a real attack.

They said to take cover on the floor of the church. Being curious, I kept looking out the window and saw the planes flying on attack runs to Wheeler Field and Schofield Barracks. To this day I swear I saw a twin-engine bomber flying on one of these attack runs, but it must have been two single attack planes superimposed on each other simulating a twin-engine bomber.

Mt. Ka`ala, in the Wai`anae Range, is the tallest mountain on O`ahu at 4,025 feet above sea level (upper, JBB, 1953) and affords a magnificent view of Pearl Harbor (lower, JBB 1962).

Planes Strafe The Streets Of Wahiawa

WAHIAWA, Dec. 7.—Ten or more persons were injured when planes strafed the streets of Wahiawa about 7 this morning. Neither the identity of the injured persons nor the extent of their injuries was immediately available.

The less seriously injured and those who could not be moved were taken to Dr. Merton H. Mack's office. Others were taken to the Ewa hospital.

About 75 planes flew over Wahiawa at 6:30 this morning.

One plane crashed into a row of houses and burned completely. Two houses were burned to the ground. The fire was brought under control by volunteers and a small fire engine from Waipahu.

Honolulu Star Bulletin

Recollections of John O'Donnell (1934-2003)

John retired as a Foreign Service Officer (1962 -1991) with the Agency for International Development in Southeast Asia and South and Central America. He was also a part-time consultant in international agriculture and rural development. He recently co-edited ***Prelude to Tragedy, Vietnam 1960-1965*** (US Naval Institute Press, 2000) which deals with the early days of U.S. involvement in South Vietnam.

My father, Raymond (Don) O'Donnell left San Francisco and moved to Hawai`i in 1927. He was hired as a statistician at Waialua Agricultural Company on O`ahu where he later became Office Manager. While staying at the plantation bachelor quarters, he met and later married my mother, Maile Bowman, a new teacher at Waialua Elementary School, who had been raised on the Big Island and had attended Kamehameha and Punahou, graduating in 1924. Her mother, Mele Pā, was full Hawaiian from Hilo and her father, Don Bowman, came to the Islands from Ohio in 1898, working first as a public health official in Hilo and later for many years with the Hawaiian Sugar Planter's Association in Honolulu.

Early Sunday morning, my father and I were in our back yard in Waialua, playing with the family dog, Kimi. My mother and sister were inside fixing breakfast. Suddenly, we saw a large group of planes flying towards us from Waialua Bay. They flew directly over our house, continuing up the Kaukanahoa gulch towards Schofield Barracks and Wheeler Field. The planes had large red circles under the wings and they made a loud, growling noise as they flew over. My father was watching them intently and then turned to me and said quietly, "Son, we'd better go inside—those are not our planes." As we entered the house, the planes had flown out of sight. Not too long after that we heard muffled explosions coming from the direction of Schofield Barracks and Wheeler Field.

We had a large radio in the living room, which we switched on. One voice I remember in particular was a quavering voice announcing that we had been attacked by the Japanese and that we all "sh..sh..should re..re..main ca..calm!." The radio remained on all day and through the night. We put blankets over the windows so that no light would shine out. The radio had short wave capability so other neighbor families—the Andersons from next door and the Davis' from up the hill came to listen with us, some remaining through the night.

The next day, our Japanese yardman, Miya, came to the house all dressed up in a black suit, white shirt and black tie. I remember him talking with my mother in pidgin English, saying several times, "Japan son ka bitch," and shaking his head.

There were a couple of other interesting incidents. According to reports that we received, the first casualty in the Islands was a Japanese milkman in Waialua whose truck was strafed by a Japanese fighter. He was hit in the leg and treated at Waialua Hospital.

In another incident, the wife of one of the Waialua supervisors who lived off the Kaukanahoa road to Wahiawā was very annoyed by the buzzing of the planes over her house and the sounds of explosions towards Schofield Barracks. Thinking that the noises were the result of an American military training exercise, she called an officer friend at Schofield Barracks to complain. She got a few words out before he said, "Pompei, get the hell off the telephone—we're under attack by Japanese planes!" and then slammed down the phone.

The waves along the North Shore (O`ahu) were always spectacular in the winter months, but few folks surfed them in the 1930s and '40s (JBB, 1962).

We will always remember those following days where there was so much uncertainty. Our lives would never be the same again.

Recollections of Delia Wilson Schmedding

I went to the University of Colorado graduating with a MA degree and later acquired a MBA from the College of Notre Dame in Belmont, California. My career was mainly in banking, both in Honolulu and the San Francisco Bay Area.

My grandfather, James T. Wilson, of Port Townsend, Washington, graduated with an M. D. degree from the University of California in 1891. In November 1894, after a tour as surgeon on a revenue cutter that was on a mission to research seals in Alaska and the Bering Sea for the consideration of their protection, he sailed to Hawai`i. His interest in Hawai`i came from his grandfather, a New Bedford whaler from 1830 to 1850, who had visited Hawai`i many times. After graduating from the Johns Hopkins nursing school in Baltimore, my grandmother, Delia Sheehy, sailed to Hawai`i as companion to the children of a local family. My grandparents were married in 1897.

Having recently returned from the Mainland, my grandparents, loaded with gifts, as grandparents are wont to be, had my brother Mike and me to their house in Lanikai that fateful morning. While we were eating breakfast (my grandmother made a mean waffle), my father, Walter Wilson, called to ask us to walk home to our house a few blocks away. He had been listening to the radio and was becoming concerned by the repeated warnings that "This is not a drill". We were being attacked. On arrival at our house, which was on the hillside between Lanikai and Waimānalo, my father, Mike and I climbed further up through a neighbor's yard and saw a Japanese plane flying over the area of our house on its way to strafe the planes neatly lined up at Bellows Air Field, located just on the other side of the hill. We were able to see the pilot and we even waved at him. The impact of what was transpiring had not hit us yet. We were very fortunate that the pilot did not have orders to shoot people like us.

As the day progressed my father went to his office at the Pacific Guano Company (later renamed Pacific Chemical Company) in Honolulu. When he determined there was not much to do there, he joined up with an FBI acquaintance assigned to ferret out spies living within Honolulu. He told us it was spooky and scary entering homes that evening arresting suspected spies. Meanwhile my grandfather was called upon to assist at an emergency clinic established at Kailua School. By then all of us in Hawai`i had been instructed not to use lights, so while he drove, my mother, India, walked several miles along the roadside guiding him in the darkness.

After the attack, a military family that had been living at the Kāne`ohe Naval Air Station moved in with us rather than be evacuated to the Mainland. Subsequently, my family moved back to our house in Woodlawn where my father would be closer to his plant, because the company was instrumental in providing chemicals to the Army. Soon, our house, like many in Hawai`i, was constantly filled with servicemen—sons, uncles, cousins or neighbors of friends—who were on their way from the Mainland to action in the Pacific.

After the Pearl Harbor attack, we often saw barrage balloons in the sky to hinder low flying aircraft (Hawai`i State Archives, 1942).

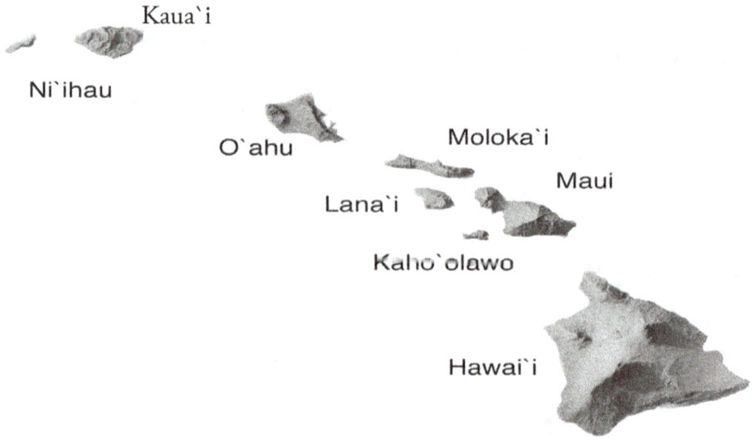

Other Islands

Jean Brown Anderson—Hawai`i
Margaret (Peggy) M. Burt—Hawai`i
Kathy Cadinha Strong—Maui
Tom Chang—Kaua`i
Shiela Cruickshank Mahoney—Maui
Eddie Hamilton—Kaua`i
Kirby C. Hanson—Hawai`i
Ellen McGillivray Luhrs—Hawai`i
Connie Ruddock Paresa—Maui
Neal T. Walker—Maui

Recollections of Jean Brown Anderson

I now live in the San Francisco Bay area with my three sons and two grandchildren living close by. I have many happy memories of times gone by in old Hawai`i.

My father, Tom Brown, went to the Islands after the First World War. As I understand it, as a soldier getting out of the British Army in 1918, he was given his Army insurance money and like many soldiers did, he took that money and went in search of adventure. Along with many other adventurers, my dad ended up in Hawai`i. His first job was on a plantation near Hilo, where he rode on horseback out to the fields to collect the time sheets of the workers. He used to say that the Hamakua Coast was known as the "Scot's Coast" because of the number of Scotsmen working there! He later moved to Na`alehu where he was the bookkeeper for the sugar plantation. Like many other young men, he lived in the bachelor's quarters and made friends with the "foreigners"—the American schoolteachers!

In 1925, he returned to Scotland for a visit where he resumed his friendship with Mary Crawford, the woman he would eventually marry. My mother refused to marry my father in Scotland as she knew in those days married women in Scotland would not be hired and that if she were married, it would be a long time before her name would come up in the quota of people to be accepted into America. She was finally accepted in 1928 and traveled by herself across the Atlantic, across the U.S. and then across the Pacific—a brave lady! My dad met the ship when it docked in Honolulu on May 28th. They went directly from the ship to St. Andrew's Cathedral, along with two of my father's friends who served as witnesses to their marriage. No living together in those days! Then it was off to the Big Island and their plantation house at Na`alehu to begin their life together. From stories I have heard, plantation life was a real cultural shock for my mother. I was born at Pāhala and later home-schooled by my mom, before moving to Honolulu in 1943 when I entered Punahou. It was a HUGE cultural shock for me!

On December 7th I remember that my dad was washing the car after breakfast when some neighbors came to tell us what they had heard on the radio. I did not understand the seriousness of the news, but I do remember the fear on the adults' faces and in their voices. My dad quickly left for the plantation office; why, I have no clue except there was a telephone there. At this point things get a little fuzzy. I remember that certain rooms in the house were quickly blacked out by hanging blue denim over the windows. There were plastic rings sewn onto the denim and these fit over the nails put into the window frames. This method allowed the denim to be taken down during the day. But where on earth did the denim come from? There was only one store on the plantation and everyone's windows were covered the same way! One of the men on the plantation acted as a warden and each night he would walk around each house. If he saw the least crack of light he, would pound on the wall outside the window—a terrifying sound. My child's mind said that if the enemy were that close, we were in deep trouble! We had huge leather suitcases packed with food and clothing so that we could flee to the hills in case of another attack. Those suitcases became so heavy that none of us could have lifted them, let alone flee with them! Good friends of ours had a son who was a boarder at Punahou on December 7th. They knew that the campus had been taken over by the military, but due to lack of communication between the Islands, it was almost a week before they were able to make contact with him and know that he was okay.

During the war, my dad and other men on each of the plantations voluntarily worked on Selective Service boards deciding who was eligible to be called to military duty. Na`ālehu and Pāhala worked together to do this and I remember evenings when Dad would drive to Pāhala with those funny blacked-out lights on the car. I have documents signed by both President Roosevelt and President Truman thanking him for the time he gave to this work. Finally, I think it was in late March, I remember standing by the main road through Nā`ālehu to welcome the American troops as they passed on their way to South Point to protect us from future attacks that thankfully never came.

Despite the confusion on O`ahu caused by the Pearl Harbor attack, the outer islands were relatively calm (JBB, 1947).

Recollections of Margaret (Peggy) M. Burt

I received a baccalaureate and Master's degree in nursing from the University of Washington and worked in Seattle except for seven years when I was teaching in Lewiston, Idaho. I enjoy retirement and do volunteer work at my church, tutor English as a second language and am a docent at the Burke Museum. I take assorted short classes, volunteer at Midway Atoll through Elderhostel, and argue with my computer.

My father was one of a number of young men who came from Scotland in the 1920s to work on the sugar plantations on the Hāmākua Coast of the Big Island. He had attended agricultural school in Scotland and first went to Honomū (the center of plantation activity along the Hāmākua Coast). For a time there were so many Scots on the Hāmākua Coast that it was nicknamed "The Scots Coast." From 1927-29 my father was on the Punahou faculty at the Farm School. My mother was a Canadian, originally from Prince Edward Island. She developed tuberculosis shortly after graduating from nursing school and was hospitalized for a year. She went to Honolulu to visit her sister while recuperating.

The call from the sheriff came to my father as we were having breakfast at our Big Island home that December Sunday morning. The sheriff reported that Japanese planes were bombing O`ahu. All Island radio stations were off the air and people were requested to keep off the highways and off the telephones. He had no other information to give us. My father was manager of Kūka`iau Ranch and we lived in the tiny community of `Umikoa, several miles above the Hāmākua Coast on the slopes of Mauna Kea. There was one other telephone on the ranch and a quick call spread the news to the dozen or so other families of `Umikoa. My father went out to confer briefly with the other families and to determine who was there that morning.

It was a long day. A card table was placed beside the radio, which softly crackled static. Talk was minimal as we played cards and board games. Occasionally, a terse phrase would burst from the radio: "Plane down off Barber's Point! Bomb on school campus!" The brief messages fed our anxiety.

Sometime in the afternoon, the sheriff called again. The attack had stopped, but there was concern for further bombings, paratroops dropping or shelling of the coastlines by submarines. Curfew was enforced along with total blackout. All schools were closed and the radio stations would continue to be silent. `Umikoa was on its own to prepare as best it could.

My father let me go with him as he made the rounds of the village with the latest news. The word on school closures brought small smiles to most children, but everyone was anxious. The men organized into shifts to watch for parachutes and to enforce blackout. Horse blankets from the stable were distributed as needed so each family could have at least one room with light on this darkest night.

There were two Japanese families at `Umikoa. The elders had lived there for years; their children and grandchildren had been born in Hawai`i. These people were part of our community but today they hung back from any discussion. My father spoke to each of them, "Has anyone been giving you trouble over the bombing?"

"No," they replied.

"If you have trouble from anyone," my father went on, "You come and tell me. I know you're not to blame. Hawai`i is your home." This brought a few soft smiles and whispered thanks.

At dusk we hung blankets over the window of one room. Even so, Mother would permit only the tiniest of lights. When it was dark my father emptied his pockets of money and identification and left the house to search the sky for the enemy. The night was quiet.

Much later when my father returned home from his patrol shift, he turned on the radio to the Island stations. They were silent. He then tried short wave; at our elevation we sometimes got distant stations at night. After several slow twists of the dial he found a station with extensive news of the attack on Pearl Harbor. The broadcast was from Bombay, India.

Throughout the war, sugar plantations (including Ola`a on the Big Island) were in operation; most are no longer in use (JBB, 1947).

Recollections of Kathy Cadinha Strong

After Punahou I graduated from Whittier College in primary education and eventually earned a master's degree from Pepperdine. This prepared me for the thirty-two years I taught kindergarten in Torrence, California until I retired. My husband Carl and I have a son and daughter and two grandchildren.

My great-grandparents arrived by ship in Hawai`i from the Azores in the late 1800s. One great-grandparent on each side came from an orphanage: my great-grandmother on Dad's side and my great-grandfather on Mother's. Thus we came by our family name, Cadinha, from the foundling home of that name. Mother mentioned that her dad worked on the sugar plantation as some kind of "luna" (foreman) and spoke fluent Hawaiian. Evidently Grandpa (Dad's father) was some sort of policeman.

Both families located on the Big Island, Dad's in Ninole, near Hilo and Mom's in Hawi on the Kohala side. Mom and Dad met in Honolulu while they were attending the University of Hawai`i (Normal School for Teachers). The night after they married, they took one of the inter-Island boats to Maui, where they stayed.

I don't think I shall ever forget December 7, 1941. My father was principal of Kamehameha III School in Lahaina, Maui. We lived in the principal's cottage on the school grounds. A low stone wall separated the front yard from the beach. Naval ships frequently passed through the channel between Maui, Lana`i and Moloka`i. The ships would often stop for a short time. During the night we could hear their engines over the sound of the waves. The ships were there the night of December 6th, but were nowhere to be seen on the 7th.

Our radio was often the first thing to be turned on in the mornings, as Dad was adamant about keeping up with the news of the day.

I knew something was terribly wrong when I walked into the living room and saw my mother pacing the floor, visibly upset, holding on tightly to my brother, who was about seven months old. Dad was trying to comfort her, but he appeared to be quite apprehensive himself. They soon told me what was happening. I also learned that Mother was worried about her three brothers who worked at Pearl Harbor. She was not able to get any news at the time, but eventually learned that one brother had been there. It was difficult for him to talk about that day, but little by little we learned that someone had pulled him behind a coconut tree during some of the strafing, saving his life as bullets hit the tree. This was so hard to imagine, as some of those trunks are so skinny! He also told about work he had to do on a ship named the *Oglala.* He decided to do another job first. When he returned, the *Oglala* had been sunk.

A few memories linger about the life changes after December 7th: blacked-out windows, air raid drills and shelter trenches camouflaged with sweet potato vines on the school grounds, gas ration stamps, typhoid shots (ouch!!) and gas masks! My brother had a full-body "bunny" gas mask—so cute! My gas mask appeared to have belonged to the creature from the Black Lagoon—(ugh!) Each day after public school closed, many of my friends would attend the Japanese school nearby. I was curious about what they did there, and wanted to go too! This became quite a bone of contention in our house. Soon this was no longer an issue, as the Japanese school quietly closed.

I still have my ID card dated March 31, 1942, complete with serial number, fingerprints and an inaccurate blood type! Thank goodness I never needed a transfusion.

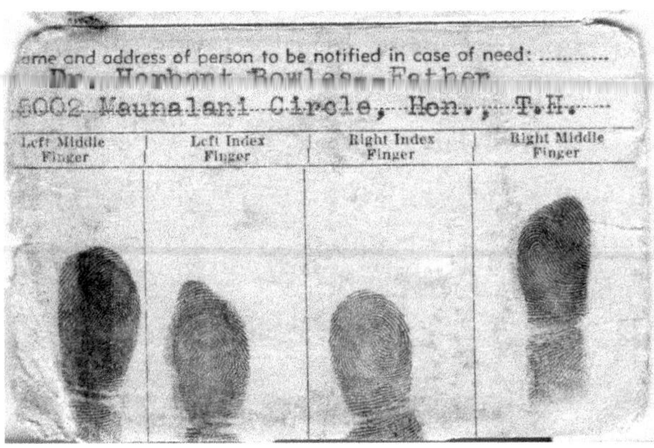

...ame and address of person to be notified in case of need: ....
Dr. Herbert Bowles--Father
5002 Maunalani Circle, Hon., T.H.

Left Middle Finger	Left Index Finger	Right Index Finger	Right Middle Finger

Shortly after December 7th, residents of all the Islands were fingerprinted and required to carry identification cards at all times (1943).

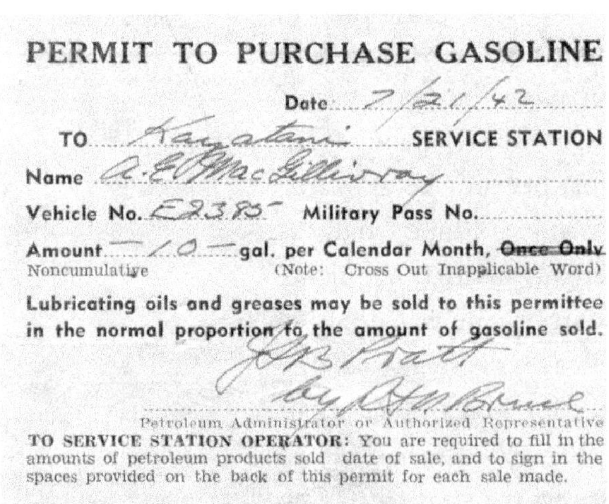

PERMIT TO PURCHASE GASOLINE

Date 7/21/42

TO Kanatani SERVICE STATION

Name A.E. MacGillivray

Vehicle No. E23 85 Military Pass No. ....

Amount 10 gal. per Calendar Month, ~~Once Only~~
Noncumulative (Note: Cross Out Inapplicable Word)

Lubricating oils and greases may be sold to this permittee in the normal proportion to the amount of gasoline sold.

J.B. Pratt
by A.H.M. Bruce
Petroleum Administrator or Authorized Representative

TO SERVICE STATION OPERATOR: You are required to fill in the amounts of petroleum products sold date of sale, and to sign in the spaces provided on the back of this permit for each sale made.

Nearly all commodities, including gasoline, were rationed throughout the war years (courtesy of E.M. Luhrs).

Recollections of Tom Chang

I was born in Līhu`e, Kaua`i. My mother, Dorothy Chock Chang, was born on Kaua`i, in Hanalei Valley. Her dad owned much of the valley at that time. His main source of income was from growing rice. He also owned a general store and restaurant. He built a lily pond next to the store and restaurant, which is still partially there. When my grandfather first arrived from China, he worked as a paniolo (cowboy), on the Big Island. Mom was one of the first graduates of Kaua`i High School. She commuted from Hanalei by horseback. After graduating from the University of Hawai`i, she taught at Līhu`e Grammar School, the same school I graduated from before entering Punahou.

My dad, Dr. Sau Yee Chang, was born in Hanapepe, Kaua`i. After graduating from Mid-Pacific lnstitute he went to Northwestern's School of Dentistry in Chicago. He practiced dentistry on Kaua`i for 50 years. A staunch Republican, he was active in politics and was once the acting mayor of Kaua`i. He was also active in the Hawai`i Dental Association and the American Dental Association, being president and vice-president respectively of those organizations. He was also president of the American Board of Dental Examiners.

I went to the University of Washington and in 1959 was ninth in my graduating class in the newly opened dental school. I returned to Kaua`i and practiced dentistry for three years with my dad. Then went to graduate school at the University of Southern California where I received a Master of Science in Orthodontics. I have practiced orthodontics in Mission Hill, California since then and am on the part-time faculty at USC, teaching Orthodontics. I met my wife, the former Jane Chun of Honolulu at UW. We married in Seattle and have three children. We still live in Mission Hill.

Not much happened on Kaua`i during the December 7th attack, but because I was only six-and-a-half years old, I was quite impressed anyway. Dad (the local dentist in Līhu`e) had taken me to the office to fix my teeth. He decided to turn on the radio to listen to some music. I remember clearly the announcer repeating over and over again, "This is not a drill; this is an attack." Since I was not really enthused about having my teeth worked on, (Dad usually worked on me without anesthesia) I was more than happy when my dad said, "We better go home!"

We lived just above Nāwiliwili, so we were close to the eastern shore of Kaua`i. All morning I heard the planes flying overhead as they headed back to the carriers. We were told that they were about 100 miles north of Kaua`i.

Needless to say, I wanted to go out and look at the planes, but my father said it was too dangerous. I remember him sitting up all night listening to the radio, as he was sure that an invasion was about to occur. Thank goodness Japan did not have that in their plans.

The most impressive thing to occur in my young life was the shelling of Nāwiliwili Harbor early in January of 1942! It woke us up in the middle of the night with first a flare, then the shelling. Our air raid shelter was already built. As I ran out to the shelter, I hit my head on a mango tree branch. Fortunately no damage was done. A shell did hit an empty Shell Oil storage tank, but it was a dud.

During the war years, Kaua`i was the training island for the Army and Marine Corps before they headed to the Pacific theater. Many of the soldiers came to my dad to have cosmetic dentistry done before having their photographs taken.

Hawi on the island of Hawai`i, like most rural Hawaiian communities, established its own military unit after the war began, in preparation for possible future attacks (courtesy of E.M. Luhrs, 1942).

The military was present on all the major islands, either as regular military personnel or as local militia like the Hawai`i Rifles at Hawi (courtesy of E.M. Luhrs, 1942).

Recollections of Shiela Cruickshank Mahoney

Retired (as of 1998) from California State University, Hayward, English and ESL teacher.

George and Agnes Cruickshank, my grandparents, came to the Islands directly from Scotland just as the 20th century began. George took a job as a luna (foreman) on a sugar plantation, having heard that the Americans were paying well for that work. A short time later, he became head overseer at Waialua Agricultural Company on the North Shore of O`ahu.

Their three sons—including my father, James—were born and raised in Hawai`i. My dad graduated from Punahou in 1922 and went from there to the University of Hawai`i, where he and his older brother Bruce played football, most notably on the Wonder Team of 1925.

On the maternal side of the family: My grandfather, Colonel Edward Schreiner, was an Army doctor who had originally come from Pennsylvania but had traveled extensively because of his work. When he came to Hawai`i with his family, he served at Tripler Hospital. His daughter Dorothy, my mother, was born in the Philippines but attended Punahou in her high school years and graduated in 1925. Punahou was actually the vehicle for their meeting.

They married in 1927; the two families, with very different pre-Hawai`i histories, converged. My sister Brucie (Dorothy Bruce) was born in 1928; I was born on Maui in 1936. Before World War II arrived, the family traveled between O`ahu and Maui. My father took a position as an assistant treasurer at Hai`kū Pineapple Company on Maui (later he held the same position at Dole on O`ahu). In 1943, the family came back to Honolulu to stay, but earlier, in 1940, my father was a captain in the National Guard. He became part of the Maui Service Command and was stationed in Wailuku, where we were living when the Pearl Harbor attack occurred.

December 7, 1941: My sixth birthday was still more than a month away, and my memories are limited to brief images that are rather like snapshots. I realized that the radio reports signaled danger and fear and I had a vague understanding of the attack, but I am sure that I didn't grasp the full meaning. Mostly I noticed the reactions of those around me. My father, tall and taciturn, was in uniform, stirring his morning coffee many more times than necessary and listening to the radio with grave concentration. My mother tried almost successfully to hide her nervousness, but her hands trembled as she took pictures with our Brownie camera that morning as she tried to keep occupied with ordinary, everyday actions. My sister Brucie, thirteen at the time, was on her way to teach a Sunday school class when news of the bombing came.

My memories of the following months and years are clearer, of course, as I got older. Rationing, blackouts, the nearby bomb shelter, the gas masks we carried to school, jeeps, the high presence of the military, even a child's quick glance at planes overhead to check for familiar markings and many other aspects of the war became commonplace, almost accepted as a way of life.

My sister told me recently that she was asleep when Maui was shelled briefly, early on, and she recalls going back to sleep with barely a moment's worry. Children sometimes have a sense of safety that might not match the facts; we never truly thought that we were in danger.

Certainly we felt that the people around us were good and protective, and there was never any question of the loyalty of those of Japanese ancestry that we knew and met on Maui and O`ahu. Our story does not reflect the drama of the tales told by many others, especially those who were on O`ahu on December 7th. Still, it is one small part of the World War II experience that had such a very deep and long-lasting effect on the people of Hawai`i.

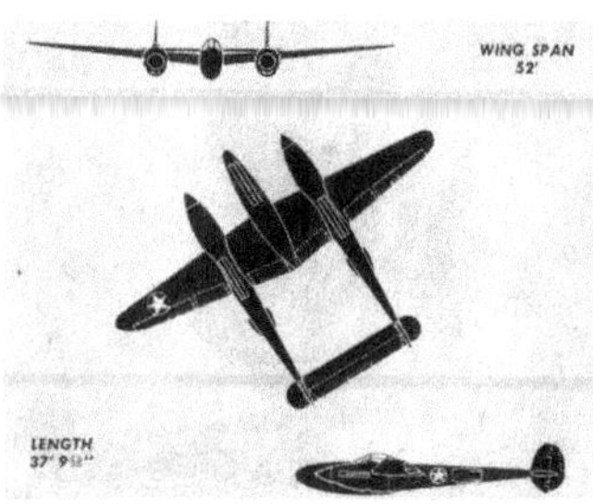

All over the Territory, kids became experts at identifying all kinds of airplanes by their outlines (*Aircraft Spotter*, by L.Ott, Harcourt, Brace, and Co., 1943 edition).

Recollections of Eddie Hamilton

I served twenty-four years in the Navy, retiring as a Captain in 1980. I then pursued a fourteen-year career as a legal administrator in Atlanta, Georgia. I retired in 1994, put my son in college, sold my house and moved to Whidbey Island in Washington state to enjoy the Northwest, be closer to my two daughters in Seattle, hike the Cascade mountains and shuttle to and from Hawai`i. In late 1999 I relocated to Georgia. I married Birdie, a widow I had known for some years on September 9, 2000, and we now reside in Griffin, Georgia, fifty miles south of Atlanta.

My father had wandered to Hawai`i in the early '30s from Nebraska via Wyoming. I guess he then got to California, and just kept going to the next spot West. My mother was born, raised, and lived her entire life in the Islands, on O`ahu and Kaua`i. Her father, Harold Jeffs, had emigrated from England to Honolulu in the late 1880s, and I understand that for a time he was the barber to Prince Kūhio. He raised and shipped orchids all over the world from his Sierra Drive home. My mother attended Punahou for a short while, with the class of '26. I guess somewhere in the early '30s she met my father, who had a job offer with the sugar company in Līhu`e as a chemist, and they moved to Kaua`i. I was born there in September 1935 and lived there until we all moved to Honolulu in 1945, via an overnight trip on the MV Hualālai. *My dad was ineligible to serve in WWII (he had a lung removed after having pneumonia); so he spent the war years as an air raid warden on Kaua`i and prepared gas masks for babies in the courthouse basement...but those are other stories in themselves!*

Following two years at Ali`iolani Elementary School in Kaimukī, I entered Punahou in the seventh grade. Several '52 classmates were in Ms. Froelich's sixth grade room at Ali`iolani.

I distinctly remember my younger brother and me playing "cowboys and Indians" in the yard of our Līhu`e Sugar Company plantation house on Kaua`i the Sunday morning of December 7, 1941. My mother frantically called us into the house where she was filling the bathtub with water. "Why?" I asked. "We had our baths last (Saturday) night!" She informed us that the Japanese had attacked Pearl Harbor and that the radio was advising Kaua`i residents to fill containers with water and to pack a box of food and emergency supplies, which she also did (where were we going to go to escape the expected invasion?) I still wonder.

Recollections of Kirby C. Hanson

Both my parents were immigrants to Hawai`i. After my dad graduated from the University of California, Berkeley, he went to Hawai`i to work six months for Standard Oil of California. Soon after his arrival he went to work for First Hawaiian Bank, in those days known as Bishop National Bank. He went from a general office boy to CEO and Chairman of the Board. His six months in Hawai`i turned into forty-two years as a resident of the Islands.

My mother was a native of Connecticut and left New England in 1930, her first time more than 100 miles from home, and headed out by herself for the Hawaiian Islands to assume the position of surgical supervisor for the Hilo Memorial Hospital. My mother and dad were married in 1931 and remained in Hilo until 1948 when they, together with my sister Faye and myself, moved to Honolulu. At that time Faye and I entered Punahou in the eighth grade where we remained until graduation in 1952.

We were living in Hilo on December 7, 1941. I remember the day distinctly. We always went to Mass on Sunday morning and that morning was no exception. As we started down Wāiānuenue Avenue to St. Joseph's Church, Civil Defense personnel met us and said we would have to return home because the Japanese had attacked the island of O`ahu. We, of course, had no alternative but to obey the directive and returned home immediately. To this day I do not understand how those Civil Defense teams were organized and put into place on such short notice. Like everyone else we were glued to the radio for the remainder of the day and many days to come. For those of us who were removed by a couple of hundred miles from the scene of action it seemed surreal. It became very real the next day when a machine gun nest was set up in our front yard and the Hilo Harbor was torpedoed by a Japanese submarine.

There is something about the bond that is Aloha that will always hold us together as a class and a group of friends.

After active duty with the military, I returned to work in the field of finance. In 1961 I was transferred to San Francisco, to the head office of the Bank of California. Finally, in 1962, I resigned from the Bank and entered seminary to study for the Catholic priesthood. I was ordained in 1969 and have had various assignments over the years. For the last seven years I have served as Pastor of St. Thomas, a small parish in the Richmond District of San Francisco. I retired from active ministry on June 30, 2001.

Kirby dedicates this story to his twin sister, Faye Hanson Schlichte, who passed away in 2002.

Recollections of Ellen McGillivray Luhrs

Graduated from Whitman College, Walla Walla, WA 1956. Recruited to work for the CIA 1956-1960. Came to San Francisco after three years in Washington, D.C. Married; have two children (Eric and Alexandra); one grandchild, another on the way. Divorced. Stockbroker since 1980.

As many of you may know, there was an influx of Scottish people into the Hawaiian Islands in the mid 1800s. This was predicated on the fact that the sugar mills were prefabricated in Scotland and shipped around the Horn with Scottish engineers who then built and ran them. They wrote back to Scotland telling of the island paradise they were experiencing and because of both weather and economics, many brothers and friends also went to Hawai`i. Daddy was one of four brothers to go to Hawai`i from Scotland in the 1920s and all ended up on the Big Island. Mother, a schoolteacher in Missouri, read with fascination a National Geographic *published in 1924 (I have the magazine), which was completely devoted to the Hawaiian Islands. She decided she wanted to go to Hawai`i and wrote to the Department of Public Instruction, asking for a teaching job. They wrote back saying there were none. She went anyway!! I think this was around 1926. (It makes me feel quite unadventurous in comparison.) She ended up with a job teaching at McKinley High School. Then (I'm not sure of the timing here) they asked her to go to the Big Island to be principal of an elementary school at Makapala. Mother and Daddy met there and married in about 1930.*

My mother was braiding my sister's and my hair, getting us ready to go to Sunday school, when our neighbor called to tell Mom that she had heard reports on the radio that the Japanese had bombed Pearl Harbor. My dad was pheasant hunting on Kahuā Ranch, so instead of going to Sunday school we went looking for Daddy. When we found him, he didn't believe Mother. But he came home, and the rest of the day is somewhat of a blur in my memory. I do remember listening to Mother and Daddy saying that perhaps they should bury their valuables in case there was an invasion. So my sister, Barbara, and I decided we should bury our valuables. Unfortunately our most valuable possessions were books. We took our favorite books and buried them in the soft flower beds. Later, when Mother noticed great gaps in our bookcase she asked about the books. Of course they were ruined from water and mud.

Like some of the other families (I think especially on the outer islands) my dad shipped my sister, Mom and me out of the Islands. He continued working and also joined the Hawai`i Rifles. I believe that was like the local National Guard. We went to Honolulu along with Marice Hind ('50) and some other kids that my mom chaperoned up to relatives on the mainland. We stayed with Mrs. John Hind in Mānoa Valley until we were notified that we could leave which was in March 1942. All evacuation was done through the Army. While we were waiting for notification there were numerous air raid alerts and we went into the underground shelter dug in Mrs. Hind's back yard (remember those?). The day after one of the air raid alerts the shelter collapsed. Very excit ing!

We were in an Army hospital convoy from Honolulu to San Francisco. It took ten days because of zigzagging to avoid Japanese submarines. We were on the main ship of the convoy and I remember that our ship target-practiced on the other ships—seeing how close they could come. It was all very exciting and not scary at all to the kids. I'm sure Mother thought otherwise. We stayed in Kansas City, Missouri, until March 1944 when we returned to Hawai`i.

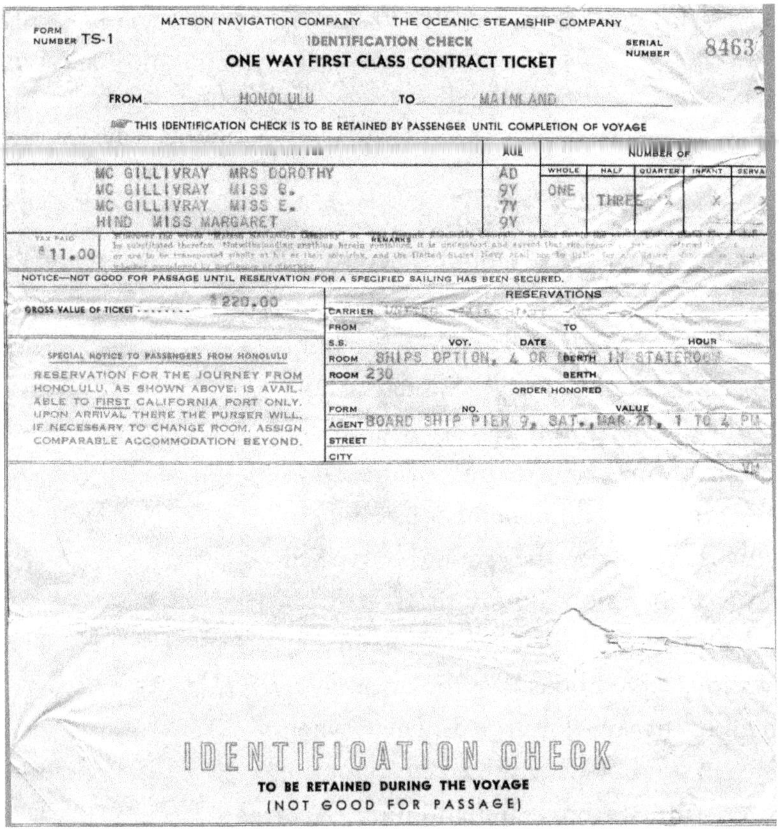

FORM NUMBER TS-1

MATSON NAVIGATION COMPANY THE OCEANIC STEAMSHIP COMPANY

IDENTIFICATION CHECK

ONE WAY FIRST CLASS CONTRACT TICKET

SERIAL NUMBER 8463

FROM HONOLULU TO MAINLAND

THIS IDENTIFICATION CHECK IS TO BE RETAINED BY PASSENGER UNTIL COMPLETION OF VOYAGE

	AGE	WHOLE	HALF	QUARTER	INFANT	SERVA
MC GILLIVRAY MRS DOROTHY	AD	ONE	THREE	X	X	X
MC GILLIVRAY MISS B.	9Y					
MC GILLIVRAY MISS E.	7Y					
HIND MISS MARGARET	9Y					

TAX PAID $11.00 REMARKS

NOTICE—NOT GOOD FOR PASSAGE UNTIL RESERVATION FOR A SPECIFIED SAILING HAS BEEN SECURED.

GROSS VALUE OF TICKET $220.00

SPECIAL NOTICE TO PASSENGERS FROM HONOLULU

RESERVATION FOR THE JOURNEY FROM HONOLULU, AS SHOWN ABOVE, IS AVAILABLE TO FIRST CALIFORNIA PORT ONLY. UPON ARRIVAL THERE THE PURSER WILL, IF NECESSARY TO CHANGE ROOM, ASSIGN COMPARABLE ACCOMMODATION BEYOND.

RESERVATIONS

CARRIER

FROM TO

S.S. VOY. DATE HOUR

ROOM SHIPS OPTION, 4 OR BERTH IN STATEROOM

ROOM 230 BERTH

ORDER HONORED

FORM NO. VALUE

AGENT BOARD SHIP PIER 9, SAT., MAR 21, 1 TO 4 PM

STREET

CITY

IDENTIFICATION CHECK

TO BE RETAINED DURING THE VOYAGE

(NOT GOOD FOR PASSAGE)

Many women and children went by ship convoy to the mainland during the first few years of the war (courtesy of E.M. Luhrs).

Recollections of Connie Ruddock Paresa

After graduation, I worked for Bishop Insurance Company. Nolan and I married in 1954. We lived on O`ahu, Maui and Hawai`i before moving to Texas in 1981. I retired from a banking job in 1996. We have a son and a daughter.

My mom had just graduated from nursing school in Canada. She and two other classmates decided to visit Hawai`i. On board the freighter* Aorangi, *my mom met my dad, who was employed on board as an electrician. They "bonded" and over a period, married and settled in Hawai`i. They lived in Kaimukī and went through the Depression. Mom gave birth to my brother, Jack, and since times were so hard and Dad was having an employment problem, Mom and Jack went back to Canada to be with her parents. When things settled a bit and Dad could afford his family, they returned. Dad was employed with Hawaiian Pineapple Company as an electrician when in 1937 we moved to Maui where he was chief electrician with Maui Pineapple Company. Mom was a nurse at Pā`ia and Pu`unēnē hospitals.

December 7, 1941, was very "memorable." Jack and I were at Sunday school when my mom came rushing over to pick us up immediately after hearing the alert, which was the reported bombing on O`ahu. This extended over to Maui, affecting Maui Pine. We lived in Sand Hills and Dad was prepared with a bomb shelter and "his" lookout spot over Kahului Harbor and the cannery. We were safe and I don't remember being afraid. What I didn't like was having to deal with the blackout and carrying our gas masks—mercy, they were heavy and ugly, although necessary. Then came the servicemen from all walks of life whom Mom and Dad befriended, opening our home to many of them. This period of my life has left me very compassionate for others not as fortunate as I. I am so grateful to our superior Being–Our Lord.

In the 1930s and 1940s, much of the rural transportation was provided by "Hilo station wagons," also called "banana wagons" or *sampans* (JBB, 1999).

Recollections of Neal T. Walker

Neal received a BS and MBA in engineering from Stanford and served three years in the US Navy. He first worked in the pre-silicon valley San Jose, then went to Hilo where he was first Treasurer and then President of the Moses Co., Ltd. In the 1970s he helped organize a California to Hawai`i boat delivery company for the sailing of new sailing vessels from California ports to Hawai`i. In 1975 he sold the company and built his own forty-two-foot sailing vessel. Neal is married to Elizabeth and they have five boys.

As a fifth generation kid born in Hawai`i (in Pu`unēnē on Maui), I endured a typically segregated (see Joan Wood Fleming's explanation of English Standard Schools) elementary school on Maui before enplaning for Honolulu and Punahou at the start of my freshman year. My father's family came to Maui after a brief but fairly successful business experience in India. My grandfather then became the "storekeeper" at Kahului Store, the plantation store in the port town of Kahului, Maui. Although my father and all of his brothers and sisters grew up in Kahului, all but the last couple were born in Alameda, California because there was no reliable doctor on Maui and my grandmother preferred the risks of a sailing voyage to and from California around the turn of the last century to the level of medical care then available in Honolulu. Also, being born in California, a US state since 1850, made them all US citizens as opposed to Hawaiian citizens. My mother's (Hitchcock) relatives came with the third wave of missionaries to Hawai`i in the 1830s settling first on Moloka`i (his church still stands at Kalua`aha) and then later in Hilo where my mother grew up. I grew up with one foot in the water. We summered at our beach house in Kīhei and my father had various small sailboats and skiffs that he encouraged me to use even as a little kid. Through the hands-on approach I developed a love of things maritime which has stood me in good stead ever since.

Every Sunday morning my father and I would listen to a radio program called "The Waterfront Reporter." It consisted of a series of short stories about things maritime, from small sailboat sagas to large steamship tales. The program always started out with the same few lines taken from "Through the Looking Glass." On December 7th I still remember the announcer saying the usual "…of shoes and ships and sealing wax and cabbages and kings. The air will be filled with salty tales and some of them mebelies ('may be lies' said as one word)" At that point he was interrupted with the first words of the attack on Pearl Harbor. From then on all I remember was the same phrase over and over, "This is the real McCoy," together with long lists of doctors and other health workers requested to report to the various hospitals.

Of course, Maui escaped attack by the Japanese, but that night the paranoia that the Japanese might return caused our family to move from our home, located close to the HC&S sugar mill in Pu`unēnē and on a direct line from the Island's only power plant to the mill, to my uncle's home, quite far from Pu`unēnē.

Mainland

Pat Clarke Clifford—Illinois
Pat Fox—Connecticut
David E. Harris—Pennsylvania
Shannon Heath Wilson—Washington
Jane Hughes Simms—California
Anne Parks Strain—Washington, DC
Barbara Rhodes Maness—Alabama
Carolyn (Connie) Schrader Peterson—California
Greg Seastrom—New York
Susan (Sooch) Wall Ludewig—California

Over Seas

Joan Maggioros Triantafyllides—Greece

Recollections of Pat Clarke Clifford

Pat received her degree from the University of Washington, and spent many years as a private secretary and administrative assistant. She now lives in Kamuela on the Big Island (Hawai`i)

Father was with Pan American Airlines and transferred to Hawai`i. We arrived in Honolulu in June of 1948 and had to have "over seas shots" and permission from the Territory to enter the islands.

I was seven years old on December 7, 1941, as were most of us in our class. Unlike those who grew up in Hawai`i, I was busy sledding, learning how to ice skate or playing with my little friends in the snow, so the bombing of Pearl Harbor didn't mean much to me. I don't think I even knew where Pearl Harbor was, but my memories of the accounts I've heard from my family and their friends have left a lasting impression.

When I think back to those war days, I remember the small town with brick streets where I was born, outside of Chicago. I can remember the pall-like atmosphere that hit the town and that nobody seemed to be happy anymore. Relatives and family friends were dressed in uniform, and I remember seeing small red, white and blue flags with one, two or three gold stars on them, displayed in windows, one star for each member of that family that was in uniform. I remember my dad being very, very disappointed that they wouldn't take him in the service at the age of twenty-eight because he had two children and a wife to support.

I remember everyone complaining because they didn't have enough food stamps or gas stamps. It didn't matter to me because I was always well fed and we didn't have a car, so what was the big deal about gas? We always walked to school, to the market and to see the relatives.

The impact of December 7th never really hit me until I started school at Punahou in 1948 and talked to my classmates about that day and realized how frightening it must have been to a seven-year-old to hear the bombing and to see the war planes flying over.

Recollections of Pat Fox

I graduated from UCLA with an art degree and then traveled the South Pacific, ending up four years later on a NATO base in France working as Base Artist for a year. After playing in Seychelles and hitchhiking down the Nile I returned to Châteauroux to marry my Air Force doctor. We returned to California, joined the Peace Corps in West Africa, back to California again, bore two children (Hanna and Sam Levitz), and then ended our twenty-two-year marriage. Now I divide my time erratically between Hawai`i, Los Gatos, and the rest of the world. I carry my paintbrushes worldwide in case I find a wall to paint on, a chair to embellish, or a banner to whip out—Got a blank spot I could fill in?

I don't remember December 7, 1941, (I was six, and have retained very few memories from those days)—maybe I would have had those Japanese planes been strafing my house, with the pilots making eye contact and dropping bombs which I could see and hear. I do, however, remember vividly, in subsequent years, sitting in the kitchen of our little house at the edge of the woods in Connecticut listening to war news every night on the radio. It was scary and it was far away.

My father at that time was superintendent of schools in East Hartford, having received his Ph.D. in Education for school administration, after reluctantly giving up the idea of coaching/recreation/physical education. He had a wife and three little girls already and needed a steady income in those post-depression years.

One of the teachers he had hired, Will Hayes, was drafted into the military, sent to Hawai`i, and attended a Rotary lunch at the Royal Hawaiian Hotel at which he heard that Punahou School was actively searching for a new president to replace retiring Mr. Shephard. Will wired the information at once to Daddy, who applied for the job. I remember both parents coaching Jeanie, Mary Bell and me to be on our absolute BEST behavior when we went to dinner at a Punahou Alum's house in Massachusetts, a sort of social interview. We passed!

My fourth grade class at Green Knoll School was electrified to learn that I was going to the Sandwich Islands to live. It was unthinkably exotic, half the world away, swaying palms, grass huts. I prepared myself to be a little white goddess (embarrassing, but that's the way little Easterners thought in those days). Daddy was able to get an air passage—difficult during the war—and wrote us enthusiastic letters from his third floor *makai* (seaside) room at the Moana Hotel, where Punahou housed him for three months before he could move into the enormous Victorian President's House on campus. He loved Hawai`i at once and forever!

Meanwhile, Mother had to sell our Connecticut house along with its contents and decide what was absolutely necessary to take with us—all her life she mourned certain things she had been hasty to give up. Then she conscripted an aunt-in-law to help drive us all across the vast country to catch a boat to Hawai`i from San Francisco. Everything was rationed. I remember weeping for celery, of all things, somewhere in Nebraska, but it was not available or we didn't have the script to buy it. I'm not sure how we got enough gas coupons to make the journey in our old Packard with fuzzy seats. We stayed with my mother's parents for a month in Lawrence, Kansas, a mixed blessing for them! That's where we got all our immunizations for the tropics, and I remember being felled by fever from the immunization for typhoid. Then onward we drove, and to keep three restless little girls from wrangling, mother promised a nickel to the daughter who could spot the first mountain as we entered Colorado. We'd never seen a mountain, ever. Hills, yes. I wanted that nickel! I searched the horizon close to the ground, looking for a mountain. Jeanie found it, not by looking close to the horizon, but by looking high up in the air! It never occurred to me that land might appear way up there. Maybe that's why high mountains have attracted me ever after.

Then we reached San Francisco and the coast: thrilling beyond words. My first palm tree (the stiff kind), the crashing grey ocean, a tiny motel on a cliff where we stayed before embarking on the boat! We sailed in early September 1944 aboard the *Permanente*, a Kaiser cement freighter. We traveled in convoy with three other ships and seven submarines, pursuing a zigzag course across the Pacific to confuse the enemy. The voyage took us eleven days, all fabulously exciting to the nine-year old that I was. We were in a cabin with bunks stacked three high, which we shared with some Gypsies in multitudinous bright satin skirts. Next door were their aquiline men—a very mysterious group—who eventually set up shop on Hotel and River streets, telling fortunes to the soldiers and sailors for the remainder of the war. That part of downtown Honolulu was colorful in the extreme! Prostitutes, servicemen, military police, gypsies, lei sellers, tattoo parlors, upstairs dives; it was teeming with riotous activity day and night.

The ship was listing dangerously, and in fact had to put in for repairs once we got to Honolulu. We greatly enjoyed the slanted decks! We could look down inside the open hold and see that it was full of Japanese, cooking around hibachi. Were they being brought back to Hawai`i from the internment camps before V-J Day? I don't know.

The ship's crew was wonderful to us—they used to serenade me with a guitar and the song "Beautiful Brown Eyes." I was smitten. Both Mary Bell and Jeanie had a birthday aboard, Jeanie first. She, as firstborn, was a model of decorum and mentioned her birthday to nobody, so turned eleven without fanfare. Mary Bell, on the other hand, spread the word over the entire ship that her seventh birthday was coming—she got a cake, special greetings from the captain, songs from the crew, and lots of attention from the other passengers. Our whole lives have basically followed these individual patterns of behavior!

Landfall Hawai`i! Millions of leis (hot, damp, fragrant) and Daddy at last. This was our new life. Growing up on campus provided me a most enjoyable childhood—I had seventy-two acres of front yard, thousands of kids around, and a fine view of the wave action at Waikīkī from my upstairs bedroom. I still shared a room with Mary Bell, but it was about 500 square feet, with a fourteen-foot high ceiling, a balcony, and a walk-in closet bigger than our bedroom in Connecticut.

That President's House is a treasure. During our twenty-four-year tenure, 1944-1968, there were no windows downstairs—everything was open to the tradewinds and sudden squalls; you just moved the *lauhala* mats and rattan furniture back a few feet til the wind and rain abated. Our screened food safe stood in tuna cans of water to foil the ants and mice. I did the dishes in the huge silver *Uluniu* punch bowl, a trophy that I guess our swim team won year after year. We had a whole big room next to the kitchen for our sewing room—I think Miss Zwilling taught me how to make dirndl skirts in sixth grade, and all the Fox girls sewed like mad and still do! My first bought dress was on the occasion of our Baccalaureate. Our phone number was five digits. My address was Punahou School, Honolulu, T.H. (Territory of Hawai`i.) Life was simple!

Daddy completely changed Punahou. He was only thirty-four when he took over, a dazzlingly handsome man with prematurely white hair. He loved Hawai`i's racial mix, he loved football and tennis, he loved hiring new exciting teachers directly after their graduations from Ivy League schools, he loved shaking up the old order and making things happen. He was controversial, charismatic, optimistic, and exactly the right man to lead Punahou in the giant postwar growth that Hawai`i experienced. Mother was gracious and warm, the perfect foil. They loved Punahou completely. At one time Daddy was offered the presidency of University of Missouri, his home state, but that job tempted him not at all.

It was hard at times to be the daughter of the president. I had to bear a lot of ragging in about seventh grade, but that eventually stopped after I threatened to tell on my taunters. (Where did that rumor come from that I wasn't allowed to date boys with lower than a B-plus average?) In preparing for our fiftieth reunion and going over all the classmates' names, I was happy to find I remembered almost everybody, and with aloha.

We were the luckiest of the lucky, growing up where we did, when we did, and with whom we did. Going to Punahou was such a head start in life, it was like being shot from a rocket!

Transportation to the Islands during the war years was either by airplane or ship, thus among the most coveted early views were of the Pearl Harbor entrance (above) and Aloha Tower (below)—the tallest building in Hawai`i at the time (JBB, 1947).

Recollections of David E. Harris

I'm "a retired baseball player," that is, I haven't picked up a bat in years I regret to say. After thirty-eight years in the ministry and social work, I retired in 1992, following some heart problems. My wife and I have been blessed with two wonderful sons. Jean and I are probably more busy now than when I was "active," with some teaching duties at our local community college, service clubs and singing groups. We attended our fiftieth reunion in 2002. What a trip down memory lane that was! Besides seeing some lovely old/ever-young faces, I breathed again the fragrance-laden trade winds.

I was not living in Hawai`i when the planes bombed Pearl Harbor. I was a mean "wittle-kid" of eight, having just moved to South Philadelphia, PA where my dad, a U.S. Navy dentist, was stationed at the Naval Shipyard. I don't remember much of that Sunday except that it seemed my whole world turned from Technicolor to four years of grays and blacks. We listened, my folks, my older brother and I, with disbelief and terrible confusion, to the news reports filtering in to our living room radio that afternoon and later, to FDR's Declaration of war before Congress. I hadn't the foggiest idea of what war was all about. I only knew how it was affecting the people I loved. It was like the whole world had come to an end. And, of course, in many respects it had.

Kindly let me jump eight years to 1949. My dad received orders to Pearl Harbor to head the dental program there. I was sixteen and remember our trip across the mainland in deep winter; arriving in San Francisco and embarking on a tramp steamer for the Islands. Two days before we arrived we could smell the flowers! Lord, I fell in love with Hawai`i before I ever saw her! We lived in Naval housing at Makalapa, just outside the Station. The next three years of my life were Punahou, Pearl Harbor, and a *malihini* (newcomer) teenager coming of age in Paradise. I felt I had come to a place that connected me with my past and which has provided me with dreams to this day. Shortly after our arrival, my dad loaded us in a launch and we took a brief cruise toward Ford Island. We came to a buoy, looked down into rippling waters, brightly colored with an oil slick. Beneath the surface lay a faint outline of a ship's deck and a mammoth gun turret. I had only seen my dad cry a couple of times in my life. This was one of them. As a young man, just married, his first sea duty had been aboard the *USS Arizona*. I've returned to that site several times over the years. I was not there when that great ship went down forming the grave for hundreds of seamen; but as a kid, then as a seaman myself and later, as a seminarian on the Island of Moloka'i, I have shared my dad's tears and the tears of all of you who remember.

Recollections of Shannon Heath Wilson

My grandfather came to Hawai`i from Aberdeen, Scotland in 1876 on the* SS Zealandia. *He was sent for by W.G. Walker, manager of the O`okala Sugar Plantation on the Hamakua Coast. After working there a short time, he decided to come to O`ahu, where he established himself as a building contractor (Walker and Olund, later Walker and Moody), married my grandmother, Sophie Klussman, who had come to Hawai`i in 1883 from Bremen, aboard the SS Ehrenfels. *They had eight children here, and lived most of their married life in the family home at the corner of King and Pi`ikoi streets. My mother, Flora, was the youngest of the children.*

After I left Punahou, I continued my high school and university education on the Mainland, eventually getting my Master's in clinical psychology. I worked in this field in institutions and later developed a private practice in Jungian based psychotherapy. I'm now retired and back in Hawai`i with my husband, Mike. We have a combined six children and six grandchildren, who live in London, New York, and California.

My mother and my sister and I left Hawai`i in August of 1941 (probably on the *Matsonia* to San Francisco and the train north) to Seattle, where my father was outfitting a ship at Bremerton, Washington, which he subsequently took as his first Naval command to the Aleutians. When December 7th came we were frantic with worry about my grandmother and many aunts and cousins in Hawai`i and about my father, as well. An announcement of the sinking of the *U.S.S. Gillis*, a small destroyer tender, had appeared in the Seattle newspaper. (My father was a Lieutenant Commander in the U.S. Navy at the time.)

Fortunately, we soon were in touch with Hawai`i and learned all was well with our family. Navy comrades of my father's called and told my mother in some kind of "code," that he was all right. We put up our blackout shades and soon had aunts and cousins and small children from Hawai`i living with us in Seattle. Not a real "Hawai`i December 7th Story," but our connection to it. The rest of the war years we saw our father for about a total of four months out of four years and my sister and I went to about six schools. Like everyone, we saved tinfoil and bought stamps and war bonds and were centered around the war, rationing, victory gardens, knitting squares for afghans and socks for servicemen and listening to FDR on the radio faithfully—not quite understanding the expressions on our parents' faces, and wishing those we loved would come home safely. Some of our Hawai`i family came to live with us for a while in South Carolina. After the war my father was stationed for a year in Washington D.C. and then we spent the next three years at (then) Kāne`ohe Air Station, which was when I had the wonderful chance for a Punahou education.

Recollections of Jane Hughes Simms

I went to college in the San Francisco area, married and had four children and have four grandchildren. I was a part time Registered Nurse for forty-five years and retired in 2002.

We were supposed to move to Honolulu in December of 1941 because my father's company was transferring him to their home office there. My parents persuaded the company to postpone the move until after Christmas.

My older brother, who was nine at the time, was very upset about the move. He didn't want to leave San Francisco. He was also a great kidder and one couldn't believe half of what he said. On the morning of December 7th, he raced into the house screaming that Pearl Harbor had been bombed. My mother paid no attention to him at the time. She thought it was just another ruse to prevent our move.

For once he was right. For three and a half more years, we stayed in San Francisco, doing all the war things: black out drapes, rationing and my father was a block warden. Our lives were fine.

In 1944, my father's company told him he had to go to Honolulu. He moved in April, and we went in May. We left on the last ship that took civilians before the war ended. We sailed on a hospital ship in a convoy of about nine or ten ships. It took ten days. We slept in large wards with bunk beds. The lights went off at 10:00 p.m. and on at 6:00 a.m. If you were on the top bunk and sat up fast, you banged your head on the steel beams.

My mother was lots of fun and "never met a stranger." The ship was full of college students, taking advantage of the last time they might be able to get home. We met many people that we stayed in touch with for years.

Upon our arrival, we had the traditional lei greeting. It was wonderful. Finding a house was extremely difficult at that time. We spent a month at the Moana Hotel. We spent most of our time at the beach and loved it. By that time (1944), things were fairly stable. My main memory is blacked out headlights with only a pinhole showing and a 10:00 p.m. curfew for everyone. Nobody could be on the streets after 10 o'clock at night.

I'll always remember V-J day in 1945. Such celebration I'll never see again. I lived in Honolulu until high school graduation 1952. It was a wonderful period of my life and I frequently reminisce on it.

Recollections of Anne Parks Strain

My father was promoted to brigadier general and was on Gen. Eisenhower's staff in England soon after Dec. 7. We spent a good part of the war in Elizabeth, NJ. We blackened our windows in Nantucket, MA where we went for the summers because of the submarines. We came to Hawai`i in 1948 when my father was made deputy commander of the US Army Pacific and we lived at Ft. Shafter.

My three brothers and I entered Punahou when I was in the 9th grade. My middle brother Floyd immediately distinguished himself by falling out of a tree outside the lower school and breaking his arm. I was in Mr. Lane-Rettiger's homeroom and sat next to classmate Dave Guard (later of The Kingston Trio). I remember bringing my portable radio and going into a closet to listen to the World Series (all were afternoon day games in those years). We must have had some groovy teachers!

I took geometry and Latin II in the senior academy. I tried to outdo Malcolm Ing and Clinton Ching in math (both include accounts elsewhere). I went to all the football games and can still sing all the songs and have a taste for "shave ice." Bonnie Edgar (see her account) lived near Ft. Shafter and we would sometimes go home on the city bus together. We were at the end of the line. She taught me how to eat mangoes.

My father's tour in Hawai`i was cut short when he was asked by the Chief of Staff to return to the Pentagon to head the new Office of Public Relations. My father really loved Hawai`i. He had been there as a Lieutenant and had worked his whole career in the hope of returning. We were all sad to leave! By the 1980's the two-room Office of Public Relations had become a corridor for the Office of Information. It was named the Parks Corridor after my father.

On December 7, I was 6 years old, living at the Army War College in Washington, DC. My father was an Army officer and I don't really know what he was doing there professionally. It was a Sunday after lunch and my mother and I were decorating a small artificial Christmas tree. It was a tradition to have it in the center of the dining room table for the season.

Suddenly one of the people who helped in the kitchen burst into the dining room and told us of the Pearl Harbor attack. I was struck most by the concern and anguish of those around me. The "attack" didn't really register. It was beyond my ken, but the fear and the anxiety were palpable. What did this mean for my father? Where would we go? We listened to the radio

I graduated from Holton-Arms, a girls' school in Washington, DC. When I started Vassar College in the fall I discovered that Bobbie Purvis (account included elsewhere) was there, too. After working in the Alumnae Office at Ethel Walker School in Simsbury, CT, I returned to Washington, DC, and was married to Richard Strain in April, 1958. We lived in Poughkeepsie and had four nice children. During that time I made some decisions which led me into paths I came to realize were wrong for me. I was divorced and remarried, only to divorce again. I realize that without these twists and turns I never would have begun the journey toward self-awareness and truth that centers and directs me now.

and they played over and over the sounds of the bombs and the planes.

Ever after when we trimmed the little tree I remembered the feelings of that day. When I was in 12th grade my parents gave a nice party for me, a dance at the officers' club. My mother used the little tree as part of the decorations. At the end of the party we found that someone had stolen the tree and its trimmings. But the memory could not be taken! It remains vivid and clear.

Parkinson's disease has crept into my body, but so far it has not progressed enough to really curtail my ability to get along by myself. It is not fun to contemplate the future in that dimension, but the future of relishing my children and grandchildren and glorying in every day as it comes seems very satisfying.

Newcomers to the Islands were greeted by the fragrance of many flowers and after the initial confusion of the attack were again given leis upon arrival—perhaps plumeria (above)—or flowers—such as orchids (below, JBB, 1962).

December 7, 1941—Birmingham, Alabama—Mom, Dad, Carol, Poochie and I came home from Sunday school and Church. A young man (friend of the family) was coming down the stairs, in full Navy uniform (he was a submariner). All I remember of his words were, "The Japanese bombed Pearl Harbor!" I think he said, "We are at war." (He survived two of three attacks on his subs, torpedoed or bombed. I still feel so sad about our loss.)

We had air raid warnings. The house went dark and we spent time in the basement. Dad was not allowed to enlist. He was German. Our name, at one time, was von Rhodess. He even told us he was watched along with a few others. Birmingham was a steel town.

In January of '46, Dad called home from the Kress annual meeting in New York. He had Mom put us on the other phones and said we're moving to Honolulu! There were two concerns going through my eleven-year-old mind —Pearl Harbor and I was too fat to wear a hula skirt. That summer we went to San Francisco on the Sunset Limited. We saw many troop trains. I thought we were entering a war zone. We sailed on the *Matsonia* for the Islands. I never unpacked my suitcases 'cause if that ship was going down, my bags were going with me! Mom was seasick the entire trip. The rest is history. My love, my dreams, my memories of my years in Honolulu and Punahou fill my heart. Outside of the years with my children and grandchildren, that was the happiest time of my life! When I say Punahou, it means "education" and wonderful friends.

Arrivals to the Islands saw many new trees, many of which had distinctive shapes (like this Monkeypod) and were easily identified (JBB, 1962).

Recollections of Carolyn (Connie) Schrader Peterson

Both of my parents arrived in the Islands in the early 1920s. My dad, who was working for an insurance company in San Francisco, was sent to the Islands to open an insurance department at Von Hamm Young. My mother and her sister, both of whom were just out of high school with a year of business school, decided on a lark to have an adventure. They booked passage on the S.S. Mariposa *with the intention of staying the two or so weeks that it would take for the liner to make a round trip to the States and back. If they could find jobs in that time, they would stay…otherwise they would return to their family in Southern California. They both found good jobs. One was at C. Brewer and Company and the other at Theo H. Davies. My dad met my mom and bingo…wedding bells and family. My aunt married a fellow who started the KGMB radio station but fell on hard times. He left the Islands leaving my aunt alone and pregnant. Consequently, she returned home to live with her parents until she could get back on her feet.*

I attended the University of Hawai`i for a year and the University of Washington one year before getting married in 1954. I graduated from the University of Washington in 1956 with a BA in Education and 1959 with an MA in Theatre. While my husband was earning his Doctor's degree in Optometry and establishing himself in the Optometric world, I taught school in the following places: Seattle, WA; Forest Grove, OR; Lake Oswego, OR; Niles, IL and Forest Grove, OR where I retired in 1995.

The interesting story is December 7th. I hope I can do it justice. When I was teaching school, I would always tell it to my students on December 7th. To preface the story…My family had a trip to "the States" planned for June 1941 through December 1941 to visit relatives in the Los Angeles and San Francisco areas. My father had to return to Honolulu a little earlier so he could get back to work, but my mom, my brother Chuck and I were scheduled to stay on a bit longer. We had reservations to return on the *Lurline* on December 10th.

Needless to say, after the war broke out, we weren't able to get home—for three years. Finally, in May 1944, we got passage on a hospital ship (that had been temporarily converted to civilian use) and spent almost two weeks in a convoy zigzagging our way across the Pacific toward home.

Now the December 7th story…for any golfers in the audience, you'll really appreciate this! My dad was an AVID golfer and this story will prove that! My father had a golf game planned for the morning of December 7th with a tee off time of 7:00 a.m. at Mid-Pacific Country Club. He and his foursome started out on their eighteen-holes as innocents. The Japanese strategy that day was not only to do away with the

American fleet at Pearl Harbor, but also to cripple the aircraft stations, which included Bellows Field, Mōkapu Naval Air Station, Kāne`ohe Air Station and others.

Unbeknownst to my father's group, their presence was right in line with the route that the Japanese aircraft would take to attempt to demolish Bellows Field. As the aircraft came out of the skies, they would fly over Lanikai's shores and strafe Bellows. As my dad and his group were playing their game, they heard loud explosive sounds coming from a distance but thought it was probably routine practice maneuvers. Soon, however, they began noticing airplanes speeding in low with bright "sun" insignias on the wings of the planes. They began thinking that perhaps serious trouble might be at hand.

But, the golfers' creed is "nothing interrupts a good game." They proceeded to shoot a couple more holes. The blasting was continuing across the bay. Soon, more planes came roaring down the fairway. They passed so low that my dad and friends could see the pilots in the cockpits, waving at them. Soon, these planes that were flying low over the golf course began strafing the greens. When this happened, my father's foursome would hide in the shrubbery until the planes were gone. They would then come out from under cover and shoot a couple of more holes. This continued for a while longer until the group finished their game. By then, employees of the club were speeding up the fairways in a truck to pick up these daredevils…who finished their golf game on December 7, 1941 under attack of the Japanese Air Force.

The *hau* tree grew near many beaches and was popular for both climbing and as canoe rollers (JBB, 1952).

Recollections of Greg Seastrom

I have been retired for five years after teaching and coaching in high school and community college for forty-two years.

In the summer of 1946, after a three-day transcontinental railroad trip and a five-day ocean voyage on the Matsonia, *which was still painted in wartime gray, we arrived in Honolulu where my father had been hired as a jeweler at Grossman Moody Ltd. I was fortunate to be accepted into the Junior Academy of Punahou to begin seventh grade.*

On December 7, 1941, we lived in a bungalow on West Lena Avenue, Freeport, New York, a quiet, suburban village on Long Island, inhabited mainly by commuters who rode the Long Island Railroad into the city. A few miles away was Mitchell Field, an Army Air Corps field, now Mitchell Air Force Base.

On that morning in a variety of places far from Freeport, people unknown to me then found their worlds greatly changed. Rollie Hughes stood on his Dowsett Highlands' lawn, watching Japanese airplanes fly over the Pali heading down Nu`uanu Valley to Pearl Harbor. John Bowles on Maunalani Heights and Jack Altman in Kaimukī heard the distant impact of bombs and saw the smoke rising out toward Ewa. In Fresno, California, Ken Zenimura and his young sons Howie and Harvey heard a solemn broadcast and knew that their lives would be radically changed. Unaware of these, I sat in our kitchen, looking back into a dark living room, hearing the somber voice of a newscaster updating my grave and saddened parents on the situation in Hawai`i, a place I was vaguely aware of because of an annual Christmas card and pictures from my dad's boyhood friend Rollie Hughes. Although I had no idea of the enormity of it all, I was a bit nervous and concerned.

A related event from a few weeks later had much more impact on me. We had just returned to school after lunch at home, when they announced a possible German air raid on Mitchell Field and instructed us to quickly return to our homes in an orderly fashion, which I did. Although this might have been a drill, as far as we were concerned it was real. After I arrived home, my mom became distraught because my younger sister Marcia, a kindergartner, had not yet arrived. In panic we climbed into our 1939 Dodge sedan to search for her. We were relieved when we found her happily skipping along with a number of her friends, oblivious to any threat, but I understood enough to be afraid. Soon after that day, we moved to the Washington D.C. area, where I remember a number of occasions when I climbed under my bed in fear as air raid sirens wailed in the darkness outside.

In thinking of December 7, 1941, I dwell on some of the people who became part of my life. Events such as the attack on Pearl Harbor tend to be points of reference, which connect us. Rollie, who had worked with George Moody and Ed Grossman since the early thirties, influenced my father to move to Hawai`i, providing for me a rich and instructive place to spend my formative years, which includes Punahou and all the friends and instructors I met there. Jack and John became lifelong friends, accompanying me through life, many times bringing comfort and instruction. Ken, who spent his early years in Hawai`i, possessed a love for baseball. He and his family were interned at Gila, Arizona, where he immediately laid out a baseball field, forming a league, which provided a needed relief from the realities of camp. In 1951 he was influential in arranging a visit to Honolulu by the Fresno State College baseball team, which led to my decision to come to the San Joaquin Valley. Playing baseball for Fresno State, I became acquainted with Howie and Harvey. Each of these friends felt a far greater impact than I, and I am grateful for what I learned from the stories they told. A vague memory of my own uneasiness enhanced by their experiences has helped me realize there is a darkness in the human soul, again realized in the events of September 11, 2001. I hope that someday we finally understand the folly of war.

Those living in Hawai`i were treated to classic Army-Navy baseball games played by major and minor leaguers. Here, Joe DiMaggio heads for first base in Honolulu Stadium during one of those games (Tai Sing Loo, Bishop Museum Archives, 1945).

Recollections of Susan "Sooch" Wall Ludewig

In 1946 my father returned to work at United Airlines (he was an original employee way back in the '30s) and was sent to Hawai`i as Operations Manager. We moved to Hawai`i in December 1946.

I went to Oregon State University and San Jose State. I married Dick Ludewig ('52, see account) and we have two children and four grandchildren. I retired August 2000. Prior to retirement I was a housewife and mother, a travel agent and cook/housekeeper. (d. 2008)

My recollection of December 7th isn't much. I was standing in the front entrance of our house in Menlo Park. It was like a long hall with windows all along the front. One of my parents started shouting, "We are at war!" I don't remember anything else of the day. Soon after that, my older sisters collected rubber items to be donated somewhere. All during the war I diligently took my coins to school and filled my stamp books until I had enough to buy a bond…a very thrilling event in my life!

Later, we moved to Millbrae, California, because my father worked for United Airlines and we would be much closer to the airport. Then my father was somehow "drafted" into the service of the Air Transport Command. It is my understanding that the ATC was a quasi-military force that enlisted civilians... most coming from the airline industry…to provide supplies to the troops overseas. It must have been a huge organization. My father had the rank of captain and I was very impressed with his uniform. He spent most of the duration of the war in the South Pacific in such places as New Zealand, Australia and islands as they were captured. He brought home a "shrunken head" one time which I think my mother must have disposed of right away…I loved it but I think it disappeared very quickly.

After the war, my father went into Japan with the occupation forces and lived in the German Embassy or Consulate in Tokyo.

How happy we were when the war was *pau* (ended, source of photograph unknown).

Recollections of Joan Maggioros Triantafyllides

*My grandfather George Lycurgus came to Hawai`i in 1889, probably to escape poor economic conditions. "Uncle George" purchased the Volcano House in 1896, and operated it and the Hilo Hotel. He lived to the age of 101 and credited his longevity to his devotion to* Pele, *Hawaiian fire goddess, whose* Halema`uma`u *home the Volcano House overlooks.*

In 1940, a fire destroyed the main building of the hotel; it was rebuilt in 1941. Through the years many people visited the Volcano House, including Queen Lili`uokalani, Mark Twain and President Franklin Roosevelt. My mother, Georgina Lycurgus, a Punahou graduate, was born and raised in Hawai`i. My father, Maggioros, was Greek. I was born in Athens, Greece.

In 1938, my mother took my sister Kay and me on a trip to Hilo, Hawai`i from Greece. There I attended kindergarten; we returned to Europe in 1939. Greece was occupied by the Germans in 1940.

On December 7, 1941, my mother was on a bus in Greece (where we lived) when she heard of the bombing of Pearl Harbor. It was a very difficult time for her because half her family was in the Islands. All I really remember that day was that the Germans came to our home and took our car. I guess they had had their eye on it, but seeing it was registered to an American (my mother), they couldn't touch it until the U.S. entered the war and became an enemy.

In 1946, we returned to Hawai`i. There I attended Mrs. Daly's school in Hilo, then Hilo Intermediate, then Punahou.

After Punahou, I went to the University of Washington, receiving a BA. I returned to Greece in 1958 for two months, where I met my husband, Pavlo. And there I stayed. We have two children and five grandchildren.

History Goes By In A Truck

History grinds by in great, green trucks
With war weary leathernecks back from the
front
Balky troop ships slip into Hawai`i
Unloading her men in our Hilo Harbor.
Back they come from landings and battles;
Truk, Peleliu and distant Spain;

Away from the stench, the noise, and the
smoke:
Okinawa, Iwo Jima, and blood-bathed Tarawa.
History grinds by in great, green trucks
Up Wainuinui Avenue, past shops and past
schools.
A convoy of ten, a convoy of thirty,
It doesn't much matter, we know where
they're
from.
In the land of Aloha, in our forests and
beaches,
They hope to find peace; at least for a
time.
History grinds by in great, green trucks;
As Children we shout and wave as they
pass.
We see those young men, in dingy fa-
tigues,
Crowded together in hot, burning sun;
They see our bare feet, laughing sun-
tanned
faces,
Of Asian, Hawaiian, European ancestory.
Sober men turn, give a grin and a wave,
And history moves on, up the street, in a
truck.

The Enemy Alien:
Recollections of Ramsay Mori

The

Enemy Alien

I set out to write a short "recollection" about a Japanese kid who becomes an American. As I got more and more involved, it became a long story of the not too obvious, indirect impact of WWII: hate, alienation, corruption, misery and death.

Although my story follows the framework of a biography, it is not a true scholarly treatise, I suppose. I am describing personal and emotionally-filled episodes from the memory of an eight-year-old. For example: when a 50-caliber bullet came through the roof of our house my brother, Victor, 17 at the time, remembers the bullet being found on a book shelf and that I took the bullet to our friend Percy's house and Percy's dad called the cops. I, on the other hand, being eight, remember the bullet coming in and spinning on the top of a glass dressing room table. I picked up the bullet while it was still hot and raced it to my friend Percy's house where his dad called the cops who came and took the bullet away from me.

Dredging up painful memories has not been an easy exercise and were it not for the urging of John Bowles and Ted Tsukiyama it would have been much easier to slowly forget that long ago war. In this age of arbitrary Preemptive War, I hope my recollections remind people that the conflicts of war go far beyond the battle field.

December 7, 1941, Sunday. I knew things were different that Sunday because I didn't have to get ready for Sunday School and nobody fussed about what I was wearing.

We lived on Wyllie Street back then, close to the bottom of `Ālewa Heights (see map on page 75), which is about half way up Nu`uanu Valley and about a mile above Judd Street. The trade winds coming down the valley really start cooling you off about there, and it's usually several degrees cooler than downtown. It rains more too.

I was aware that my parents were involved in very serious, quiet discussions and weren't paying much attention to me so I got on my bike and peddled my way up `Ālewa Drive and up to the intersection where Twin View Drive drops away towards Saint Francis Hospital. It's kind of a lookout from there and you can see over the roof tops to Punchbowl and then on to Diamond Head and Waikīkī.

The sky was full of hundreds of black puffs of anti-aircraft fire. It was an unnatural contrast to the normal white tradewind cumulus clouds that pile up around the top of the mountains and break off once in a while on the lee side.

There was another kid from the neighborhood who was a little bit older at the lookout. He was pretty excited about what was going on and we both decided to pedal up to "Tootie" McCandles's big brown house on the corner and down Auli`i Road all the way to Makanani Drive. You could see everything that was going on from there, Waikīkī to downtown all the way to the Wai`anae Range.

Pearl Harbor and Ford Island are about 7 miles away from there, and we could see lots of black smoke towering up and blowing out over the ocean. There were lots more black anti-aircraft puffs too, but it was too far away to see much detail. Other people started gathering at the vantage point and pretty soon a big Hawaiian cop drove up and told us all to go home and stay home.

People had radios on and the broadcasts were all the same—*This is an air raid. This is the Real McCoy. Take Cover.*

We could hear sirens on a few patrol cars wailing in the distance, probably Nu`uanu and Liliha streets, but they were distant.

War had no meaning to an eight-year-old like me. It just wasn't something I could conceptualize. In fact I never became aware of the politics or the violence of war till many years later and I still can't say I understand it.

Why were they talking about an *air raid* on the radio? We didn't see any airplanes flying around. What did we need to *take cover* from? There were no bombs dropping down on Wyllie Street. It was just a quiet boring Sunday in a quiet boring residential neighborhood.

About mid-morning, two FBI agents came to take my father and grandfather away. The agents were both thin young haole (Caucasian) guys dressed in suits and were visibly officious and nervous the whole time they were there. They were accompanied by a Honolulu Police detachment. The FBI men drove my father and grandfather away in a dark sedan; the police detachment followed.

In the evening the FBI returned to take away my mother and my half-brother, Victor, who was 17-years-old and a Punahou senior.

My parents never returned home till after the end of the war in 1945.

My oldest half-brother, Arthur, was at Yale University in New Haven, and he remained on the mainland for the duration of the war eventually getting involved as a language instructor at Camp Savage, Wisconsin; Fort Snelling, Minnesota and finally the Presidio of Monterey, California. My brother, Arthur, was eventually commissioned as an Army intelligence officer during the Japanese occupation.

In the early afternoon something dropped on the `Ālewa hillside, close to where Senator Fong later built his house, making a heavy sharp thump. I immediately thought, bomb, so I made my way up the trail at the end of Wyllie Street to see if it was so. By the time I got half way up the cactus and *haole koa* covered hillside I noticed there were several other neighborhood kids up the hillside looking for the bomb. We looked for at least an hour but we never did find anything. Much later on, one of the fathers of one of the kids told him the thump was from an undetonated anti-aircraft shell that Army Ordnance had recovered. Of course we were disappointed, we never even got to see it.

Sometime later while we were having dinner, we heard a bang upstairs. I ran up to my parents' room and found a big bullet spinning on the glass top of my mother's dressing room table. It was still hot. The bullet had come through the roof and the ceiling, piercing two one inch-thick shelves before dropping to the table. I took the bullet to show my friend Percy (Percy Torres). Later, a policeman came and took the bullet away from me. I found out later that it was an American-made 50-caliber tracer round. It had probably been shot off in a nervous burst of machine gun fire by some jittery sailor or soldier at Pearl Harbor or Hickam Air Base.

My grandfather, Iga Mori, arrived in the Kingdom of Hawai`i in 1890 during the early period of Japanese immigration as a physician for the Bureau of Immigration. He came to the Islands as an Imperial Navy surgeon having been educated at the Naval Medical College in Japan, Cooper Medical College in San Francisco and had taken post-graduate studies at University Hospital in London. Iga Mori's fluency with English was probably a significant factor in his appointment to the Kingdom.

I'm sure my grandfather's initial responsibility was for the medical well-being of the early immigrant population and as their liaison with the Kingdom. He was eventually licensed to practice in the Kalākaua Era Kingdom and went on to established a large medical practice in Honolulu.

My father, Motokazu Mori, received his medical training as a physician and surgeon at the Kyushu Imperial University in Japan. After coming to the Territory of Hawai`i in 1918, he went on to the Mayo Clinic in Rochester, Minnesota, for further study. He then returned to Hawai`i in 1920 to join his father, Iga, with his practice. When my mother arrived in the Islands in 1927, she told me she found at least a third of the patients at the Japanese Hospital (later Kuakini) were Mori patients.

My grandfather had been in the Islands for over 51 years and was very active in the Honolulu community and politically well-connected. Among his influential acquaintances were: Frank C. Atherton, Dr. W. D. Westervelt, Syngman Rhee, Chung K. Ai, Dr. Albert Palmer, Theodore Richards and Gilbert Bowles.

It was pretty obvious that my 77-year-old grandfather was not a serious or eminent threat to the United States or the Territory of Hawai`i. The shortsighted military authorities would look like fools if he was kept in detention. My grandfather was at Sand Island on December 24.

By the same token, it was absurd to consider my 17-year-old half-brother, Victor, a threat to the community or America. He was born and raised in Hawai`i and a United States citizen. There was no good reason to throw my brother in jail in the first place. My brother came home from jail after ten days of hard tack and lukewarm coffee with a dark shadow of beard growth and a look that was sullen and embittered.

The military authorities that had taken charge of Hawai`i were clearly confused, threatened by the large number of Japanese people in Hawai`i and were definitely not taking any chances.

My mother and father had been detained (a War Department euphemism for imprisoned) for far more serious considerations than my brother and grandfather. My mother, Ishiko Shibuya Mori, had been a special Hawai`i Society correspondent for the *Yomiuri Shimbun* in Japan for many years.

On December 5, 1941, two days before the Japanese attack, the political correspondent at the Yomiuri Headquarters in Japan radio-telephoned my mother and began asking about American troop strength and the number and kinds of ships berthed at Pearl Harbor. My mother had no interest or knowledge of ships or troops and decided that my father would be better equipped to handle questions of such a technical nature.

Missing the political nature of the radio-phone call from Japan, and because of his nature of being a thoroughly methodical and theoretical sort, my father anticipated that the ordinary reader of the Yomiuri in wintery Japan would be most interested in the contrast of climate and the balmy conditions of Hawai`i compared to wintery Japan. He accordingly began talking about the weather and then describing the well-tended garden, the flowers and their colors and the abundance of flowering trees in our yard.

Meantime, eavesdropping U.S. Intelligence agents immediately made direct correlations between flowers and trees and battle ships and cruisers. The intrigue of the Flower Message of December 5th had been conceived.

The whole situation engulfing my parents was far-fetched and unlikely, but nevertheless, they were placed under a heavy cloud of suspicion that they had passed strategic military intelligence to their homeland, Japan. The FBI was quick to follow up on their suspicions and imprisoned my mother and father immediately after the Japanese attack.

I never fathomed the chilling thoroughness and intrusiveness of the wartime detention of Japanese by the Army until 1984 when historian, Michael Slackman, published his article "Patton and the Orange Race". It comes as no surprise that many American of Japanese Ancestory (AJA) veterans of World War II think of George S. Patton as an "Arrogant Genocidal Bigot."

In the aftermath of December 7th, everyone had to adjust to wartime conditions. There were blackouts, restrictions and rationing, and a whole bunch of new wartime rules, which for the most part were not things I had to worry about. My sister Pearl and I had to go back to school, although school was now being held in large private homes in various parts of the city.

My half-brother Victor went to work at the Dole cannery to generate some kind of income for family survival. The Draft was a huge threat to my brother's ability to work. Mr. Gilbert Bowles, a prominent missionary of the American Society of Friends (Quakers), intervened on behalf of my brother before the Draft Board arguing that, "This family has been left without parents." He instructed the Board that they were not to draft my brother for military service "under any conditions." My brother obtained a deferred classification until after the war.

Grandfather Iga went back to the old Nu'uanu office to take care of my father's patients. My 73-year-old grandmother, Yaye, who had lived with the vicissitudes of uprooting from the home country and learning the foreign ways of a new country, now stayed quietly and efficiently as usual in the background making sure things got done her way. I can still imagine her grumbling quietly about how difficult it was to do things with the war going on.

Meantime, my 16-year-old half-sister Margaret tried to get the household organized with elaborate schedules and work assignments. I remember she tried hard to make things work but I was too young to pay much attention. Besides, she wasn't my mother or father and couldn't make me do things.

Being suddenly separated from my parents was not anything tragic or life threatening like a suckling baby being torn from its mother's breasts. I was, after all, an energetic, uninhibited eight-year-old who chafed at being constantly restrained by conservative, rule-waving, discipline-oriented Japanese parents. I found myself suddenly unbound, unrestricted and free. I spent a lot more time out in the streets unsupervised, and that experience brought with it a lot of bad habits.

One Portuguese kid used to make it a point to tease, "Nyah-Nyah-Nyah! Yo Fadda One Spy." I'd get mad and chase him up the street and when I caught him I would put one of those Tarzan-style full-nelsons on him and make him cry. Sometimes his mother would come after me but she was so fat and heavy that she could never catch me; besides her kid was wrong for teasing me in the first place. It wasn't as if she could come complain to my parents and she knew that.

There were other kids that would ask me whether we had spy radios in the house. When I told them "No," the kids would say, "Oh yes yes yes you do, so-and-so saw the wires!"

We did have an intercom system in our house (which may have given some weight to the whisperings), but it definitely was not short wave capable.

Curiosity and questioning was only normal among neighborhood kids but the everyday notoriety that was forced on me kept me constantly on the defense and I would end up being hostile all the time.

There were other things that worry an eight-year-old like being called "Jap" and the propaganda posters that started cropping up showing Hideki Tojo and Emperor Hirohito with huge buck-teeth and slitty, slanted eyes and huge round glasses like my grandfather used to wear. The posters cropped up everywhere. The caricatures were skinny and bandy legged, so evil and bad and so unlikely; I knew Japanese people didn't really look like that, but it still bothered me, especially the glasses because my grandfather had a pair that looked like that.

There were more subtle attitude changes that bothered me. The Green Hornet always depended on his faithful, resourceful Japanese servant, Kato. All of a sudden Kato became Cato the faithful Filipino servant. Even Superman and Captain Marvel hated the Japanese and flew around bashing slant-eyed, bucked-toothed, round-eyeglassed, bandy-legged caricatures.

My mother had constantly reminded me to be proud of being Japanese, but the wartime hostility was so pervasive, so overwhelming, that it was impossible to feel that way. I had to learn to keep my feelings to myself and not let anyone see that my feelings had been hurt. All that made me less sensitive and less tolerant of other people around me. I didn't want to be around people.

Spending time out in the streets requires hard, fast rules that do not help in building good social character. If you've got a ball or something and a bigger kid wants it, you give it to him. Of course if you're the bigger kid, you get to take the ball. That rule applies to everything: money, candy, toys and clothes. You don't ask for stuff: you take it. You take stuff even if you don't need it, and you don't bother with "Thank You," or thoughts about, "what's right or what's wrong." You learn to run fast, to be wary of trouble and to get away in a hurry before you're caught. You become attuned to opportunity the same way wild animals are. Conscience doesn't belong out there on the street when survival is the basic need. You yourself are the only important justified thing. You end up being a loner because that way you don't have to share.

When the war started some kids were no longer permitted to play with me. On the few occasions when I ran into some of these kids, they would say their parents had told them not to play with me. For the most part those guys and I never did get to be good friends. Friendship, after all, does require trust.

I had a handful of good friends, though, and I really know they and their families helped me keep some normal perspective. "Mangee"(Lester Sen) and Leonard (Meek) lived in the neighborhood, and the three of us would find most of our adventures up on top of `Ālewa Heights playing *Tarzan of the Apes* predator and prey games or at other times down in the Waolani Stream bed, fishing for sword tails, crayfish and *o`opu* (small fish).

Sometimes we'd shoot doves with our BB guns and cook them over an open fire in the Tarzan way. The birds were a mess to clean and were wild and gamey tasting, but we knew Tarzan would have eaten them, so we did too.

Once in a while "Mangee's" mother or Leonard's mother would let us have hotdogs or even teriyaki meat sticks. We'd get a can of beans and left over rice and we'd have a feast that we knew was better than anything Tarzan ever ate.

Dougie Ackerman ('52), and Albert Lemes ('53) were after school friends that took me home and treated me like I was a regular kid. Dougie's mother would fix us wonderful sandwiches with home baked bread, and she'd always have fresh fruit for snacks. Being brought up in a rice culture, it was a whole new way of eating.

Dougie's father built miniature trains and had a special room with tracks laid out and tools for building things. We didn't have access to the delicate stuff in the room, but it gave us both an early influence about patience and craftsmanship that was to play a part in both our later years.

Albert and I would walk up to his house in Dowsett Highlands after school. Albert's mother was a pretty lady with big brown eyes and pretty brown hair, and she'd always ask Albert if we wanted anything. Of course, it was more than likely that Albert would reply "Naw" with that sleepy, shy, myopic look he always had. We didn't usually get anything unless we asked on purpose. Mrs. Lemes usually brought out cookies and stuff anyway if she had them. It wasn't really that important, though, because we usually had a good time telling each other stories. Most of the stories we made up were nonsensical and weren't told for critical appraisal or competitive reasons so it was just fun listening to each other.

Sometimes, Dr. Lemes, Albert's father, would come home early and find us hanging out. He always had a nice word for us and always took an interest in what we were doing.

None of the parents of the kids I hung out with ever questioned me about being Japanese or my political leanings if I had any, and they all must have tried very hard to be very sensitive and considerate about not talking about my parents' problems or about the war. The grown-ups just treated me like any other kid and I was a lot more comfortable that way.

Albert, his brother John and I would just *talk story* to while away the time, and then I'd walk back home to Wyllie Street when it got late.

Of course most everyone else knew "Japs" weren't good people anymore. I had a few friends that kept telling me that they didn't think of me as being a "Jap" but that did not give me a whole lot of comfort.

The idea of being an enemy alien was even worse. It was conceptually more personal, very official and so profoundly bad that I had difficulty understanding the full implications. How could they have let me into this country in the first place? How was it I hadn't been shot on the spot? Of course, thinking like that was demoralizing; it really wore down my confidence and it really made me be a lot more careful about whom I spent time with. I had to watch my back. I couldn't trust anyone anymore.

I first arrived from Yokohama, Japan, at the port city of Honolulu in the U. S. Territory of Hawai`i on July 5, 1934, as a year and five month old baby. My mother, my sister Pearl Toshiko and I were admitted into the Territory as temporary visitors for one year under the provisions of the U. S. Immigration Act of 1924.

1934 with mother and sister, Pearl

It didn't matter that our mother was married to my father, who was a permanent resident of the Territory and a prominent medical doctor who was already father to three children born in the Territory. Sections of the Immigration Act permitted only one-year visits to the Islands. It meant that the three of us had to spend alternate years back in Japan, then we could return for another year in Hawai`i.

My mother was outraged by the Japanese exclusion provisions of the Immigrations Act of 1924 and resolved not to let her children become Americans because, "America did not want my children." For both my sister Pearl's birth on November 13, 1930, and mine on February 23, 1933, she returned to Japan. Of course, her strong reaction was idealistic and impulsive and would eventually become a problem for me in later years; then again, she really didn't have too many other options.

Shuttling back and forth between countries and cultures did not present much of a problem for my sister and me while we were young, but as we approached school age, the sudden cultural changes became more difficult to adjust to.

I remember being placed in 1st grade in 1940, when we returned to Hawai`i, and the only words of English I could say and understand were "yes" and "no." I wasn't dumb; I had attended Japanese school the prior year, and I already understood math concepts quite well.

With little means to communicate, the first year at an American school was a lonely, embarrassing experience. Of course my sister was almost three years older than me and probably a lot more sensitive to the changes, but she never complained.

My mother's life and character were chiseled and formed by events and history like no other person I have ever met. She was born on July 21, 1899, in a little town that she called *Boshu* at the southernmost tip of the Chiba Peninsula. She used to tell me that it was an area of rocky beaches and rough seas where you could see Mount Fuji across the stretch of waters entering Yokohama Bay to the west on clear days. She remembered that the fish catch of the area was the best in the world.

My mother came from a family of physicians that extended back for three generations. She had dim memories of her own mother being sickly and inaccessible, spending much of her time quietly in a special room. She remembered her father as being a kindly, warm sort of man. Both of my mother's parents died by the time she was eight. As an orphan, my mother was sent to live with a strict aunt and uncle to be raised in the traditional manner for girls, learning to be a housewife.

By the time my mother was 13, her family had decided that a marriage should be arranged with a 50-year-old doctor in order to preserve the tradition of having a doctor in the Shibuya family.

My mother rebelled and declared that she would become a doctor herself if it was so important for her family to have a doctor. With a determination and ambition that was rare for a Japanese woman of the time, she entered the Tokyo Women's School of Medicine and graduated in five years.

There were only a few women doctors back then and they were given little or no status or consideration. The only possibility for work as a doctor was in Manchuria or Hawai`i and in due course Dr. Ishiko Shibuya arrived at the Japanese Hospital on the island of O`ahu in the U.S. Territory of Hawai`i in 1927.

Dr. Shibuya was young, well-educated and attractive and soon drew the attention of Dr. Motokazu Mori. (Dr. Mori's first wife had died, leaving him with three young children.)

As my mother described the courtship, young Dr. Mori, dressed in his best touring clothes (riding breeches and a roadster cap), would drive up to the hospital in a huge two-door Packard Roadster. His eldest son, Arthur, dressed in his best sailor suit, and rode chaperone in the rumble seat. Dr. Shibuya would be escorted to the passenger seat, and off they would roar to the Pearl City Sanitarium that Dr. Iga Mori owned. They would spend many idyllic hours reading poetry and high-toned literature beside the sea.

Again in due course, Dr. Shibuya and the young Dr. Mori were married on April 19, 1930. My sister, Pearl Toshiko, was born on November 13, 1930.

In conversations with me, my mother made it sound as if she had been slyly seduced by my father, but once I grew up I began to realize that feminine modesty must have had a lot to do with that notion. Besides, my parents were both doctors and would have known what they were doing.

It's for certain, though, that my five-year-old half brother Arthur didn't do too good a job as chaperone.

My mother cherished a dream of someday taking her first born son, grown up and schooled in the best traditions of medicine and surgery and personally groomed to Shibuya manhood, back to *Boshu* at the tip of the Chiba Peninsula to confound and amaze her relatives and to finally fulfill *her promise* and *the tradition* of a doctor to head the Shibuya family.

To serve that end, my mother had my father's approval to be responsible for the upbringing of my sister and me.

My parents were released from "internment" at the end of the war. They both returned to Honolulu, December 7, 1945. The Justice Department finally cleared them both of spy accusations that were raised at the start of the war. There were no apologies; after all, they were enemy aliens.

Their war time odyssey had taken them from barbed wire prison camp on Sand Island, across the Pacific on a troop steamer to Angel Island in San Francisco Bay (Oakland Army Base). The crew of the troop ship, fearing a "Jap" torpedo attack, would muster the prisoners out on the cold, wet, windy deck in the middle of the night and line them up around the flood-lit rail so that any attacker would know that they were torpedoing civilians, their own people.

They stayed on Angel Island in another prison camp for a short time then they were ferried to a temporary camp at Sharp Park in Millbrae, then another temporary camp at San Mateo Raceway Park. They were then moved by rail to the Santa Fe Relocation Camp, New Mexico, then finally by rail to Crystal City, Texas.

My parents were "interned" by the Justice Department out in the desert in Zavala County in an old labor camp. They stayed in tents surrounded by a barbed wire enclosure and watch towers. My mother told me she would go to sleep listening to the coyotes' lonely howling out in the desert night.

The "internees" were a resourceful, talented group and much of the routine work at camp was done by prisoners. By the time the war was over, they had hand dug a community swimming pool, built a hospital, a community center and decent housing for themselves.

I have an old letter and photos sent me in December 1990, from my half sister, Margaret, that reported nothing left at the "internment" camp site now except for a school yard, remnant house foundations and a small monument erected by "internment" survivors.

When my parents first returned from Texas after the war, I don't think they fully realized the changes that I had gone through. Besides, my parents were busy trying to get their own interrupted lives back together. My parents could see that I had grown physically but not everyone can readily interpret attitudinal changes. You have to wait for social situations to occur. Then you see subjective responses, and then you began to realize how much you actually know about a kid. Of course like most kids, I had learned to obscure a lot of my bad behavior by acting like a normal kid. I could still speak Japanese, which was a reassuring comfort for my parents and a good cover for me.

You must consider that I had experienced four years of freedom and I was already street-wise and opportunistic. I had been exposed to an American school, the American culture and had absorbed the ideas of being American. I was no longer malleable like I was at the start of the war, and no one could make me morph back to that condition. Even if I was my mother's first born son, I did not want to be a "Jap" anymore and I did not want to live out my life back in the "old country" rusting away in a small seaside village with relatives I did not know or care about. Furthermore, I did not want to be a doctor. I wanted to be a plain ordinary American.

I was adventurous enough and uninhibited to the point of getting into trouble fairly frequently. One time I got caught stealing model airplanes by sneaking them into my friend's school book satchel at Kress Store. We both made a huge fuss, crying our hearts out and making sad penitent faces for everyone to see. Of course adults are always embarrassed by kid behavior like that and will usually do anything to mitigate the situation and make you stop fussing: "You promise never to take anything again? Will you?" or "You don't want your mom and dad to find out you did this thing do you?"

Detective Hussy wasn't easily fooled, though. He asked me: "Why you teach dat haole boy how fo steal? "He delivered me officially to my father's office with more strong admonitions, and I had to stage another crying fit for my father. I was more careful not to get caught after that, especially by Detective Hussy. My very stern, authoritative father handed me off to my mother for discipline.

By 7th grade I was smoking cigarettes fairly regularly and experimenting with booze and beer. My sister's friend, Napela, would tell me in later years that I was rude and unruly back then and used to push old ladies out of the way to get on the bus first.

Then by 8th grade, when I was 15, I got my driver's license, my mobility increased and there was no stopping me.

I had made it from "Fresh Off the Boat Immigrant" in 1940 to "All-American Juvenile Delinquent" by 1948. It had taken me nine years.

By the time my mother was fully aware of the extent of my Americanization and my corruption, she went totally frantic. Not only had the war taken four years of her life, the American post-war subculture was now robbing her of her first born son and her daughter, as well. My mother now marshaled all of her formidable drive and determination to taking back her children.

At first my mother tried being subtle. She, like most other Japanese mothers, wanted her first born son to grow up a *Samurai*, a warrior in the finest Japanese tradition. She casually talked about Mifune (Toshiro Mifune, the famous Japanese motion picture star)—how manly he was, how handsome and how Japanese. Of course she was referring to the actor's portrayal of *Samurai* Attitude in films, not the arduous years of patient training and discipline that are actually required and which finally show in the up-front appearance of a real warrior. *Bushi-do* is, after all, the Path of a Warrior.

If I was working on a surf board and wading around in wood shavings or greasy from head to toe from working on cars, my mother would make it a point to mention what wonderful hands I had that could perform miracles in surgery.

My mother's pointed messages were persistent, presented at every available opportunity and finally became an unbearable nagging presence.

I went completely negative; I did everything I could to displease my mother. If she liked something I was doing, I immediately stopped it. If she expressed displeasure about something I was doing, I insisted on doing even more of it. She wanted me to be a doctor; I expressed an interest in becoming a mechanic or a surfboard maker.

By 1949 I was hanging out with a different set of friends, Hawaiian *hapa* (part) *haoles* for the most part. I was uncomfortable with haoles, after all, they had won the war; I was uncomfortable being with Japanese, after all, they had lost the war.

Hapa Hawaiians made me comfortable; they understood discrimination first hand from the inevitable friction of their own parenting. They were aware of the Hawaiian subjugation in their recent history and their attitudes showed it. They had lost their own country, and their culture had been nearly wiped out by dominant Christian Missionary influences. Their attitudes reflected that too. For the most part, instead of being angry, the *hapa* Hawaiians showed me warmth and humor, they gave me understanding and friendship, *and* they welcomed me and were generous. The *hapa* Hawaiians provided the shelter I needed.

My mother mistrusted Hawaiians; they were people of the agricultural frontier, primitive natives at best. They were dark, savage people (*dogin*), a mystery in her mind. In fact my mother hated Hawai`i because it was a place that had entrapped her and had prevented her from achieving her life goals. She missed the changing of the seasons and the food and the intense cultural climate of Japan. Hawai`i had none of that but she couldn't go back to Japan. The only hope she had was the future potential in her children. It was the key and she was determined to shape that future potential.

My mother had uncommon notions about how to raise us. For the most part, she was indulgent, letting my sister and me do what we wanted, but if we crossed some imaginary forbidden line of behavior, she could be very harsh. Other times, her concepts about raising us were more Spartan and arbitrary in the sense that she was willing to expose us to the wildness of things, to make us deal alone with natural threats, and if we survived, it would prove us strong and worth nurturing.

My mother grew up independent, assertive and strong-willed because she had to be. It was these very qualities that had helped her survive as an orphan. Many people admired my mother for those very qualities, but there were also facets of contradiction in her behavior. There were times when she acted more like an isolated lonely dreamer, aimlessly making her way through her own idiosyncratic cosmos.

When I was five or so and in Japan, I wanted a train window opened, and I remember fussing about it. My mother refused to open the window for me, telling me that I had to learn to open the window myself. That wasn't the way I expected the task at hand to be accomplished so I increased the tempo of my fussing till I was screaming and crying and attracting the attention of a number of people who rushed in to assist me. My mother refused to permit anyone to open the window for me, and she sat steadfast until I finally and resentfully opened the window for myself. It wasn't that she had forced me into being self-sufficient. She had won a personal battle of wills, and I remembered that and resented it. She was smug afterwards, and I had to open my own train windows after that. I never forgot.

In an even earlier time when we were in Hawai`i, my mother threw me in my grandmother's old chicken coop at night for some transgression. The coop was in the backyard and was dark and oppressive and scared me so that I had to escape, but each time I did so my mother would catch me and throw me back into the coop. The fear of the dark got worse with each time she threw me back in the coop till I finally gave up in a catatonic clutch. I could not move for fear and I could no longer cry out. She left me there to fend for myself.

To this day, I sometimes start out of deep sleep in the middle of the night to find myself soaked in cold sweat and fear. Of course there is nothing there that wakes me and nothing there to fear. It takes a while to calm back down. The irony is that I never have been able to figure out what I did to get punished like that in the first place.

By 1950 I spent as little time at home as possible. It was too contentious, and the struggle to maintain my own agenda, which was mostly to thwart my parents' wishes, required more and more effort.

In a desperate attempt to separate me from what she determined were my bad influences, my mother began phoning my friends' mothers to tell them that their sons were bad and that she did not want their sons associating with me.

I was furious when I finally found out about my mother's betrayal. I could not apologize or explain my mother's behavior to my friends because I didn't understand her destructive irrational course. The alienation between my mother and me had become complete. She was now my enemy.

The first time I realized my sister Pearl was having serious trouble with her life was when I came home late one night and found her burning her personal papers. She had set up a thick pile of papers that was smoldering on the outside. I took a bunch of kindling and aerated the pile, and it began burning brightly. She didn't say anything to me and, considering my own problems, I didn't pry. I told her to mix in kindling with the paper to keep the fire going, and she nodded to let me know she understood. I went inside and upstairs to bed. I don't know how long it took her to burn all those papers.

I came home late another night and smelled gas as soon as I walked in the door. The kitchen windows and doors were all closed. All the gas range knobs were on high and the oven doors were open.

I turned all the range knobs closed and methodically opened all the windows and doors from the windward side to the lee. I could see my sister lying quietly in the dark in the maid's room, but I wasn't too sympathetic that night because she could have blown up the kitchen and burned us all up in the process. We didn't exchange any words that night either, and I heard her come quietly upstairs to her bedroom an hour or so later.

On March 25, 1951, Pearl drank down a small bottle of Black Leaf 40 (Nicotinic Acid), convulsed and died. She was twenty years old.

My mother had heard her calling and, expecting the worst, came to get me. By the time we got to my sister's room, she was very pale, comatose and unresponsive. Her final breathing was rasping out of her throat, and her eyes had turned back up into her head. My mother, with all her medical training, could do nothing. She sat by my sister for a long while as if in deep shock and said nothing.

I stayed with my mother and sister with my mind full of thoughts. I hadn't been the only person that was aware of my sister's desperation. I now felt a deep sympathy for my sister's decision to die. Her actions somehow seemed so justified. I knew she had been corrupted in the same manner that I had been. I knew now she had always been more sensitive and had surely been hurt more deeply by the war, by our parents' attitudes, and all the sudden post-war changes. I had just never thought about my sister's problems. I had too many of my own.

My sister's funeral was held at the house on Wyllie Street. We had a large living room and a connecting library. The dining room also adjoined so there was lots of room. My sister looked very small and fragile dressed in white in a white brocaded casket. All the wreaths and flowers were white. There were white sprays of phalaenopsis and dendrobium, calla lilies, white *obake* anthuriums and delicate white cattleyas showing purple and yellow throats of color.

The mourners were young, in their twenties like my sister, and they truly mourned the loss of one of their own with pain-filled hearts and bitter tears. There were few dry eyes. There were classmates from Punahou and the University of Hawai`i. Her boyfriends came with tears in their eyes and murmured earnest condolences given with cold clammy handshakes. There was a young university professor, and Jocko, the gambler from up the park. There was a local Japanese guy that I had never met before and there was *Mohammed*, an Iraqi exchange student, who kept murmuring, "Berlante Berlante," oblivious to the crowd of mourners.

I felt emotionally removed from the funeral proceedings and I did not cry. I had difficulty accepting my sister's death, and for several years I would walk into her room talking to her before I realized there was no one there to listen.

My mother was grim and stoic and blamed my sister's death on the war. There were others that blamed my mother.

My mother seemed apathetic for a few months after my sister's death. Then she approached me carefully to see if I would see a psychiatrist. I told her quite pointedly that I wasn't crazy and I wasn't going to kill myself. I felt a little guilty, just a little sadistic, telling her that so soon after my sister took her own life, but she only became more insistent. I could tell my mother wasn't going to give up so I finally went to see Dr. Haruki.

Dr. Haruki was a dumpy, middle-aged Japanese woman who dressed in a nondescript professional, beige, brown and gray, sort of way. She hid behind thick glasses and a bare minimum of make-up, and she seemed as desexed as anyone could possibly be. She talked in a soft, penetrating, nonprovocative sort of way, asking: "How are you? How do you feel?" Not emphatically enough to provoke me but with just enough emotion to get an answer. Of course her professional manner made me moody, maybe even a little emotionally explosive, but she seemed to be aware enough to skirt real issues so that I didn't explode. She didn't ask me if I hated my mother, and she didn't ask me if I missed my sister. She just sort of asked around important questions. I tried to be as forthright as possible, true to my feelings, but I rarely got any kind of emotional reaction. Talking to Dr. Haruki was about as satisfying as talking to an upholstered chair, but I went anyhow because I thought the situation required the meetings.

I went to see Dr. Haruki about four times. I was late for appointments twice. Each time I went to see Dr. Haruki, she was careful to tell me I wasn't crazy, and she always gave me her best professional smile, nothing spontaneous as if she really felt like smiling, just one of those practiced in-the-mirror smiles.

By the end of the month Dr. Haruki and my mother decided that I should be talking to a man, and they sent me to talk to a professor at the University.

Dr. Walker was a Negro. He was a small, thinnish man, and he wasn't real dark-skinned; he was more grayish. He didn't have thick lips like I would have imagined but had thin sensitive ones that shaped words carefully. Dr. Walker's kinky hair receded way back to the top of his high forehead. He showed quite a bit of gray along his temples, and he had high cheek bones and a thin tall elegant nose which supported close-up glasses, which he intently peered over. Dr. Walker's eyes were deep set, dark and penetrating, almost invasive. Dr. Walker didn't smile as much as Dr. Haruki; he just kind of gave a nod of approval if he liked what you said or if he wanted you to feel at ease. Other than the nod, Dr. Walker rarely telegraphed any personal feelings. He was just an intense presence. If looks were the criteria, Dr. Walker was an archetype psychiatrist, scary even.

By the time I went to Dr. Walker, I already had the hang of psychiatric interviews. I would just walk in, make myself comfortable, then just unload whatever thoughts or feelings I had on the top of my head. Dr. Walker would just give me the nod if I was doing good; then he'd frown if I got off track, so I suppose he sort of steered me into whatever kind of discussion he wanted to hear. I knew my habit of coming late to appointments irritated Dr. Walker but on the other hand, I didn't really want to meet with him or Dr. Haruki anyway, and I really resented the time spent and the intrusion into my head, which was my business and nobody elses. It wasn't anything like going to the regular doctor's office when you were sick and you got a shot that made you better. These psychiatrist things kept going on and on with no substantial relief. Of course my intermittent efforts with Dr. Walker ended up in a long rambling report that I found among my mother's effects many years later. From what I read, I think he stopped our interviews because he detected that I had some hostility toward Negroes. He never told me that, but he did tell me I wasn't crazy. When I think back, I had never met or talked to a Negro before.

I took every opportunity to get drunk the summer of 1951. The more I thought of my life and my involvement with psychiatrists, the more resentful I got. Drinking dulled the senses so that you didn't feel so bad all the time. It made you feel oblivious and dulled your self-consciousness. You could do crazy things that you normally wouldn't do. If you drank enough, you would pass out for an hour or two; then when you woke up you felt so bad that other things that might have been bothering you didn't matter too much any more. If you felt bad enough, you could start drinking again, and it would send you right back to oblivion. I knew drinking wasn't the right thing to do, but it sure seemed to help sometimes. Drinking was a method that accomplished a desired end.

By the time school started in September, I found myself in a serious funk. I felt torn by erratic floods of feeling that I really couldn't put my fingers on. I was sad sometimes, then angry the next time. I would hate everyone one day and the next day no one mattered. I'd feel like breaking stuff one day then I'd feel fear and impotence the next. When I had rational periods, I really didn't care any more about anything. Dropping out was easy after that.

By mid-term in the school year I had attended very few of my classes and had done none of my assigned work. School counselors told me I could stay in school if I got all my work caught up. That was impossible, an unacceptable alternative; it was much easier to go drink and forget it. My parents were very concerned but there was little they could do. They had already passed me off to third-party professionals, and they hesitated to interfere with that relationship. I took the remainder of the school year off.

I went back to school in the fall of 1952. Taking the year off had helped to get my head screwed back straight and find some inner perspective, but I still had no real motivation. I had to take English and History to graduate, and I had enough other credits to carry me through. I took lots of mechanical and wood shop, especially because those classes were my kind of saneness therapy. Study Hall filled out the rest of my schedule, and I more often than not left campus early to do whatever I had to do.

My school counselors, my teachers and my parents gave me lots of leeway that year, and they must have held their collective breaths while they watched me. I'm sure the bitter thought of having another miserable suicide on their watch crossed a few minds. I still didn't much care about anything.

The final high school year went very slowly for me, but I still had difficulty getting the few assignments in that I needed to. Deadlines mean nothing when you don't care. Two weeks before graduation the Army tried to draft me. After my parents talked to the draft board, they let me graduate in June of 1953. I had to report to Schofield Barracks right after graduation.

One would immediately expect that an alien resident would be exempt from the draft but that was not so. The Army didn't care about your citizenship, loyalty, feelings or attitude. They knew they could change all that. They only wanted your body. Once I asked the question, I found I had two real hard choices: either stay in the Army or go back to Japan. I had lived most of my life in Hawai`i. It was the only real life I knew. It wasn't really much of a choice. I stayed with the Army.

The Basic Training process started when they clipped off all our hair. Then they yanked out all our bad teeth. They gave us uniforms and shoes that didn't fit. Then they finally inoculated us for every known disease in the universe. Half the guys got sick from the inoculations, and the other half couldn't eat for lack of teeth.

The Army put us up in large rooms with cots, that they called "bays." There were about 60 of us, two platoons, with communal wash basins, showers and toilets. You had to line up side by side all in a row to go pee in a long stainless steel trough. When you made "number 2," there were bare partitions between the toilets, but no doors. You waited till you really had to go bad, and that way you spent the least possible amount of time sitting on the throne exposed to hazing and public ridicule.

The Army made us run double-time all over Schofield Barracks, all the way up to *Kolekole* Pass and all around East Range. We ran to every training class and every weapons range. The cadre exercised a diabolical range of epithets and personal insults, all designed to destroy our sensitivity. If you made a mistake or fell asleep in class, the cadre made you do 20 push-ups. By the end of the first week, the Army had systematically destroyed any ego, pretensions or individuality that we might have developed during the first part of our young lives.

I spent 16 weeks in Basic Training then another six weeks in Leadership Training. I was then assigned overseas to K Company of the 11th Infantry Regiment, Third Division, stationed in Augsburg, Germany. I stayed for 15 months, participating in tactical infantry maneuvers, carrying around an 18 pound Browning Automatic Rifle and slogging around in Rhine River mud with big tanks growling all around me.

No other experience in my life would ever be as dirty and degrading and purposeless as the Army had been.

I had gone from a comfortable, permissive, upper-middle class private school environment straight to complete immersion into the lowest form of reality in an instant. Only the U. S. Army could make life that miserable.

Yet, it was clear that the Army had pitted me against a cross-section of American men from all walks of life, all of us about the same age and thrown into the worst possible situations the War Department could devise. Furthermore, it was clear to me that I had done better than most of the men that were there with me. In fact I could even say that I had thrived in that constantly challenging environment. I hated the experience, but it had given me a self-confidence that I had never felt before, and it definitely made me feel older.

The Army took about a week to process me out of active service. Then I headed down to the beach. The beach had always been my place of refuge. I would borrow a surfboard and paddle out to the surf-line and wait for waves, surf till my hands and feet got that wrinkled waterlogged look and I got so hungry and cold, I had to come back to the beach for food. I'd paddle back and sit in the sun till I was warm again and watch young girls and fat tourists, the surf, and the shimmer on the water. I sunburned the first couple of weeks, and then I got good and brown like I used to be.

In the summer of 1955 I finally had a chance to relax. I had been away from my parents for two years now, and the notion of being my own man was beginning to take hold. I now had school benefits as a veteran, and although I still had no motivation, I registered in September and started going to class at the University of Hawai`i. I was now much older than the rest of the freshman, and they all seemed so young and silly, so I started hanging out with some of the other veterans and the upper classmen. I immediately adopted all their bad habits.

We'd go out and buy *Vino da Tavola* by the gallon. I can still remember the label design: red-and-white checkered table cloth. We all learned to drink the wine right out of the gallon jug while we had it slung over one shoulder.

Breakfast was always a sixty-five cent stew and rice at a place in Moili`ili. By afternoon we were back on the *Vino da Tavola*. It gave a nice buzz if you drank enough; besides it was really cheap. Everybody read Sarte, Camus, Kerouac and Ginsburg and listened to bad recordings of Brubeck and Thelonius Monk on bad phonographs. We were all convinced that we were engaged in deep intellectual exchanges by the time we had consumed a quarter gallon of that *Vino da Tavola*.

We would feel so lousy the next day with that thick sour tannin taste on the tongue that we'd show up for stew and rice washed down with strawberry soda in Moili`ili, then the whole cycle would start over.

The life style was so unhealthy that one guy got beriberi, with aches all over and bleeding from the gums. Some of us took vitamins daily so we wouldn't fare so bad, and we felt just a little smug about cheating the malnutrition problem.

Academically none of us did too well, but for some reason or another we really were convinced we were getting smarter.

I stayed a Freshman on the GI Bill for about two years before I decided I didn't like the pretentious poverty or the life style anymore and went out to look for work.

I found work at the airport and went successively from Hawaiian Airlines to Japan Airlines and finally to United Airlines, where I started work as a swing-shift clerk down at the hangar. United paid me $290.00 per month, but you've got to understand that it was almost three times the amount of my GI school allowance and enough to live on. I immediately bought myself a "baby window" Volkswagen "Bug," and I started feeling very independent indeed.

My father died on January 21, 1958, after an extended illness with cancer. He was 67 years old. My mother tended to his needs at home the last year with a devotion and tender sensitivity that I found touching. My mother and father clung to each other for solace even as the final awful end approached, and their lives together as life partners for 28 years slowly crumbled. They had been through so much together, of time, events and history. Death, the final event, seemed to only drive them desperately closer.

When I left for work in the early afternoon of the day my father died, I heard my father murmuring as if talking to someone else: *Iya-da, Iya-da* ("No! I don't want to. No! I don't want to"). When I stopped by the master bedroom, he stopped his verbal complaint and pretended he was all right. When I returned home after midnight that night, my mother met me to tell me he had passed on. She had been with him when he died.

My father's funeral was a huge event at home on Wyllie Street. Thousands of people came to bid him a final goodbye. It wasn't just the high and the mighty that came because he was a cultural leader in the Japanese community. He had been an early leader in the medical community as well, and that brought all his peers. He had touched many through the day-to-day contact of his medical practice and these grateful people came. Only my grandfather Iga Mori's funeral on May 12, 1951, shortly after my sister Pearl's death, had been bigger.

As huge and as obvious as the personal loss was to my mother, she remained silent and grim and stoic.

My father's death was the first of a series of events that served to harden the alienation between my mother and me. My half-brother Arthur came to the funeral from Japan, where he now practiced law. With the formal wisdom of the law and of his profession, Arthur now began to organize the disposition of our father's estate with the best interests of the whole family in mind. The immediate problem was the lack of a will. Without the specific instructions of such a will, my father's estate needed to be administered according to the law. As things fell into place, I was the only heir and sibling at home in Honolulu, and I became the Administrator of the Estate. My half-brother Victor was in Indianapolis finishing up his medical residency at the General Hospital and my half-sister Margaret was busy in Michigan raising her growing family. They had both sent written regrets and had not been able to return to Hawai`i to attend our father's funeral.

The first order of administration was to close down my father's old Nu`uanu office. The office was a steady drain on the estate, with lease payments and a multitude of small expenses. My father's secretary and his nurse were still there like faithful feudal servants waiting for the master to return. Even after I had dismissed them and signed certifications for unemployment benefits, they both returned for months after to look for things to do.

There was a two-generation accumulation of medical odds and ends that simply needed to be thrown away. My grandfather, being an old time Navy surgeon, had the habit of pickling any curious organic object, diseased or otherwise, that he had surgically removed from the ill or injured, in formalin solutions sealed in glass jars.

His office as I remembered it as a child was lined with shelves upon which the specimens were placed like trophies. My father was not quite so morbid in his displays, but he did keep the instruments of his profession displayed in locked glass faced cabinets of the waiting room along with petri dishes full of kidney and gall stones that he had removed from hapless patients. For both my father and grandfather, the medical displays must have been a show of professional pride but for an ailing patient seeking relief the office must have been a fearful place.

There was a *monooki* (storage shed) in the back of the lot, full of old newspapers, old copies of the *Lancet*, my grandfather's pickled specimens and old medical texts in German, Japanese and English. When I opened a small, old-fashioned medicine cabinet I found four small bottles of USP heroin. The drug had been outlawed in the mid-forties but was still quite clearly listed on my father's narcotic inventory. It had never been collected or returned. In my grandfather's day, he had concocted a very heady, very effective cough medication with the stuff. When I finally turned the drug in to the Federal Narcotics Office along with a shoe box full of ampules of morphine, codeine and cocaine, the Federal Agent shook his head in disbelief. When the agent finally wrote up a receipt for me, he explained that the heroin would have generated twenty thousand dollars out on the street if it had been cut and sold in capsules. It probably was a good thing I didn't know about that. In the late 1950s you could buy a house for $20,000 dollars.

The second story of the Nu`uanu Office was full of laboratory equipment. My father had once set up a medical laboratory for the use of the medical community of the time, but it had not been financially viable. The labs at the hospitals had been more convenient. There were zinc lined sinks, large and small centrifuges, bunsen burners, unused flasks, and test tubes still in their boxes. One room had been set up as a photo lab with enlargers and big trays, photo papers and photo chemicals.

I phoned Dr. Walter L. Curtis, the principal at Punahou School, whom I had only known as the iron-jawed, steely-eyed, top-most authority dispensing discipline at school, to see if the school had any use for the equipment.

Dr. Curtis showed up at the Nu`uanu Office the next week dressed in dungarees and work shirt with a crew of Punahou workmen and a big truck. Together, they carted off most of the still-usable equipment. Dr. Curtis sent me a nice letter of thanks and appreciation which eventually got filed away as one of the probate papers.

Breaking the lease for the Nu`uanu Office was a lot more complex, and this time my brother Arthur had to pull strings to get the property condemned by the Redevelopment Agency. Once that was accomplished, I could move on to concentrate on the Wyllie Street property.

By April of 1959 my involvement with the estate was so demanding that I quit my United Airlines job. I wrote a long, complicated letter to my boss, and he reluctantly released me with a recommendation for rehire.

"On the first day of May in the year of our Lord nineteen hundred and fifty nine, and of our Independence the one hundred and eighty third, having complied with all applicable provisions of the Naturalization Laws," I was admitted, *"as a citizen of the United States of America at the U. S. District Court of the District of Hawai`i."*

I had already lived so many years like an American that it seemed anticlimactic to suddenly be a real one. Citizenship had been such a long bumpy road for me, and I had wanted the status so badly at one time. It marked a mile-stone in my life but I was much too busy to celebrate. As for my mother's reaction, her feelings for my achievement were bitter, dubious and mixed with her own loyalties and nostalgic sentiments of her own family and Japan.

My mother had been working as a research assistant in epidemiology for a cancer research group at the University of Hawai`i, and our involvement was infrequent as long as I was working on the Nu`uanu Office. Once I started working on the Wyllie Street house, the situation changed dramatically. I would start in the morning and immediately begin sifting through the accumulation of two-and-a-half generations of family things. Some items were trivial: a magazine, a newspaper, a tooth brush or a comb, a paperback book. Others things were more personal: photographs, written notes, letters and diaries. These things needed to be segregated so they could be looked at carefully later.

It's funny how inanimate objects began to acquire character the instant someone owns them. A stain or a strand of hair immediately makes things personal with a stamp of time and place, a memory of time gone by. It seemed everyone in my family kept things and of course the things they kept began to read like a diary of what kind of person they were. Even my sister Margaret and my brother Victor, who both had been away so many years, had left their own personal collection of things. My grandfather Iga's and my sister Pearl's rooms were just as they had left them, almost eerily untouched except for the layers of accumulated dust. Memories of both of them hung thickly there in their rooms. It seemed almost sacrilegious to break their personal order, the spirit that they had left there.

If you spent time ruminating, you got nothing done. You had to put aside feelings and thoughts and just do things mechanically. I would put all the throw-away items in garbage bags and the keep-things in separate piles. When the piles got big enough, I'd take the throw-away bags out to the upstairs veranda and throw them down in a pile on the driveway. Then when the driveway pile got big enough, I would borrow a truck and haul it away to the dump. I put the other save stuff in boxes with labels so I knew where they came from and what was in them.

My neighbor, "Bully" Phillips, who lived across the street, would tell me in later years that everytime I threw stuff out onto the drive way, he would see my mother scurry out as soon as I went back inside, to check the rubbish I had left. Then she would scurry back inside with stuff she wanted to save before I brought out another load of throw-away rubbish.

My mother wanted nothing more than to live out the remainder of her life in the Wyllie Street house because it was the reservoir of all her living memories. Every nook and cranny had memories of family, events, of happiness and sorrow. That was an entirely impractical, near impossible expectation, and I tried to explain that to my mother, but it all went very badly.

My father had built the family complex in the mid-1930s for nine family members, and in the old days there was usually one live-in maid and a day maid that helped my grandmother maintain household order. My two brothers and my grandfather stayed in the smaller two-bedroom house. It had a special Japanese room that had been built for my grandfather. It was floored with *tatami*, which are traditional thick straw mats. The room contained a *tokonoma*, an alcove for objects of art, and a separate shelved area where *Ojiisama* (grandfather) could display his swords and other *samurai* (warrior) accouterments. There was an *engawa* (outer passageway) on two sides of the room that made the room airy and open and there were *shoji* (sliding partitions) around the central room that could be closed for privacy and sleep.

The rest of us lived in the main house, which was built with large common areas: a family dining area with large curved glass outer wall; a formal dining area with a long *koa* dining table and adjoining living room with a descending quarter-round staircase naturally lit by a glass brick wall. The east end was a book-lined library with comfortable chairs and sliding glass doors to let in the light. The rest of the first floor consisted of a large kitchen, a large bathroom and a number of utility areas. My parents were comfortable having large parties and meetings here.

The second floor consisted of four large bedrooms and a bathroom. A veranda curved around the street-side of the house.

The house was a wonderful place to grow up, with a large yard and lots of well-maintained plants and trees, but the whole complex was now run down, termite-ridden and in need of major repair and paint. Without the constant attention required, the yard had become overgrown and unkempt.

With my father's long illness, no one had even attempted to keep the place clean. It was a massive repair and maintenance project. One old woman living in the complex would be overwhelmed. It just was not feasible for my mother to continue to live here, especially alone.

We both talked about the situation often, and the more we discussed the problem of my mother living in the Wyllie Street complex, the more polarized our positions became. I was no longer just a kid. I had grown up and I had the logic and the justice of the Estate Law on my side. Besides, my brother Arthur was around to supervise. My mother knew she had rights and she was now suspicious and defensive. She would argue that if my father were still around she would be able to live here.

Suddenly, I became the oppressor. I was the "Administrator," the official destroyer of her tranquility, the official destroyer of her most cherished memories.

My mother had been a faithful and loving wife to my father. She had tended to her husband and our father to the very end with loving, caring hands. Now she was being treated shabbily, without concern or respect by her very own first-born son. The argument and confrontations continued with varying intensities for months. My emotional tolerance grew thinner and thinner, until one evening after an especially tiring day the confrontation began again. The accumulated rancor spilled over into a rage, and only in an instant of rational evaluation, I realized the rage would overwhelm me uncontrollably. I walked out of the house abruptly and into the evening air, and I aimlessly walked and walked. The coolness of the air and the darkness of night seemed to gradually transform the overflowing rage to feelings of guilt and fear and even when I got home hours later, I could not sleep for the emotional turmoil. The next morning I left in my car and drove aimlessly along the shoreline roads and the countryside. When I got home that night, I dropped off to sleep instantly from sheer physical and emotional exhaustion. By the time I woke the next morning, I knew with a certainty that I had to avoid confrontations with my mother at all costs, to stay away from her.

As for my mother, I think she realized that there had been a change in me. I think she began to understand that her arguments would not prevail.

By 1960 my brother Arthur's international cliental had increased to the point that he made as many as two or three trips through Honolulu a year. He was now better able to supervise the disposition of our father's estate. My brother made arrangements with a contractor-client to undertake repair and renovation of the Wyllie Street complex. Carpenters and eventually painters, began arriving every morning for the work on the property. I had done enough clean-up and throw-away for the work to proceed. I went back to United Airlines for my own work. United rehired me as a passenger agent in March of 1960. I transferred to a rapidly expanding Flight Steward Service in May. It was the beginning of jet aircraft service and unprecedented growth for the company. I remained in the In-Flight Services Division for 36 years till retirement in 1996.

United provided a normality for me that I had never experienced before. I met Judith Ann Tate in 1960, then married her in 1962. Judy gave birth to David Lindsey in July of 1962. Lyra Hiromi followed soon after in January of 1964. When I look back, it seems too evident that I had rushed into normality with the same helter-skelter intensity that had occurred in the earlier part of my life.

In late 1959 my mother made a pilgrimage back to Japan. With my brother Arthur's sponsorship, she stayed there for a year. We never discussed her visit back to Japan, but I knew it was not the same country that she had left in 1927. Japan was experiencing the rapid rise of her post-war economic boom and everything was brand new and fast-paced. My mother probably never completely reconnected with neither her family nor her mother culture. She must have felt left behind.

In September of 1960 the Wyllie Street property was sold. My brother Arthur had obtained the release of my mother's dower interests in the property and had made acceptable arrangements for her financial upkeep. It was no small achievement as I was well aware, and I was grateful for everything that my brother had done.

In the following year my mother made arrangements with my brother Arthur to sell her family property in *Boshu* at the southern-most tip of the Chiba Peninsula. Her physical ties to the mother country would be permanently severed.

My mother and I now lived separate lives. My mother found an apartment on Keanu Street in Kaimukī with a friendly, worthy landlord and good neighbors. By 1962 Judy and I were involved in our own family. I would see my mother at least once a month usually for lunch, or other convenient occasions. She knew well enough to leave me alone with my growing family.

My mother kept busy with cultural activities. She belonged to the *Dokushokai* (the Reading Group), the *Go* (chess-like game) Society and wrote cultural articles and poetry for the Japanese daily. My mother indulged herself in Japanese movies, becoming a film critic and regular reviewer.

I will never know if whim, nostalgia, boredom or just plain compulsive indulgence drove my mother to smoking cigarettes. I was a smoker, and my father and grandfather had smoked at one time or another so the habit was nothing new, but my mother suddenly began smoking in 1966. She would tell me that smoking reminded her of my sister Pearl, who was a moderate smoker. She would puff away with stylish mannerisms that she had learned from watching cinema, and she feigned enjoyment without ever once inhaling the smoke.

I once visited her apartment during this period, and there were packs of cigarettes, ash trays, matches, scattered ashes and half-smoked butts at every one of her favorite places of relaxation. Of course, she was old enough to do what she wanted, and I was not about to start arguing about contrary behavior with my mother, so I kept my mouth shut and worried about the fire hazard.

By 1968 my mother had developed bronchial cancer, and her doctors began the arduous process of treatment.

Dr. Gebauer (Paul W. Gebauer MD) operated on my mother in October of 1968, removing the right side of her lungs. When he came out of surgery, he told me: "You know? Your mother's lungs are pink like a country girl's, like she's never smoked before, but the cancer is in the roots of the lungs, the bronchia, and I just couldn't remove those." Then Dr. Gebaur told me the medical team would use radiation and finally chemotherapy to further relieve my mother's condition. Then he told me the cancer would probably redevelop in about 5 years. My mother was released from the hospital on November 30, 1968, and she began the long road toward recovery.

By mid-1970 my mother was beginning to feel herself again. In a compulsive, assuredly-self-destructive impulse, my mother began smoking cigarettes again. It was suicidal.

By mid-November of 1971 my mother's cancer had redeveloped to a completely debilitating degree. We placed her in a hospital and finally a care home.

My mother died on January 6, 1972. Her bronchial cancer had made it difficult for her to breathe, and in the last days, even with additional oxygen, she labored for breath. In the final minutes of life she suddenly seemed to relax and even her facial expression became calm and peaceful. Her breathing became almost regular and effort-free. Her breathing slowed and finally stopped, and all I could see of life was the artery in her neck, pulsing strongly with the beat of her heart. I watched her face, finally at peace, and the beating artery for what seemed like minutes, and then even the pulsing slowed and stopped.

I walked out onto an adjoining terrace, looked up at a starry, clear night sky, and in an overwhelming moment of emotion, I finally cried.

I wasn't crying because I had lost my mother, and I wasn't crying because I had lost someone I loved. I cried because my lifelong conflict was finally over. To this very day, I cannot say with any certainty that I loved my mother, nor can I say with any certainty that I hated my mother. I only know that there must have been large measures of both passions to have caused the kind of conflict that we lived through.

I had survived.

The Ice Cube Press began publishing in 1993 to focus on how to live with the natural world and to better understand how people can best live together in the communities they share and inhabit. Since this time, we've been recognized by a number of well-known writers, including Gary Snyder, Gene Logsdon, Wes Jackson, Patricia Hampl, Greg Brown, Jim Harrison, Annie Dillard, Ken Burns, Kathleen Norris, Janisse Ray, Alison Deming, Michael Pollan, and Barry Lopez. We've published a number of well-known authors as well, including Mary Swander, Jim Heynen, Mary Pipher, Bill Holm, Carol Bly, Marvin Bell, Debra Marquart, Ted Kooser, Stephanie Mills, Bill McKibben, and Paul Gruchow. As well, we have won several publishing awards over the last seventeen years. Check out our books at our web site, with booksellers, or at museum shops, then discover why we are dedicated to "hearing the other side."

Ice Cube Press (est. 1993)
205 N Front Street
North Liberty, Iowa 52317-9302
steve@icecubepress.com
www.icecubepress.com

thinking of waves and Hawai`i
hugs, kisses and cheers to
Fenna Marie & Laura Lee

Printed in the USA
CPSIA information can be obtained
at www.ICGtesting.com
LVHW051516050624
782366LV00005B/105

9 781888 160116